Democracy and Legal Change

Since ancient Athens, democrats have taken pride in their power and inclination to change their laws, yet they have also sought to counter this capacity by creating immutable laws. In *Democracy and Legal Change*, Melissa Schwartzberg argues that modifying law is a fundamental and attractive democratic activity. Against those who would defend the use of "entrenchment clauses" to protect key constitutional provisions from revision, Schwartzberg seeks to demonstrate historically the strategic and even unjust purposes unamendable laws have typically served, and to highlight the regrettable consequences that entrenchment may have for democracies today. Drawing on historical evidence, classical political theory, and contemporary constitutional and democratic theory, *Democracy and Legal Change* reexamines the relationship between democracy and the rule of law from a new, and often surprising, set of vantage points.

Melissa Schwartzberg is Associate Professor of Political Science at Columbia University. She received an A.B. from Washington University in St. Louis in Classics and Political Science in 1996 and a Ph.D. in Politics from New York University in 2002. From 2002 through 2006, she was an Assistant Professor of Political Science at George Washington University in Washington, DC.

CAMBRIDGE STUDIES IN THE THEORY OF DEMOCRACY

General Editor
ADAM PRZEWORSKI   New York University

OTHER BOOKS IN THE SERIES

Jon Elster, ed., *Deliberative Democracy*

Adam Przeworski, Susan Stokes, and Bernard Manin, eds.,
Democracy, Accountability, and Representation

Adam Przeworski et al., *Democracy and Development:
Political Institutions and Well-Being in the World,
1950–1990*

Robert Barros, *Constitutionalism and Dictatorship:
Pinochet, the Junta, and the 1980 Constitution*

José María Maravall and Adam Przeworski, eds.,
Democracy and the Rule of Law

For my family

Democracy and Legal Change

Melissa Schwartzberg

Columbia University

CAMBRIDGE UNIVERSITY PRESS
Cambridge, New York, Melbourne, Madrid, Cape Town, Singapore,
São Paulo, Delhi, Dubai, Tokyo

Cambridge University Press
32 Avenue of the Americas, New York, NY 10013-2473, USA

www.cambridge.org
Information on this title: www.cambridge.org/9780521146579

First published 2007
First paperback edition 2009

Printed in the United States of America

A catalog record for this publication is available from the British Library.

Library of Congress Cataloging in Publication Data

Schwartzberg, Melissa, 1975–
Democracy and legal change / Melissa Schwartzberg.
   p.   cm. – (Cambridge studies in the theory of democracy)
Includes bibliographical references and Index.
   ISBN-13: 978-0-521-86652-1 (hardback)
   ISBN-10: 0-521-86652-9 (hardback)
   1. Law reform. 2. Law reform–History. 3. Democracy. I. Title. II. Series.
K552.S29   2007
340'.3–dc22   2006031900

ISBN 978-0-521-86652-1 Hardback
ISBN 978-0-521-14657-9 Paperback

Contents

Acknowledgments

I began writing this book in New York City, where (much to my surprise) I finished it. Many of my debts are thus to New York institutions – to NYU, where I wrote the initial dissertation; to Columbia University, where I finished the book; and to the New York office of Cambridge University Press.

Virtually every idea in this work has been improved through conversations with Bernard Manin, a model of intellectual generosity and personal graciousness. I am profoundly indebted to him both as a student and as a friend. Adam Przeworski's support for this project from its inception gave me the confidence to pursue it, and I am honored to have it in his Theory of Democracy series. John Ferejohn's energy and insightful criticisms spurred me along, and Pasquale Pasquino and Jeremy Waldron helped shape the scope of the project in fundamental ways. Jon Elster offered detailed comments on the original dissertation for which I am especially grateful, for they served as a critical guide to my subsequent revisions.

Jack Knight set me on this path when I was an undergraduate at Washington University in St. Louis, and he continues to ensure that I do not wander off into the brambles. I will resist the impulse to shift all blame for the deficiencies of this work to him and instead just thank him for those dimensions of my career and scholarship for which he will acknowledge responsibility. Conversations with Christopher Eisgruber, James Johnson, John McCormick, Andrew

Rehfeld, and Bernard Yack, among many others, shaped my thinking about these questions in fundamental ways.

At NYU, a McCracken and a Bradley Fellowship supported my research. My colleagues Suzanne Fry, Jennifer Gandhi, Sona Golder, Wonik Kim, Dimitri Landa, Jeffrey Lax (now a colleague at Columbia), Carmela Lutmar, Patricio Navia, Sebastian Saiegh, Loretta Sorensen, Christian Stracke, and James Vreeland – among others – helped to develop this work in various ways through their insights and their friendship. My new colleagues at Columbia – including Jean Cohen, Tanisha Fazal, John Huber, David Johnston, Ira Katznelson, Samuel Moyn, Annie Stilz, and Nadia Urbinati – asked important questions that helped me to think through the final revision of the manuscript. I am grateful to Lewis Bateman and Ciara McLaughlin at Cambridge University Press for their help and their support for the project, as well as to Stephen Calvert for his careful work as copy editor and to Navdeep Singh at TechBooks for his attention to the manuscript.

Most of the book was written at The George Washington University, where I spent four years as an assistant professor. Ingrid Creppell was a marvelous interlocutor and friend, and Nathan Brown provided detailed comments on the manuscript and shaped my thinking about constitutional scholarship in countless ways. Sarah Binder, Chris Deering, Henry Farrell, Steven Kelts, Forrest Maltzman, Kimberly Morgan, Elliot Posner, Chad Rector, Lee Sigelman, Erik Voeten, and Bill Winstead offered advice and friendship throughout my time in Washington. I also received a University Facilitating Fund Award, enabling me to hire a GW undergraduate, Laura Blessing, who collected pamphlets and other primary sources for the seventeenth-century chapter.

Along with talks at NYU and GW, I presented elements of this work at the American Political Science Association (APSA) Annual Meeting, the Midwest Political Science Association Annual National

Acknowledgments

Meeting, the Northeast Political Science Association, and the Institute for Constitutional Studies Summer Seminar on Slavery and the Constitution (as well as a special Institute session cosponsored by the APSA, for which I am grateful to Maeva Marcus). I thank the chairs, discussants, and participants at all these sessions for their advice. Nathan Brown's graduate seminar in constitutionalism at GW read an early version of the manuscript, and Mark Tushnet's constitutional law seminar at Georgetown Law read a very condensed version of the work. Students in these seminars wrote response questions and essays on this work, which guided my final revisions; the condensed paper was widely circulated, and I appreciate the many comments I received (particularly those of Benito Aláez Corral).

Jennifer Gandhi has been the first and last reader of my work since graduate school; her patience is, almost, unbounded. For that, for her capacity to recall details of our shared history and of my own historical arguments, and for her friendship, I thank her. I also wish to express my appreciation to my non–political scientist friends (from my youth in Albany, from Washington University, and from our years in the District of Columbia and Baltimore) who occasionally expressed polite interest in the progress of the book but who usually goaded me into forgetting about it for a while.

I dedicate this book to my family. My parents, Rosalyn and Barry Schwartzberg, have encouraged my intellectual interests since childhood, and my sister Debbi has kept me from taking them too seriously. My wonderful in-laws, Nina and Howard Jones, and the entire Jones clan tolerated with very good cheer my work on this project during our "Jonesfests." Most of all, I thank my husband, David, for his support for my academic career and for his efforts to bring balance and relative calm to my life. This undertaking should have induced everyone I love – including our cats, Sully and Otto – to flee. I am very fortunate that they did not.

Permission to reprint material is gratefully acknowledged. Chapter 2 appeared, with slight modifications, as Melissa Schwartzberg, "Athenian Democracy and Legal Change," *American Political Science Review*, 98:2, 311–25, © American Political Science Association, published by Cambridge University Press.

Chapter One

Introduction: Explaining Legal Change and Entrenchment

Since ancient Athens, democrats have taken pride in both their power and their proclivity to change their laws. For centuries, political theorists have recognized the distinctively democratic tendency to modify laws, yet this very capacity has given pause to democrats, and they have sought to restrict radically their ability to exercise this authority. As a consequence, democrats have resorted to "entrenchment" – the use of irrevocable laws – as a means of countering their tendency to engage in legal change.

Although today inflexible law is considered a hallmark of democracy, the process of modifying law has a distinguished democratic pedigree of its own. At critical moments for the development of democracy, debates about the appropriate scope and locus of legal change have come to the fore. Political theorists have shaped the ways in which we have conceptualized the nature and the limits of the power to modify law during these disputes. Through retrieving a set of arguments on behalf of the democratic ability to change law, and through analyzing the circumstances in which democracies have restricted this power through the use of entrenchment, we can revisit the question of the relationship between the rule of law and democracy from a variety of fresh vantage points.

The form that legal change has taken, and the logic underlying the modification of law, has of course varied over the centuries. The Athenian embrace of legal change derived from an ideological commitment to pragmatic innovation more broadly. This may be distinguished from seventeenth-century English republicans, who saw the possibility of legal change as a means of affirming popular consent to legislation by wresting the power away from the artificial reason of judges and, in turn, from the American framers, who situated the power of amendment on the grounds of human fallibility. Nor have defenses of immutability remained consistent across the centuries: Whereas the Athenians sought to make their commitments credible to allies, Cromwell used entrenchment to protect religious freedom for Christians (not those engaged in "Popery," however) and to regulate the sale of the crown lands, and the Americans sought to make equal suffrage of states in the Senate and – for a limited time – the slave trade substantively immutable.

Today, the best-known example of entrenchment is the protection granted to human dignity in the post–World War II German Basic Law. This usage has given it remarkable moral standing among contemporary constitutional framers and political theorists. However, entrenchment serves as a means by which legislators can seek to protect not only those rules that they regard as most important or those that serve a "constitutive" purpose – securing the conditions of democratic decision making, or preventing democracy from revising itself into tyranny – but as a means of preserving privileges and power asymmetries. Thus, entrenchment betrays one of democracy's most attractive legacies: the ability to modify law.

My aim in this work is twofold. First, I seek to retrieve and defend the ability to modify law as a quintessential and attractive democratic trait. Second, I explain the use of entrenchment as a response to this fundamental activity: I argue that democrats have long had recourse to entrenchment – both in response to their own anxiety about the consequences of legal change and because of particular interests in protecting certain laws against revision – but that these efforts are futile at best and pernicious at worst.

Defining Legal Change and Entrenchment

In this work, I seek to analyze the choice of mechanisms to alter and to entrench law at key turning points for democracy, and to retrieve the arguments surrounding these decisions about legal flexibility. Through examining the means by which democracies have chosen to enable and to restrict their power to amend laws – and through highlighting the ways in which political theorists have conceptualized these decisions – I hope to defend legal change as a distinctive and appealing democratic activity, and to provide reasons for resisting the historically salient decision to entrench. Although my aim is not to offer a comprehensive overview of the methods by which laws may be modified or protected, to sharpen some of the distinctions I draw here and to identify idiosyncratic uses of terminology (e.g., "entrenchment," which typically refers to any norm that is procedurally difficult to amend) – a brief overview of the relevant concepts may be helpful. In this section, I highlight and define the major mechanisms of legal change and the approaches to entrenchment that will occupy the rest of the book.

Legal Change

Legislative (Statutory) Change
Although this is the oldest and most fundamental version of legal change – characterized by a legislature's decision to alter a preexisting rule – it is also perhaps the most controversial type of modification. H. L. A. Hart recognized that legislative enactment and legal repeal were impossible in the absence of a rule of change, and this specific dimension of legal change – as deliberate and legislative, rather than interpretive and judicial – shall be taken up in our discussion of legal reform in seventeenth-century England. Recent work by Jeremy Waldron seeking to restore "dignity" to legislation and the legislative process is of great importance to this

account, though in this work I focus on mechanisms and conceptions of alteration rather than on law making (or on the nature of democratic autonomy in general, for that matter). Accounts of statutory change are intimately linked to accounts of assembly decision making more generally: to critiques, on the one hand, of legislatures as passionate or self-interested or to laudatory accounts of the epistemic quality of democratic deliberations. Yet embracing the power of legislatures to enact law may be distinguished from affirming their power to reverse themselves, displacing traditional commitments and breaking deliberately with their past ideals. Although amendment receives more scholarly attention today, the idea that an assembly can modify law in a deliberate (and a deliberative) fashion has been a critical feature of discussions of popular government for centuries.

Interpretive Change

Today, most scholars, even those who are not red-blooded positivists, accept the idea that judges may change law through the process of interpretation. Legal scholars such as Bruce Ackerman and Sanford Levinson have encouraged us to think more broadly about the concept of amendment, arguing that judges via interpretation can effect constitutional change under certain circumstances.[1] Depending on the extent to which the entrenched law is "open-textured," it may be susceptible to significant modification over time.[2] Yet the distinction between deliberate and interpretive (i.e., "unintentional") change still has currency. Friedrich Hayek famously praised the spontaneous order by which the common

---

[1] Levinson (1995: 13–36); Ackerman (1998: 269–274).

[2] As Hart (1994: 128–36, 272–3) noted, the "open texture of law" leaves considerable scope for judicial interpretation, to the point of requiring judicial legislation; even if we regard this legislation as limited or "interstitial" – indeed, even if we dispute Hart's claim that judges must sometimes make law – that interpretation may lead to substantive changes in the law will, I hope, be granted.

law arose and endured independently of anyone's will. Whereas human agency in creating legislation would inexorably lead to the perversion of that design for evil purposes, a law produced "unintentionally" – or, in the language of the common lawyers, fined and refined through the wisdom of generations – could serve as an effective constraint on power. I shall suggest that through interpreting immutable law, judges do indeed modify it: Entrenchment, rather than restricting the possibility of amendment, shifts the locus of this change away from legislatures and toward the judiciary.[3]

Constitutional Amendment

Amendment clauses, for my purposes here, are constitutional provisions specifying the mechanism by which textual changes to a constitution may legitimately occur. There may be multiple procedures specified, with different procedures governing different clauses or delineating alternative methods for enacting change. The focus on textual changes may appear to be a reductive and perhaps simplistic way of addressing the question. Clearly, Levinson is right that there is an important difference between "a genuine change not immanent within the preexisting materials," a change that is "congruent with the immanent values of the constitutional order," and a change so at odds with the immanent order as to be "revolutionary."[4] Given the need to contrast amendment with alternative mechanisms of change, however, I hope the uniform heading will clarify rather than obfuscate the matter at hand.

---

[3] As I wrote these words, Senator Arlen Specter (R–PA) invoked the idea of "super-duper precedent" as a means of seeking to restrict the power of the Supreme Court to reverse itself on *Roe v. Wade*. Concerns that judges may engage in "legislating from the bench" reflect the increasingly widespread view that judges are capable of modifying law in fundamental ways and that this power ought to be checked rather than enhanced – however, entrenchment of abstract rights will not suffice to do so.

[4] Levinson (1995: 20–1).

It is sometimes argued that these clauses may not specify the exclusive means by which constitutional change can legitimately occur, because the alternative method of recourse to the people is always an implicit alternative. Bruce Ackerman is the best-known proponent of such a theory, arguing that Article V of the U.S. Constitution provides procedures that are "sufficient, but not necessary, for the enactment of a valid amendment"[5]: In the presence of a robust popular mandate for change, Ackerman has suggested, "revolutionary reformers" may take up the mantle of constitutional amendment through other means. Similarly, Akhil Amar has argued for the nonexclusivity of Article V, suggesting that constitutional change could occur legitimately via a mechanism reflective of popular sovereignty, such as a national referendum, because the constitution does not specify that it is the *only* means by which amendment may occur.[6] Yet the argument that constitutional provisions in general ought not to be taken to be exclusive may have disturbing implications – should we take "the executive power shall be vested in a President of the United States of America" clause to suggest that a dual kingship is a legitimate alternative? As David Dow has argued, *expressio unius est exclusio alterius* ("the expression of one thing is the exclusion of another") is a well-established statutory and constitutional principle.[7]

Yet even if we are reluctant to adopt the nonexclusivity argument, Ackerman and Amar touch upon a particularly important idea: The ability to engage in constitutional change is a fundamental act of popular sovereignty, and ought not to be alienated to judges nor subject to extraordinarily strenuous procedures. Indeed, as both Ackerman and Amar suggest and I shall argue as well in Chapter 4, the framers were abundantly aware of the importance of constitutional change (though here I suggest that the framers' defense was

[5] Ackerman (1991: 15).   [6] Amar (1995: 90).
[7] Dow (1995: 127).

primarily on the grounds of fallibility, an argument that also proved instrumentally valuable as a cloture device). My aim here is to avoid the standard dichotomy of constitutionalism versus popular sovereignty or majoritarianism and instead to retrieve other, frequently overlooked democratic defenses of legal change. However, the belief that amendment was inevitable, paradoxically, gave rise to efforts at entrenchment, and indeed it continues to do so today. American attempts to restrict the capacity to change ought not to be overlooked in our constitutional theory – if only as a cautionary tale.

Constitutional Revolution

Sweeping constitutional or regime change is not my focus here, although the concern that democracy, perhaps through its tolerance of antidemocratic forces, will harbor the forces of its own destruction has been a concern since Plato. We shall engage this argument most thoroughly in discussing the jurisprudential origins of the decision to entrench human dignity in the German Basic Law, particularly in the work of Carl Schmitt, as a claim on behalf of entrenchment. In the absence of entrenchment, it was argued, democracy would lack the stable core necessary to foreclose the possibility that authoritarianism could be imposed through democratic means – that is, a majority vote. Here, I refer to such arguments as relying on the "logic of democratic autophagy" – that is, that unfettered democracy will "consume itself."[8]

Comprehensive constitutional change also constitutes an implicit response to concerns about entrenchment. However, the rejoinder that a determined citizenry can always revoke entrenched provisions through recourse to constitutional revolution – while obviously correct – makes light of the costs entailed in recourse to constitutional conventions. This is the case even if we embrace

---

[8] Such an argument has taken many forms, most famously perhaps that of "militant democracy," as in Loewenstein (1937).

the possibilities of ongoing constitutional change. Regular recourse to constitutional conventions – to revisiting the fundamental commitments of a community, including the type of regime – would indeed crowd out the possibility of any other governmental activity. Further, although constitutional conventions should not be feared, the process of radical alteration in order to make a relatively minor adjustment to a constitution may indeed lead to instability. This instability may be desirable under certain circumstances, but, again, the loss of security of expectations could be disastrous for a society, particularly one undergoing transition. If the presence of entrenched clauses – often posited as desirable, particularly in countries undergoing transition – could induce recourse to constitutional conventions or inspire claustrophobic panic (as, we shall learn, it did in Athens), the costs of immutability could be grave.

Entrenchment

Although entrenchment as I define it here usually entails textual irrevocability, it can also take a variety of different forms. Entrenchment may be temporally limited or unlimited, formally specified, or implicitly enforced. It raises distinctive issues, as we shall see, from the typical problems associated with constitutional legitimacy, but examining entrenchment also constitutes a means of placing these questions in stark relief.

Formal, Time-Unlimited Entrenchment

This is, so to speak, the benchmark case of entrenchment. Although, as I shall demonstrate, it has existed in some form for over 2,500 years, over the past 50 years constitution makers have increasingly turned to entrenchment clauses as a means of securing fundamental norms, such as basic rights. Most Western European constitutions since the end of World War II – including those of

France, Germany, Greece, Italy, and Portugal – use entrenchment, if only to protect the form of regime (as in France and Italy), though Greece and Portugal protect extensive lists of rights and institutional arrangements. Many of the post-Soviet constitutions – including Armenia, Azerbaijan, Bosnia-Herzegovina, the Czech Republic, Romania, and Russia – feature entrenchment clauses, as do many African and Latin American constitutions. As we shall see, although democrats have regularly turned to the use of formal entrenchment as a means of checking their impulse toward change, entrenchment poses distinctive problems from those generated by ordinary constitutionalism. Further, the use of immutable laws has a long and distinctive history of criticism in political thought.[9]

As we shall see, a motif for critics of entrenchment in Anglo-American political thought is the denigration of the "laws of the Medes and the Persians." The likely source for these references is biblical, either from the Book of Daniel or the Book of Esther. The Book of Esther tells a tale in which Queen Vashti refuses to submit to the King's wish to display her nude body to his drinking companions, and the King creates an unalterable edict, in keeping with the laws of the Medes and the Persians, banishing her from the throne and asserting husbands' authority over their wives.[10] In Daniel 6:8 and 6:15, King Darius, urged on by his "presidents and

---

[9] Like most constitutional scholars, I do not insist that for a clause to be entrenched the entrenchment clause governing the law itself must also be entrenched, as formal logic might demand. Nor do I think that entrenchment clauses can obviously and legitimately be modified by "popular sovereignty"; they have binding force in constitutions and give rise to real obligations, and it is for precisely this reason that I argue against them in this work. Peter Suber (1990) offers an important and fascinating discussion of logical puzzles involving amendment and entrenchment; see also Ross (1969) and Da Silva (2004), among others, for the implications of the presence of an "immutable core" for paradoxes of amendment.

[10] This story is cited in Vile (1992: 3). Vile offers a brief (several-page) overview of the development of theories of amendment in the history of political thought.

princes," enacts a decree prohibiting petitions to God or man for 30 days, upon pain of being thrown to the lions. The presidents and princes remind him that the law of the Medes and the Persians prescribes the inalterability of his decrees or statutes. Daniel, caught praying by these men, is cast into the lion's den; the king had wished to free him, but the men again remind him of the immutability of the law. God sends an angel to shut the lion's mouth, and the king has the captors themselves (as well as their wives and children) thrown to the lions instead. The implication in this passage is that only God can create an immutable law, as the men are hoisted by their own petard: They die by the immutability of their maxims.

References to the laws of the Medes and the Persians were always critical, even when used – as by Cromwell – in a context generally defending the possibility of enacting immutable laws. As we shall see, Cromwell invoked these laws in a speech to Parliament, distinguishing the fundamental laws that ought to be unalterable from those circumstantial rules that should be changeable, and Rev. Samuel Stillman at the Massachusetts Ratifying Convention argued that the constitution ought not to be like the laws of the Medes and the Persians. Jeremy Bentham, too, referred to the Medes and the Persians in his criticism of entrenchment in the constituent assembly of the French Revolution: "The attempts made by Lycurgus, of Numa, the Medes and Persians, by the lovers of raree shows among the Athenians, and so many other pretenders to infallibility with or without inspiration, have been hitherto quoted only for the absurdity, as so many imitations of Salmoneus who, by making a noise, thought to rival Jupiter, the King of gods and men, and as so many attempts to transform finite power into infinite."[11]

---

[11] Bentham, *Necessity of an Omnipotent Legislature* (2002: 265–6); Schwartzberg (forthcoming).

Yet Bentham's discussion in "Necessity of an Omnipotent Legislature" focused on the entrenchment of the 1791 French Constitution for a limited period of time: The entire constitution was entrenched for 10 years, and after that only an Assembly of Revision could amend the constitution – and only then after three successive legislatures had approved the proposed amendment. Although we might agree with Bentham that this move on the part of the constituent assembly in essence amounted to entrenchment, there are two important features of this claim that are different from "time-unlimited" entrenchment: the 10-year sunset clause on entrenchment and its procedural rigor (which we may term "*de facto* entrenchment"). We shall take up both of these variations in turn and then turn to two more complicated issues: "implicit entrenchment" and, briefly, natural law.

Formal, Time-Limited Entrenchment

The best-known case of "sunset clause" entrenchment, entrenchment for a definite period of time, is undoubtedly the U.S. Constitution's protection of the slave trade through 1808; however, such clauses date to ancient Athens. Herodotus' tale of Solon, the great legislator of Athens, demonstrates how early in the history of democracy this struggle emerged. Before Solon gave the Athenians their laws, they had to promise not to modify them: They "bound themselves by great oaths for ten years they would live under whatever Solon would enact."[12] Despite the Athenians' promises, their inclination toward legal change was so persistent that Solon feared that if he remained in Athens the citizens would persuade him to modify the rules – and so he went abroad.

Time-limited entrenchment clauses are still used in constitutions today: For example, the entire 1992 Paraguayan Constitution was

---

[12] Herodotus (1972: 1.29).

under a sunset clause for three years. Although in some respects these clauses do not pose the challenges to democratic legitimacy that unlimited entrenchment clauses do – after all, there is a definite point in time at which the matter can be reconsidered – these clauses do raise particularly interesting and complicated questions about the logic of democratic transitions. The implicit assumption behind the use of time-limited entrenchment is, as I shall argue in Chapter 4, that something significant will change during the period of entrenchment. One possibility is that the norms will acquire such widespread legitimacy that they will not require formal entrenchment to protect them. A second is that although protection of some provision is essential for democratic consolidation, after a prescribed period of time change of these norms will no longer lead to dissolution or extreme destabilization. Third, drawing from the American use of entrenchment for the slave trade, the need for a "gag rule" may diminish over the entrenched period, perhaps through circumstantial change or the cooling of the heads involved in decision making.

De facto *Entrenchment*

A *de facto* entrenched provision is one in which the possibility of amendment is virtually impossible because of exceptionally high procedural barriers to change. For example, I take the clause protecting the equal suffrage of states in the U.S. Senate to be *de facto* entrenched. The amendment provision in Article V of the U.S. Constitution, as Chapter 4 will discuss, specifically excludes the possibility of modification to this rule without unanimous consent. I regard the chance that a state would agree to the elimination of its equal voting power in the Senate as insignificant. Although it is clearly true that such an event *could* take place, it is likewise the case that the framers of the U.S. Constitution did not take it to be a real possibility. Thus, the absence of a specific entrenchment clause, particularly given its presence in the amendment provision of the Constitution, is almost insignificant. Many unanimity rules amount to *de facto* entrenchment; however, it is worth noting that distinguishing between those that are and are not entrenched requires attention to whether a given power would need to be self-abnegating or suicidal to accept such a change, or whether the relevant agents might reasonably choose to modify the law, though it would be quite difficult. If the latter is the case, then the line between normal constitutionalism and entrenchment is blurred.

The normative arguments in this work will generally extend to strenuous forms of constitutionalism. However, as a means of moving beyond the standard questions of "constitutionalism versus popular sovereignty," I have sought to place the commitments to legal revision and to immutability in the starkest possible relief. Thus, we shall see how democracies have chosen to disable amendment, rather than merely to complicate the process of enacting such changes. By turning to the preconstitutional world, as the discussion of Athens demonstrates, we are able to retrieve precisely the nature of the democratic commitments and the choice to entrench without the preconceptions of modern-day constitutionalism.

Implicit Entrenchment

I distinguish between implicit and *de facto* entrenchment in the following way. A *de facto* entrenched provision, as I have suggested, is a law that is so procedurally difficult to change that amendment is simply unattainable. Implicit entrenchment, on the other hand, can exist even in cases in which amendment is quite easy from a procedural standpoint. Claims on behalf of implicit entrenchment may be normative or positive. The normative version may entail the argument that such a norm could not be modified if the coherence or justice of the overall constitutional order is to be maintained. The positive variation suggests that such a norm is so deeply embedded – it has such a high degree of legitimacy as a *social fact* – that change is literally unthinkable.

Normative arguments on behalf of implicit entrenchment have received pride of place in the past 20 years or so, though they date at least to the work of Lester Orfield in the 1940s. Scholars such as Walter Murphy and Stephen Macedo, seeking to defend the idea of implicit limits to constitutional change, have deployed the example of a racist amendment. Murphy, drawing on the German Basic Law, suggests that the American constitutional system of values precludes the possibility of adopting an amendment that would be an affront to human dignity.[13] Macedo argues that an amendment denying blacks a host of basic civil and political rights ought to be struck down: "Why should the Supreme Court allow that amendment to override the Constitution's basic and pervasive commitment to equality?...An 'amendment' that sought to expunge [basic structural commitments to institutionalizing a process of free and reasonable self-government] and to wipe out basic political and personal freedoms intrinsic to self-government suggests a desire to revolutionize rather than correct and amend."[14]

John Rawls likewise defended such a view, arguing that the First Amendment, as well as the rest of the Bill of Rights, "[is] entrenched

---

[13] Murphy (1980); see also Murphy (1995).

[14] Macedo (1990: 183). William Harris offers a more subtle formulation of the account of limits to constitutional change: In Harris's version of the "interpretable constitution," sovereignty is "a function of the Constitution, created by it for its own enactment and sustenance....As a Constitutional People, it is constrained to act in ways that preserve and fulfill its collective identity, the core of its character as solemnly announced now in its self-revealing text." (Harris 1993: 202) When we are operating *under* constitutional politics, "when the *machinery* of government is acting as the *agent* of the people in its sovereign capacity, the notion of limits not only makes sense; it is necessary." (Harris 1993: 193) But when the sovereign constitution maker is acting *qua* sovereign, "on a view of its whole enterprise...the notion of limits on constitutional change is inapposite." (Harris 1993: 193)

in the sense of being validated by long historical process. . . . The successful practice of its ideas and principles over two centuries place restrictions on what can now count as an amendment, whatever was true at the beginning."[15] Rawls argued that although these provisions could be amended in the sense that they could "adjust basic constitutional values to changing political and social circumstances, or . . . incorporate into the constitution a broader and more inclusive understanding of those values," or that "basic institutions" could be "adapt[ed] in order to remove weaknesses that come to light in subsequent constitutional practice," they cannot be "simply repealed and reversed. Should that happen, and it is not inconceivable that the exercise of political power might take that turn, that would be constitutional breakdown."[16]

Yet the ambiguous nature of purported implicit entrenchment may lead to graver consequences than formally entrenched provisions – in particular, the power to determine which provisions are "implicitly entrenched" in a given regime may give rise to an expansive understanding of "unconstitutional constitutional amendments." In the case of formally entrenched provisions, a constitutional court may strike down a proposed amendment in the presence of clear textual support for its illegitimacy: In other words, the presence of a textual standard provides at least some constraint on the court. A doctrine of implicit entrenchment, on the other hand, would give constitutional courts sweeping power to determine what are the essentially immutable features of a regime

[15] Rawls (1993: 239). Rawls also draws on Samuel Freeman, who suggests that entrenchment may be necessary in some nations depending upon their recent history, such as in Germany; in the American context, Freeman argues that an entrenchment clause is unnecessary because of the historical commitment to democratic rights. Yet even on Freeman's account, entrenchment clauses are supererogatory: Either they simply secure that to which all could reasonably accept, or they will inevitably fail as a means of thwarting a determined populace hell-bent on tyranny.

[16] Ibid., 238–9.

in the presence of demands for their revocation and the absence of any specific prohibition against amendment.[17]

Likewise, positive arguments that such norms are, *qua* social facts, unamendable in a given society – their legitimacy is unquestioned, and their change is literally unthinkable – have negative implications. Although few would argue that democratic societies should regard high degrees of constitutional legitimacy with suspicion, democratic decision making may depend upon a certain critical disposition with respect to constitutionalism; as we shall see, Jürgen Habermas is a proponent of this view. Widespread regard for constitutional provisions as unchangeable may indeed represent popular support for these norms; but unless the support for such norms is in some sense explicit, a positive argument may have difficulty distinguishing tacit consent from constitutional alienation. This is a particular concern if, as H. L. A. Hart argued, amendment is particularly difficult to achieve.

A Note on the Immutability of Natural Law

Given the scope and complexity of natural law theory, no sustained treatment appears of the topic in this work, though questions related to the relationship between natural and positive law will lie close to the surface of many discussions. The classical distinction between natural law and human, or positive, law is the unchangeable and eternal nature of the former and the changeable and temporal nature of the latter. Yet positive law, to have the status of law, must cohere with the principles of natural law – that is, share in practical reason and promote the common good. Citing Augustine in *On Free Choice*, Aquinas supported the idea that "temporal

---

[17] Walter Murphy approvingly discusses the *Bundesverfassungsgericht* doctrine on this matter (1995: 177).

law, although just, can be justly revised over time."[18] In Aquinas's own formulation, "The natural law is a participation in the eternal law...and so the natural law remains immutable. And the natural law has this immutability from the immutability and perfection of the divine reason that establishes human nature. But human reason is mutable and imperfect."[19] Note that although the human law *qua* law must promote the common good – that is, share in practical reason – for Aquinas, even this stringent requirement did not entail the entrenchment of a particular positive formulation of these norms. Two critical reasons why human law ought to be subject to change (again, within the bounds of natural law) are the limits of human reason and the status of human affairs as essentially in flux.

Thus, although human law is not susceptible to change in the natural law tradition strictly because it emerges from fallible legislatures, Cicero's account of natural law nevertheless suggested that a reason for adopting a defense of immutable law might be the tendencies toward legal change in a republic. In *De Republica*, Philus' defense of injustice rests in part on the constant change that the laws undergo: "[T]hey were changed a thousand times, so that our friend Manilius here, the interpreter of the law, would recognize one set of laws now concerning legacies and inheritances of women, but when he was a young man used to recognize something quite different before the passage of the Voconian Law."[20] Laelius defended the "true law" in response to Philus, suggesting that "[i]t is not permitted to abrogate any of it; it cannot totally be repealed."[21] In *De Legibus*, a discrediting feature of the laws of Livius was the fact that "in a single moment they were removed by a single word from

---

[18] Aquinas, *Treatise on Law* (2000: 63).
[19] Ibid.
[20] Cicero, *On the Commonwealth* 3.17 (1999: 64–65).
[21] Ibid., 3.33 (1999: 71).

the senate," whereas natural law "can be neither removed nor abrogated."[22] Cicero's impulse to adopt the Stoic account of natural law could, perhaps, be traced to concerns about the mutability of law in the Roman republic.

Our focus, however, shall be on the latter-day implications of natural law for the hard case in favor of entrenchment: Should transcendent norms, whether in the form of rights provisions or, for example, the German Basic Law's human dignity clause, be subject to amendment? I shall suggest that we ought not to embrace immutable positive law as a solution to the pressing problem of violations of these rights. To recognize the "core" of these norms as essentially immutable, as reflecting inherent truths about the duties of mankind, does not demand that we regard any particular positive formulation of these norms, set down at a given moment in time, as equally durable. We might wish to expand or refine our concept of who constitutes a "human being" worthy of dignity in light of moral or perhaps technological progress to include or to exclude, for example, animals or fetuses or clones or Martians. These sorts of developments are inevitable, and there is no reason to believe that the people or their legislators could not engage in morally serious deliberations on these subjects and revise the constitution based on the outcome of such considerations. But through the use of immutable law we may impede our ability to address these matters without engaging in constitutional revolution – or, perhaps more plausibly, we may find ourselves compelled to shift the decision to a constitutional court, subject to revision only through the decision of a later court. Defending revision "all the way down" to fundamental principles does not mean that we cannot take rights seriously. It

[22] Cicero, *On the Laws* 2.14 (1999: 134). Note that Cicero also related the Pythian Apollo's advice to the Athenians: The oracle told the Athenians to preserve ancestral custom, but when they replied that the customs had changed frequently, the oracle told them to preserve the best (2.40) (2000: 145).

does mean, however, that we must emphasize the possibility of a gap between the positive formulation of constitutional rights as the product of constituent assemblies and the moral commitments they ought to embody. If we preserve a vision of a constituent assembly as at its core a legislature – with the strengths and weaknesses associated with democratic decision making – the notion that fundamental constitutional norms ought to be entrenched becomes much less attractive.

Linking Democracy and Mutability

Two central questions frame the debates under consideration here: Who ought to possess the authority to modify the law, and should the scope of these changes be restricted? Although these issues have framed, perhaps disguised, struggles over political power, the way in which these arguments have unfolded illuminates some of the fundamental challenges facing democracy. In particular, debates over legal change have repeatedly raised three central issues – trustworthiness, competence, and justice – that I shall address in turn (though they are only imperfectly separable).

The ability of democracy to abide by its commitments remains as live a question today as it was in ancient Athens. Scholars of international relations, for example, regularly investigate whether democracies are capable of making their commitments credible. The power of future legislatures to undo decisions of past legislatures – and of assemblies to simply change their course – has vexed allies since ancient Athens: The risk that the assembly would decide to reverse treaty decrees placed allies in a particularly vulnerable position and induced Athens to use entrenchment. The impulse to modify laws has broad implications for the commitments that citizens can make to each other as well, and clearly the impulse toward constitutionalism more generally has emerged from the risk that an unfettered legislature could undo the rights protections, in particular, on which the durability (and justice) of democracy depends.

19

Yet although the reputed inconstancy of democracy has provoked dramatic efforts to bind legislatures, entrenchment has not succeeded in thwarting determined assemblies – nor should it, I shall suggest. There is an important difference, as Jeremy Waldron has argued, between passion-driven inconstancy and a rational decision to change course, and in viewing legislatures as driven by the former we may wrongly inhibit their ability to do the latter.

This points us toward the second matter: the competence of legislatures. The ability of the many to engage in the creation and revision of law has been denigrated since Plato; the notion that the incompetent many should have the authority to enact binding legislation, however, is not strictly the provenance of critics of democracy. Contemporary democratic defenders of judicial review often highlight the risk that the majority, left to its own devices, would be not only inconstant but unable to ensure the quality (in terms of compatibility with constitutional norms) or coherence of legislation. This argument, I suggest, reflects a long-standing dispute over whether the authority to enact legal changes is better situated with lawyers and judges than with parliaments. The struggle over legal reform in the seventeenth century largely hinged on this question: Is law that has been "fined and refined" by judges who possess artificial reason superior to law created by parliaments acting deliberately at a specific point in time? Even if we defend the wisdom of legislatures against courts, we may still argue (with utilitarians such as Jeremy Bentham and John Stuart Mill) that competence matters for the creation and abrogation of law and that committees of experts ought to draft and revise legal codes. Although, as I have already suggested, struggles for power often underlie debates over the appropriate locus of legal change, arguments on behalf of the competence of legal experts – in part, because of their supposed independence – have proven remarkably effective. Entrenchment's appeal is likely due in part to the fact that the power to enact changes is shifted toward the interpretive judgments of courts and away from the meddling hands of legislators.

Turning to the third defense, democrats might find themselves attracted to entrenchment as a means of ensuring that our laws secure just procedures and our most important substantive commitments. It may be thought that through entrenchment, fundamental democratic norms such as rights provisions can be made immune from revision. The logic is clear: In the absence of such procedural barriers, democracy might choose through democratic means to turn itself into tyranny, thus acting in an "autophagous," or self-consuming, fashion. Even when scholars do not claim that the U.S. Constitution has explicit, formal limitations to change, they often suggest that the Constitution has implicit limits to change and that such limitations ought to be recognized by the Supreme Court.[23]

Bruce Ackerman has argued that the absence of entrenchment clauses in the U.S. Constitution excludes the possibility that it could be "rights foundationalist." Indeed, because of this, he has recommended that Americans adopt the German example and "finally redeem[] the promise of the Declaration of Independence by entrenching *inalienable* rights into our Constitution."[24] Yet even a robust rights foundationalist, grounding her conception of rights on her commitment to moral realism, can embrace the morally serious activity of improving and further specifying these rights as an essential feature of our constitutional practice, instead of seeking to make unalterable one potentially imperfect formulation. The logic of rights foundationalism – that the priority of the constitution is to protect rights first, and democracy second – should not lead us to place undue confidence in a given constituent assembly's capacity

---

[23] Defenders of so-called "positivist" accounts – rejecting nontextual limits on the scope of Article V – are, as James Fleming has noted, uncomfortable bedfellows; see in particular Bruce Ackerman (1991:14–15) and Robert Bork (1990: 214–16), cited in Barber and George, ed. (2001: 99).

[24] Ackerman (1991: 321).

to frame rights in an optimal fashion, nor to exclude the capacity of the amendment process to alter rights that are found wanting.

Entrenchment reifies a particular formulation of rights that, emerging from political processes of deliberation, negotiation, and bargaining during constituent assemblies, may be normatively attractive or unattractive, adequate to their challenges or inadequate. Further, instead of inhibiting legal change altogether, entrenchment shifts the authority to alter the law away from legislatures and toward courts. That is, entrenched rights are not, in fact, immutable, because they remain subject to interpretive change by judges – and these alterations may be both substantial and themselves immutable except through subsequent decisions, given the inability to revise these norms through the amendment process. Rights foundationalists should not take comfort in granting unchecked interpretive power to judges – who may act to harm rather than enhance these rights – any more so than they embrace granting such authority to legislators.

Entrenchment may also be defended on "enabling" grounds: That is, entrenched liberal rights secure the minimum conditions of democratic decision making.[25] Even scholars such as Stephen Holmes and Cass Sunstein, who endorse highly flexible constitutions in the transitional context and who defend a collapse of the distinction between constitutional and ordinary legislation, nevertheless turn to entrenchment as a means of securing the grounds of political cooperation. In their view, "a specified list of individual rights should be made immune to revision. This list should include, first and foremost, rights that are indispensable to democratic legitimacy."[26] For these reasons, entrenchment may seem like a humane and pragmatic solution to the problems of majoritarianism. Yet the need to ensure the institutional preconditions of democracy does

[25] See, for example, Holmes and Sunstein (1995: 297).
[26] Holmes and Sunstein (1995: 297).

not require a turn toward entrenchment. To adopt Habermas' language, the co-originality of democracy and rights – that democracy and rights originate simultaneously, and that rights both enable the conditions of and are given shape through the democratic process – does not require entrenchment. Instead, Habermas emphasizes the importance of preserving the possibility of revision at every stage: from the initial choice of procedures to the outcome of political deliberations to the commitments of the individuals participating in communicative action.[27] In his words:

> The character of constitutional foundings, which often seal the success of political revolutions, deceptively suggests that norms out of time and resistant to historical change are simply 'stated.' The technical priority of the constitution to ordinary laws belongs to the systematic elucidation of the rule of law, but it only means that the content of constitutional norms is *relatively* fixed. As we shall see, every constitution is a living project that can *endure* only as an ongoing interpretation continually carried forward at all levels of the production of law.[28]

Further, Habermas embraces the possibility of "interpreting and adapting rights for current circumstances (and, to this extent, levels off the threshold between constitutional norms and ordinary law)" and argues, "this fallible continuation of the founding event...can be understood in the long run as a self-correcting learning process."[29]

We thus can take rights seriously from a variety of perspectives without resorting to entrenchment, and through embracing the capacity to revisit these choices. When we consider the potential for democracy to create just institutions, it is critical to bear in mind the circumstances under which constitution making typically occurs: transitional settings, heavily marked by power asymmetries

---

[27] Rosenfeld (1996: 812).   [28] Habermas (1996: 129).
[29] Habermas, with Rehg (2001: 774).

and distributive conflict.[30] In conceptualizing the demands of justice in democracies, regulative ideals can be tremendously valuable, yet once we move into the *realpolitik* of institutional arrangements – through discussing the virtue of entrenchment clauses or through defending particular accounts of constitutional interpretation – we must be cautious not to allow these heuristics to distort our thinking about what constitution making actually entails, lest we adopt a sanitized view of constituent assemblies. It is true that framers may appreciate the gravity of their responsibility and embark upon the process with greater moral seriousness than ordinary legislators do; it is also true that if ratification requires widespread support, framers may be induced to ensure that their provisions have broader justifiability. Yet empirical accounts of constituent assemblies clearly demonstrate the ubiquity of bargaining, logrolling, and issuing of threats. Framers have, as Jon Elster has emphasized, both institutional and individual interests in seeing their power protected, some of which may hold over from the *ancien régime*, and regularly seek to secure these interests in the construction of constitutions. Even equal constitutional rights of political participation may reflect power inequalities subject to exploitation by framers, through, for example, the protection of official languages. For instance, the list of fundamental provisions protected by entrenchment in the constitutions of Azerbaijan and Romania include official language rights: Although Azerbaijan specifically also entrenches the "free use of and development of other languages" alongside Azerbaijani, Romania does not extend such protection to Hungarian in particular, impeding the capacity of minorities to participate in the political process.

Constitution-making assemblies, far from resembling agents in an original position or ideal deliberative forum, are first and foremost legislatures, both for good and for ill. In the chapters that

---

[30] Elster (2000: 160–161); Knight (1992).

follow, I present a series of historical accounts of the ways in which legislators, while recognizing the value of a commitment to mutability on several different grounds, turned to entrenchment. What we learn, once we retreat from contemporary discussions linking entrenchment to rights foundationalism, is that immutability has a rich legacy of protecting narrow, instrumental decrees, such as treaties, and unjust laws against religious toleration and, most notoriously, slavery. Its contemporary use for rights provisions is historically anomalous, but even in these circumstances, entrenchment poses problems for democratic legitimacy, as I shall outline below.

CHAPTER 2: INNOVATION AND DEMOCRACY: LEGAL CHANGE IN ANCIENT ATHENS. The first substantive chapter of the book suggests that democracy, since ancient times, has been regarded as a regime characterized by constant legal changes. Athens prided itself on its ability to innovate in all areas, especially in the realm of law, and this trait was widely known throughout the Greek world. Indeed, a key distinction between Athens and its rival Sparta, in the fifth century, was the Spartans' conservatism with respect to law and the Athenians' tendency to modify their rules. Although the Athenian capacity to confront contingency by modifying their laws was often envied, it was also criticized both by other Greeks and by such philosophers as Aristotle, in part because the innovativeness that made Athens formidable also made it an untrustworthy ally, inclined to amend treaties and alliances.

As a result of this reputation for inconstancy, the Athenians used entrenchment clauses to make some of their decrees and laws immutable. Through analysis of a collection of entrenched laws and decrees from Athens in the fifth- and fourth-century B.C.E., I argue that entrenchment enabled the Athenians to signal their intention to uphold certain rules and therefore make their commitments more credible. In maintaining that unamendable laws, from ancient times, have been used for narrow and instrumental purposes, I highlight the uneasy relationship between the democratic commitment to innovation and the use of immutable law. Chapter 2 therefore emphasizes innovation as one democratic defense of legal change.

CHAPTER 3: LEGISLATION AND LAW REFORM IN SEVENTEENTH-CENTURY ENGLAND. Whereas in ancient Athens democracy and innovation were prized, in seventeenth-century England both concepts were disdained, and for an analogous reason. To be a "democrat," or to be an "innovator," was to be accused of believing – in the extreme of hubris – that a man guided solely by his native reason could rightfully alter existing institutions. In contrast, the common lawyers of the period sometimes argued that the common law ought not to be changed at all, but typically held that the law, as a body of customs, might undergo change through interpretation by judges guided by "artificial reason," the product of advanced legal training. Thus, as long as the legitimate scope of legal change was held to be either primarily restorative or interpretive, common lawyers could retain their authority over the deliberate change enacted by untrained parliamentarians. Yet once the ancient constitution appeared to have been sundered and legal change could be characterized as unashamedly progressive, the possibility of legal change occurring through legislative means emerged as a viable alternative. Drawing on political pamphlets, I demonstrate that the most important efforts at law reform during the Civil War and Commonwealth periods emerged as a function of "quasi-democratic" developments: one through the programs of the Levellers and a second, more sophisticated undertaking by the more radical members of the Hale Commission under the republican Rump Parliament. Chapter 3 also discusses the use of unamendable law in Cromwell's *Instrument of Government*, demonstrating yet again entrenchment's purpose as a strategic device. In conclusion, I take up three arguments distinguishing judges from lagislators – intent, interest, and expertise – to challenge the claim that constitutional change is more safely situated with judges than with legislators.

CHAPTER 4: FALLIBILITY AND FOUNDATIONS IN THE U.S. CONSTITU-TION. The framers of the U.S. Constitution deployed the language of fallibility frequently during the Federal Convention, most strikingly in the discussions over amendment. Both in abstract analyses of the nature of legal change and in debates over proposed amendments, speakers regularly referred to the imperfection of man and the inevitably defective products of his reason. This view was remarkably robust, in part because it served a variety of purposes for the actors who deployed it; in particular, it was an efficient means of bringing debate to a close. Yet the decision to secure two items against amendment – one temporarily (the slave trade through 1808), one permanently (equal representation of states in the Senate) – had nothing to do with the view that such norms were infallible.

As in Athens, entrenchment was a purely strategic device: It took the two most difficult compromises off the table prior to ratification. Was this a necessary move for the Constitution to be accepted, as some have suggested? Although this is a difficult counterfactual to assess, there is some empirical evidence to suggest that entrenchment would not have been required and that a morally regrettable outcome might have been avoidable. Yet entrenchment has enjoyed a revival of interest in American constitutional scholarship: Influenced by the German Basic Law, contemporary scholars have increasingly defended the presence of substantive limits to amendment in the U.S. Constitution, an approach I reject in this chapter.

CHAPTER 5: PROTECTING DEMOCRACY AND DIGNITY IN POSTWAR GERMANY. Again, the protection of the clause enshrining human dignity in the post–World War II German Basic Law is the best-known and most-praised example of an entrenched provision in the contemporary world. However, the origins of the decision to protect this clause are typically simply assumed to be a response to the atrocities of Nazism and the failures of Weimar. Although this is in some sense correct, it is undertheorized in many respects – and it imputes inevitability or necessity to the outcome. To challenge such an approach, Chapter 5 examines both the jurisprudential and political bases of the decision to entrench, with an eye toward demonstrating the contingent character of the decision to entrench in the face of alternatives. In particular, it focuses on the possibility of adopting Hans Kelsen's views on legal immutability, rather than Schmitt's, and the nature of the bargains that gave rise to the decision to entrench.

Chapter 5 highlights another influential formulation of the relationship between democracy and legal change: Because democratic majoritarianism should preclude limitations on the ability to change law, democracy contains within itself the seeds of its own destruction – this is what I will term "the logic of democratic autophagy." The response to this theoretical insight has been the use of immutable laws. However, the entrenchment of the human dignity clause has also shaped the distribution of political authority, as it leaves interpretation and specification exclusively in the hands of judges. Further, the consequences of protecting human dignity have not been uncontroversial, politically or morally: For example, it has enabled the German Constitutional Court to determine that "human dignity" extends to fetuses.

CHAPTER 6: CONCLUSION: DEFENDING DEMOCRACY AGAINST ENTRENCHMENT. The conclusion highlights the four ways of thinking about the relationship between democracy and legal change: from the perspective of innovation, of deliberate agency and deliberation, of fallibility, and of majoritarianism and pluralism. In Chapter 6, I suggest that entrenchment not only tends to serve a strategic purpose, but also perhaps more importantly betrays attractive democratic traits that are embodied by and reaffirmed through legal change. I then discuss the implications of these arguments for constitutionalism more generally.

A Note on Methodology

The work in the chapters that follow is partially historical and reconstructive and partially normative and prescriptive. The source materials include classical political theory texts, primary-source documents (e.g., ancient decrees, political pamphlets, transcripts of constitutional debates), and secondary historical works, as well as contemporary works in normative political and legal theory. Given the scope of the project, my accounts of these matters could hardly be exhaustive, but I have sought to draw on a wide variety of sources to reconstruct the ways in which relevant actors, at particularly salient moments for the history of democracy, sought to defend the ability to change laws and to identify laws that they wished to make irrevocable.

My treatment of foundational texts takes two forms. In some chapters, the case for using these texts is easy: I argue, for example, that Carl Schmitt's legal theory influenced the decision in the German Parliamentary Council to entrench human dignity; and to suggest how this might have occurred, I turn in part to *Legality and Legitimacy* (Schmitt, 2004). In other chapters, however, these texts serve a different purpose. In my chapter on Athenian legal change, for example, I discuss Aristotle without arguing that he actually shaped decision making in the *ekklesia*. Instead, Aristotle offers a critical appraisal of the inclination of democracies to rely on decrees, providing us with theoretical insight into the ancient view of democracy as a regime that relies on the use of particular and changeable norms.

Because my primary focus in this work is on the theoretical underpinnings of the creation of institutions regulating and restricting legal change, the choices that legislators made in designing these institutions are of primary importance. Certainly, the reconstruction of such choices must be done with great care. Here, I try to argue that the way in which legislators conceptualized their available options was shaped in part by ideas at the time about legal change and in part by their interests in ensuring that particular laws remained flexible or inflexible. Such a focus on ideas as well as interests may help us to explain some apparently paradoxical choices: for example, why the Athenians chose to retain relatively flexible laws in the fourth century B.C.E. after disastrous consequences. Though I also seek to dissuade contemporary constitutionalists from defending (or adopting) entrenchment, this normative project first requires a better understanding of the reasons why framers might seek to entrench. Hence, the bulk of the normative and prescriptive work is located toward the end of each chapter and in the conclusion. Finally, through historical and empirical research into the creation and conceptualization of flexible law, I hope to sidestep some of the standard debates over popular sovereignty and constitutional authority and to reveal new dimensions of the relationship between democracy and the rule of law.

Chapter Two

Innovation and Democracy: Legal Change in Ancient Athens

Ancient Athenians regarded the capacity to change laws and, generally, to confront contingency with new institutional solutions as a defining characteristic of their democracy. The Athenians' ability to respond to problems by modifying their laws was a source of pride and was widely known throughout the Greek world. Although the Athenians had access to a variety of institutions by which they could have made their laws inflexible, they generally chose not to do so, even in the face of disastrous consequences at the end of the fifth century. The explanation for this choice is found in the Athenian attachment to the progressive ideology of *pragmatic innovation*, the desirability of modifying institutions in light of new information or changing circumstances, a belief that proved remarkably resilient.[1]

In apparent contrast to this commitment to mutability, the Athenians occasionally used entrenchment clauses, provisions that make laws unamendable. Why would the Athenians, given their attachment to changeable law, choose to restrict themselves in

---

[1] The language of pragmatic innovation is not intended to suggest that the Athenians were forerunners of Peirce or Dewey – although some may find commonalities – but instead to affirm the specific and situational nature of Athenian decision making. In Greek, *pragmata* (plural noun) means "things," "matters," or "deeds"; in the political realm, "affairs" or "interests."

such a stringent fashion, even prescribing death for those proposing modifications? Here, I wish to suggest that the Athenians used entrenchment in highly restrictive contexts: to protect certain financial decrees and alliances and treaties.[2] Although today entrenchment clauses are typically seen in the constitutional context, where they serve to make individual rights and other fundamental institutions unamendable, the Athenians used these provisions exclusively for narrow, strategic purposes in both international and domestic contexts and did not extend them to laws regulating the democracy.

The flexibility of Athens' laws generated problems for Athenians in the international arena. Potential allies were skeptical of Athenian commitments, given Athens' propensity to change course; indeed, international-relations scholars continue to investigate the extent to which democracies are capable of credible commitments.[3] As a consequence, the Athenians required a device to signal their seriousness to prospective allies and to those who might seek to exploit informational asymmetries, such as financial officers. The use of entrenchment to enhance Athens' credibility in the eyes of potential allies, however, should be distinguished from the potential use of these devices for "precommitment" more generally.[4] The Athenians generally did not use entrenchment in this latter sense as a means of self-binding, so that a temporary passion would not overwhelm them; the single case of such an attempt, I will demonstrate, resulted in the suspension of the entrenchment clause. Entrenchment was instead used as a sign of Athens' grave

---

[2] To the best of my knowledge, the only extended treatment of the topic appears in a 1974 article by David Lewis, summarized in Rhodes with Lewis (1997). Their book also offers a catalogue of decrees of the Greek states, excluding Athens, which includes entrenchment clauses in its index. Alan Boegehold also briefly discusses the use of entrenchment clauses in "Resistance to Change in Athens," in Ober and Hedrick, ed. (1996).

[3] For example, see Gaubatz (1996); Kennan (1996); Reed (1997); Gartzke and Gleditsch (2004).

[4] See Elster (1984); Holmes (1995); Elster (2000).

intent to retain a particular policy, given its propensity to modify other laws. The need for entrenchment in the international arena seems to have persisted into the fourth century, suggesting that Athens required this additional signal despite the presence of procedural checks designed to make legal change more difficult.

The analysis here is broken up temporally, due to the importance of distinguishing between the legal systems of the fifth and fourth centuries. The account of fifth-century institutions focuses on the creation of the ideology of "pragmatic innovation" and the crucial difference between Athens and Sparta in this regard; it is followed by a discussion of the use of entrenchment in the fifth century. After a brief discussion of the revision of laws at the turn of the century, fourth-century legal institutions are addressed, paying particular attention to the philosophic conceptualization of legal change in the period, notably by Plato and Aristotle. This consideration provides the context for a discussion of entrenchment's use in the fourth century, followed by a conclusion, which highlights the distinctively democratic quality of the capacity to modify law and the limited and strategic purpose that entrenchment may serve for democracies, even in the constitutional context.

Fifth-Century Institutions and "Pragmatic Innovation"

Although we know significantly less about fifth-century institutions than those of the fourth century, the general institutional role of the bodies is reasonably well established.[5] Legislation was purely a function of the Assembly and the Council of 500. The Council deliberated on legislation prior to the Assembly and had important agenda-setting power. Although the Council could enact decrees of its own on minor matters,[6] the major legislative function of the

[5] Ostwald (1986); Hansen (1991: 27–52).
[6] Rhodes and Lewis (1997: 13).

Council, known as "probouleusis" by modern classicists, can be separated into two types: open and specific *probouleumata* (plural noun). In an open *probouleuma* (singular), the Council instructed the Assembly to debate a certain issue and, if deemed necessary by the Assembly, to pass a decree. A specific *probouleuma* was, in essence, a bill, subject to amendment, if necessary, and to ratification by the Assembly. The creation of *probouleumata* was passed by a single simple-majority decisive vote.

The 500 members were composed of 50 from each of 10 tribes, chosen by lot from those who put themselves forward within the tribe (*ho boulomenos*, or "the one who wishes"). These groups of 50 took turns serving as the prytany (*prytaneia*), the committee of the council that performed the actual function of *probouleusis*. Each day, one member of this prytany would serve as chairman (*epistates*), and a third of the prytany would remain on duty for the entire 24-hour period. From the time of Ephialtes (ca. 463/462) until early in the fourth century, the prytany and the chairman would preside at meetings of the Council and of the Assembly. Both citizens and noncitizens could apply to the prytany to bring a motion before the Council, but in general the Council was independent with respect to its decision-making process (although the *strategoi* – the generals – served as advisors, notably at the time of the Peloponnesian War).

The Assembly met at various points during the period of a given prytany, although the precise number of meetings is controversial.[7] All citizens – that is, all free, adult males satisfying the current Athenian-descent requirement – could attend the Assembly, and any *probouleuma* approved by a simple majority of the Assembly, even if it contradicted an existing provision, became a *nomos–psephisma* (law-decree), a fully valid law: The hierarchical

---

[7] Ibid.

distinction between laws and decrees, crucial to fourth-century legal history, did not exist in the fifth century, and the two terms were used synonymously.[8] Although the laws were publicly available on stone *stelai* (slabs), the *stelai* were scattered throughout the city in the fifth century, and the revision of prior law by enactment of new legislation was therefore virtually undetectable; to the extent that a procedure for resolving incoherence even existed conceptually, *lex posteriori* seems to have prevailed. Moreover, the absence of jurists was extremely important for the development and practice of law in Athens, especially in the fifth century: Law was exclusively the stuff of amateurs, and the reforms at the turn of the century were designed to remedy some of the incoherence that resulted from the lack of systemization.[9] This aversion to professionalism in law endured, however: Even in the fourth century, litigants regularly appealed to their amateurism (as in Demosthenes, 54.17).

The difficulty in ascertaining what the law actually was at a given moment was deeply problematic for litigants and for the jury courts as a whole, naturally. The absence of a police force and the reliance on private individuals for prosecution lent an additional dimension of whim to adjudication.[10] Pericles introduced pay for those serving in the jury courts (*dikasteria*), which Aristotle recognized as a democratic move inasmuch as it included those who would otherwise lose wages and would attract the impoverished more generally (Aristotle, *Constitution of the Athenians* [hereafter, *Ath. Pol.*], XXVII; *Politics*, VI, 2); members of the Assembly were not paid in the fifth century, but magistrates and Council members were. The jury courts heard *dokimasiai*, prospective reviews of one's eligibility to hold office in the polis (but not one's competence), and *euthynai*, retrospective renderings of accounts, of magistrates.

---

[8] Todd (1993: 57).
[9] Ibid., 54.
[10] Todd (1993: 79).

The flexibility of the law in the fifth century had the consequence of unpredictability, because the laws were changed so frequently that it was difficult to anticipate the consequences of actions. However, this appears to have been an unintended result of regular modifications. The public placement of *stelai* with inscribed rules would seem to have been intended to enable a person to determine whether her behavior, or the behavior of others, complied with the law and therefore to anticipate the consequences, positive or negative, of her actions. Certainly, there may have been various reasons for the display of inscriptions. Through analysis of "formulae of disclosure," statements on the inscriptions addressing the political reasons for the inscriptions, Charles Hedrick demonstrates that the erection of honorary decrees, for example, was intended to serve as an incentive for others to emulate the honorees' actions, while other *stelai*, including financial documents, included a phrase indicating that the inscription was offered "so that anyone who wishes can see it."[11] Although one might suggest that publicity could have been window dressing on the part of the Assembly, signaling publicity as it acts in a covert fashion, this explanation seems at odds both with the enormous size of the Assembly (Hansen suggests that six thousand attended on average in the fourth century, although perhaps fewer during the Peloponnesian War) and the Athenians' general ideological commitment to transparency, as demonstrated by institutions such as the *euthynai*.

The charge of *graphe paranomon*, by which a proposer of a decree could be prosecuted for a proposal deemed at odds with the legal standards of Athens – even if these principles were not always transparent – also suggests that the Athenians were not interested in instability for its own sake. Although *graphe paranomon* was frequently used as a political weapon, the Athenians nevertheless had a strong enough belief in the continuity and stability of their laws

---

[11] Hedrick (1999: 411).

over time – and a commitment to the view that their laws ought to cohere with the legal and social order as a whole[12] – to give sense to the charge of unlawful amendment. It does seems clear that the public display of inscriptions had at least the purpose of making their contents generally accessible to the population; and given the costliness of erecting *stelai*, there is little reason to suspect that the Athenians actively preferred unpredictable rules. So if the Assembly did not wish to make its laws unpredictable, then why did it feature such a simple mechanism for legal change in the fifth century?

Especially in contrast with the conservative Spartans, Athenians took great pride in their ability to confront the unexpected with modified rules and institutional novelty: innovation, in the pragmatic sense of creating novel institutions and tools to confront new challenges, was an important element of the Athenian self-conception.[13] The dichotomy between the innovative Athenians and the conservative Spartans was widely known and was a source of pride for Athens. Athens claimed to have invented virtually everything. "Even the method of sowing grain was supposed to have been passed on from Eleusis," Christian Meier writes, and he cites a late fifth-century song by Timotheus that highlights this boast: "I do not sing old songs; my own are much better. Young Zeus is in charge now; Cronos is dethroned."[14] The innovatory ways of Athens, however, were sometimes regarded as a liability: The selection of a Spartan, Eurybiades, instead of an Athenian as commander of the Greek forces at Salamis in 480 B.C.E. was due to what was

---

[12] Ostwald (1986: 135–6).

[13] Saxonhouse offers a thoughtful account of the ability to change policies as characteristic of democracy in Thucydides in *Athenian Democracy: Modern Mythmakers and Ancient Theorists* (1996), pp. 59–86, and Meier's recent narrative history of Athens from the seventh century through the end of the fifth century, *Athens: A Portrait of the City in Its Golden Age* (1993), emphasizes the importance of innovation, both institutional and technical, for the development of Athens.

[14] Meier (1993: 407, 411).

perceived as Athenian instability, which "generated anxiety if not outright distrust among their allies. . . . With a Spartan commander they could at least expect courage and decisiveness. . . ."[15]

Thucydides highlights the Athenian attachment to innovation and the democratic nature of that commitment, contrasting it with the Spartans' conservatism. The Mytilenian debate, for example, offers a look at the democratic character of the ability to change course. Although this is slightly distinct from innovation, part of what the Athenians understand as democracy, on Thucydides' reading, is the freedom to be unbound by prior decisions and, given new information, to redirect. Encouraged by Cleon, the Athenians decided to punish the revolt of Mytilene by slaughtering the entire adult male population and enslaving the women and children. However, by the following day the Athenians were struck by the cruelty of the decision, and an assembly was called to debate the motion. Cleon admonished the Athenians to remain undeterred, arguing that the greatest weakness in a democracy is "the constant change of measures" (Thucydides, 3.37.3).[16] Instead, citizens should strive, in accordance with their rejection of expertise, to stick with good laws, which they know to be wiser than intellectuals: "[B]ad laws which are never changed are better for a city than good ones that have no authority . . . ; [More-gifted fellows] are always wanting to appear wiser than the laws, and to overrule every proposition brought forward, thinking that they cannot show their wit in more important matters and by such behavior too often ruin their country" (Thucydides, 3.37.3–4).

For Cleon, decisiveness was crucial, whereas debate was both vain and ruinous; as a result, he believed that democracies are incapable of governing others (Thucydides, 3.37.1). In contrast, Diodotus argued that reopening deliberation permits was a

---

[15] Ibid., 21.

[16] Translations are from the revised Crawley edition (Thucydides 1996).

better answer to be reached, assuming that debate was not hindered by charges of corruption. On substance, Diodotus claimed that the decision ought to depend on expected future benefits, rather than on the desire for revenge for earlier deeds; as the Mytilenean democrats did not support the decision to revolt, by killing them, the Athenians would deprive themselves of potential allies. Diodotus, and the ability to change course, narrowly carried the day, and only one thousand members of the upper class were killed.

The Corinthian speech at Sparta in 432, which led to the declaration of war against Athens, similarly contrasted the competing modes of decision making, emphasizing Athenian innovation and Spartan conservatism. The Corinthians, attempting to persuade the Spartans to act against Athenian aggression, portrayed the Spartans as excessively cautious and the Athenians as foolhardy in their daring:

> The Athenians are addicted to innovation, and their designs are characterized by swiftness alike in conception and execution; you have a genius for keeping what you have got, accompanied by a total want of invention, and when forced to act you never go far enough. Again, they are adventurous beyond their power, and daring beyond their judgment, and in danger they are sanguine (Thucydides, 1.70.2–3).

The Corinthians described the Athenians as persistent and as remaining undeterred even by a series of defeats as they tried to achieve their ends. However, they were restless and desirous; as soon as they accomplished their goal, they set another before themselves. The Spartans' reluctance to act, rooted in their desire for peace and stability, placed them in jeopardy as they confronted the ingenuity of the Athenians, the Corinthians maintained:

> It is the law, as in the arts so in politics, that improvements ever prevail; and though fixed usages may be best for undisturbed communities, constant necessities of action must be accompanied by

39

the constant improvement of methods. Thus it happens that the vast experience of Athens has carried her further than you on the path of innovation (Thucydides, 1.71.3).

Conservatism was the best response to stability: The Corinthians did not praise innovation for its own sake. When circumstances remained constant, the sedentary Spartans might enjoy the predictability of their lives, marked by rigid adherence to custom. But the Athenians learned how to confront contingency with creative action. The diversity of their obstacles proved to be edifying: Progress, on the Corinthians' reading, derived from encounters with the unknown and the need to develop new tools to conquer misfortunes.

The belief in Spartan stability was both well established and enduring: One of the few good sources on Spartan institutions, Plutarch's *Life of Lycurgus*, was written in the beginning of the second century of the common era, more than five hundred years later.[17] Although, as Plutarch himself acknowledged, "There is so much uncertainty in the accounts which historians have left us of Lycurgus, the lawgiver of Sparta, that scarcely any thing is asserted by one of them which is not called into question or contradicted by the rest" (Plutarch, *Lycurgus*, 52), the legend of Lycurgus was undoubtedly known to the Athenians[18] and affected their perceptions of the Spartans. The dating of Lycurgus's creation of the

---

[17] MacDowell (1986: 14–22). Because of the time gap, Plutarch may not be the best source for the fifth- and fourth-century Athenian beliefs about the system, but his reliance on Thucydides, Xenophon, and Plato allow us to draw some inferences; moreover, MacDowell emphasizes, contra Gomme in *A Historical Commentary on Thucydides* (1945), 1.84, that his textual evidence was rather good.

[18] There are certainly problems with attempting to ascertain the knowledge of the average Athenian, but Herodotus, Thucydides, and Xenophon all visited Sparta. Given the context of the Peloponnesian War, it is reasonable to assume that the average Athenian knew something about the enemy (MacDowell, 1986: 15).

Spartan institutions is uncertain, but Thucydides places it at more than four hundred years since the end of the Peloponnesian War (Thucydides, 1.18.1). The structure of Spartan institutions is not important here, but the laws to which the Spartans, as the enemy, adhered was a matter of considerable interest to the Athenians and served as a competing conception of legislation.

Herodotus, for one, believed that Lycurgus "took care" to ensure the endurance of his laws (Herodotus, 1.65): In fact, Plutarch reported that when Lycurgus died in Crete, his Cretan friends followed his request and scattered his ashes there for fear that "if his relics should be transported to Lacedaemon, the people might pretend to be released from their oaths, and make innovations in the government" (Plutarch, *Lycurgus*, 80). Perhaps the plan worked, because the Spartans were thought to have been profoundly law-fearing (Herodotus, 7.104);[19] in Plato's *Laws* (written in the 350s and 340s, some hundred years later), the Athenian Stranger commented that one of the best laws of the Spartans was that "which does not allow any of the young to inquire which laws are finely made and which not" (Plato, *Laws,* 634d–e). Archidamus, in the debate at Sparta, maintained that their steadfastness was attributable to their training: "And we are wise, because we are educated with too little learning to despise the laws, and with too severe a self-control to disobey them" (Thucydides, 1.84.3). Whether these laws were unwritten is uncertain, but Plutarch wrote that there was even a *rhetra* against writing them down (*Lycurgus*, 63);[20] it appears safe to say that although the bulk of

---

[19] For Aristotle, the Spartan constitution's stability is owed to its status as a mixed regime (*politeia*) (*Politics*, IV, 9, 1294b13–5a1).

[20] The "Great Rhetra," as it is known, is generally accepted as an early written law. Gagarin asserts that "Sparta appears consciously to have rejected the use of written laws and to have relied on an increasing degree of control over the educational system to achieve…authority over its citizens" (Gagarin, 1986: 140).

Lycurgus's laws remained unwritten, some laws were codified, and later laws certainly were. But that the Spartans had an aversion to changing their institutions and a fear of their corruption is well documented (Aristotle, fr. 543; Plutarch, *Lycurgus*, 80), extending to a ban on foreign travel and to the expulsion of aliens for fear that foreigners might have a pernicious effect on the citizens or the laws.

Whereas the Spartans wished above all to protect their institutions from change and undue influence, the Athenians prided themselves on their ability to both revisit their decisions and to modify their institutions to fit their current needs and to innovate when necessary. Rather than remaining bound by custom or tradition, the Athenians viewed change as an affirmative good, not as a weakness; the Athenians' prior decisions were valuable only insofar as they helped them to address new problems. Yet in this context, the decision to make certain laws unamendable is surprising: Why would they inhibit their ability to modify their institutions, given the importance of this mechanism for their self-conception? One answer may be that the Athenians were well aware of the costs associated with their innovativeness, both in the domestic context and in the international arena. Thucydides suggests that although the creativity of the Athenians served them well in war making, the tendency toward inconstancy ultimately led to domestic strife. Moreover, he suggests that the Athenians were blind, perhaps willfully so, to the risks associated with their flexibility and were therefore surprised when their changes of direction led to poor consequences (as at Thucydides, 8.1.1–4).[21] However, the use of entrenchment indicates that the Athenians were conscious of the pitfalls of their commitment to flexibility, particularly with respect to their alliances. The Athenians used entrenchment clauses strategically, it appears, as an occasional corrective to their

---

[21] I am grateful to an anonymous reviewer for the APSR for drawing my attention to this point.

propensity to redirect in light of new information and to appease allies who might view Athens as untrustworthy.

Fifth-Century Entrenchment

The beginning of Athenian democracy is marked by entrenchment and apparent attempts at self-binding, though in a time-limited form: The Athenians "bound themselves by great oaths that for ten years they would live under whatever laws Solon would enact," and Solon left the country for 10 years so that he could not be persuaded to modify the laws (Herodotus, 1.29). A closer look at entrenchment clauses in the fifth century shows that entrenchment typically served a strategic purpose, an empirical finding which is at odds with our contemporary conception of entrenchment as a device designed to protect the most salient or salutary legal provisions. In addition, the liberal usage of these devices today is starkly at odds with the penalties attached for introducing a proposal in contrast to these clauses, ranging from *atimia* (loss of citizen rights) to death.

Identifying the provisions that remain flexible is somewhat simpler than categorizing the entrenched.[22] Neither honorary nor dedicatory decrees, which tended to recognize a particular good deed or set of good deeds to the city, were ever entrenched, perhaps because of a recognition that an honoree could commit an offense and deserve punishment severe enough to nullify the prior honors. Rules regulating offices were not entrenched, neither in Athens nor in other parts of the Greek world, although the actual

---

[22] The major sources for the decrees and laws are standard reference works of inscriptions in translation – Fornara's *Archaic Times to the End of the Peloponnesian War* (1983) and Harding's *From the End of the Peloponnesian War to the Battle of Ipsus* (1985) – to ensure comprehensiveness and consistency of translation (the author's Greek is not expert level). The sources were checked against Tod, vols. 1 and 2 (1946–8) and Meiggs and Lewis (1969).

case number is extremely small and therefore somewhat less reliable. The absence of entrenchment clauses attached to "constitutional provisions," however, might hint that these positions, and their duties, were among those institutions that the Athenians, at least, wished to keep flexible. Decrees relating to sacred matters were also not entrenched; whether or not they were actually changeable, however, is not clear.

The most commonly entrenched provisions are those relating to alliances and treaties, both in Athens and throughout the Greek world.[23] Non-Athenian decrees offered other forms of entrenchment: For example, an alliance between Elis and Heraea was bounded by a sunset clause, indicating that it would last for one hundred years, but additionally prescribed that "if anyone does harm to this writing, whether private citizen or official or community, to the sacred penalty [a talent of silver] shall he be liable which is here written down" (Fornara 25). The use of sunset clauses in this period is somewhat ambiguous, because all peace treaties included sunset clauses in the fifth century[24] and because the period of one hundred years is often taken by scholars to mean forever.

The explanation for the entrenchment of alliances and treaties may well be located in the belief by the Greek world that Athens could not be depended on to keep its promises. A passage from the Old Oligarch's *Constitution of the Athenians*, perhaps written toward the end of Pericles' career, illustrates the claim that democratic cities have a tendency to defect from alliances:

> Further, for oligarchic cities it is necessary to keep to alliances and oaths. If they do not abide by agreements or if injustice is done, there are the names of the few who made the agreement. But

---

[23] As Rhodes and Lewis confirm (1997: 16). They argue that the only entrenched decrees in Athens are ones of alliance and treaty, which seems incorrect given the evidence here.

[24] Ryder (1965: 5)

whatever agreements the populace makes can be repudiated by referring the blame to the one who spoke or took the vote, while the others declare they were absent or did not approve of the agreement made in the full assembly. If it seems advisable for their decisions not to be effective, they invent myriad excuses for doing what they do not want to do. And if there are any bad results from the people's plans, they charge that a few persons, working against them, ruined their plans; but if there is a good result, they take the credit for themselves (Old Oligarch, 2.17, in Xenophon, 1984).

Because assessing responsibility in oligarchies is easy – the number of agents is relatively small – the incentive to fulfill obligations is high, lest one be punished personally by pro-alliance forces or by the wronged ally. However, in large democracies like Athens, determining who was culpable was more difficult: The composition of the assembly changed constantly, and decisions were made by simple majority, allowing a substantial minority to claim that they did not support defection and that they were therefore blameless. As a result, the Old Oligarch claimed, Athens was a less reliable ally. Because a simple majority of the Council and the Assembly could revoke any decree, including those specifying relations between Athens and another state, potential allies were fearful that the Athenians might violate a treaty. Although the benefits to an ally might have made entering into a treaty worthwhile, even if the risk that the Athenians would later defect was relatively high, the Athenians may have needed to signal an intention to comply, at a minimum. This attempt at credible commitment may explain the presence of entrenchment clauses in treaty decrees.

Which treaties were entrenched? Given the problems of epigraphic evidence,[25] it is impossible to know for certain, but investigation of the extant decrees indicates that alliances with Rhegium and Leontini almost certainly were. Although modification of the law

---

[25] Finley (1975); Todd (1993: 30–44).

was not subject to a penalty, the references to the alliance lasting "forever" were intended to be taken literally and ought therefore to be counted as entrenched (Rhodes and Lewis, 1997: 524).

The decrees read as follows, as translated by Fornara:[26]

Athenian Alliance with Rhegium (433/432) (Fornara 124):

Alliance shall be made between the Athenians and the Rhegians. The oath shall be sworn by the Athen[ians so that everything will be] trustworthy and guileless and straightforward on the Athenians' part, *forever*, in relation to the Rhegians. They shall swear the following: '*As allies* we shall be *trustworthy* [and just and] *steadfast* and reliable [forever to the Rhegians and] we shall provide them with aid *if* [.] [- - -]

Athenian Alliance with Leontini (433/432) (Fornara 125):

Alliance shall be made between the Athenians and Leontinians and the oath shall be given and taken. [The oath shall be sworn] by the Atheni[ans as follows:] '*As allies we shall be* [to the Leont]inians *forever* [guileless] *and reliable.*' [The Leontinians likewise shall] *swear*: ['As allies we shall forever be to the Athenians *guileless* and reliable.]'

Why were some treaties left without entrenchment clauses? In the first place, again, as the treaties are in generally poor condition, it is difficult to determine in several cases if they do lack entrenchment clauses. However, the decree establishing a treaty between Athens and Egesta, for example, is in reasonably good

---

[26] I follow the symbol usage of the Fornara volume; [] "enclose letters or words that no longer stand in the text as it survives, but have been restored by modern scholars"; [...] "indicates by the number of dots the exact number of missing letters where no restoration is attempted"; [–] "indicates an indeterminate number of missing letters"; *vacat* "indicates that an entire line or space between entire lines were left vacant"; *lacuna* "indicates that a portion of the document is missing"; and italics "indicate that only a part of the original word is extant on the document" (Fornara, 1983, xxi–xxii).

condition (except for a lacuna) and does not have an entrenchment clause.

The decree reads as follows (Fornara 81):

> *That* it [be] sworn [by everyone shall be the] *generals' responsibility* [- -] [-14-] with *the* oath-commissioners *so that* [- -] [-11-] *This decree* and the [oath shall be inscribed on a marble stele on the] Akropolis by the Secretary of the Boule. [The Poletai are to let out the contract.] The Kolakretai *are to provide* [the money. Invitation shall be offered for] hospitality to the embassy of the E[gestaeans in the Prytaneion at the accustomed time. Euphe[mos made the motion. Let all the rest be as (resolved) by the] Boule, but in future, when [-9-} [-19-] herald shall introduce [-14-] [- - -}

If, in fact, this decree lacks an entrenchment clause (as it is commonly considered to have done), and if, in fact, the dating of the decree to 418/417 is correct, instead of an earlier alliance at 458/457 in the time of Laches,[27] why might this be? One explanation might be that the Egestaeans were extremely eager to secure Athenian support in their war with the Selinuntines and their allies, the Syracuseans (Thucydides, 6.62), and, as a result, they were comparatively weak from a bargaining perspective. The Athenians wished to conquer Sicily, "though they had also the specious design of aiding their kindred and other allies in the island" (Thucydides, 6.6.1) and therefore were willing to ally themselves, although the need was not nearly so immediate. Because the Athenians preferred to keep their alliances flexible, as the discussion of the Athenian interest in flexibility showed, they would, in general, like

---

[27] That is, as Mattingly (1996) argues against the more conservative dating of Lewis and others. Lewis, among many other classicists, is typically inclined to date decrees including a three-bar sigma as earlier, but this is one of the most controversial points in epigraphy. Given the Thucydidean context, the preponderance of the evidence (with the exception of the sigma) is in favor of the later date.

to operate without the use of entrenchment clauses. When the Athenian bargaining position was weaker – a more pressing need to reach agreement, a more powerful potential ally – and they needed the allegiance of a recalcitrant state, the entrenchment clause might serve to signal Athenian commitment. But when the advantage was overwhelmingly on the side of the Athenians, as may have been the case with the Egestaeans, they could frame the treaty as they preferred and thus could refuse to include an entrenchment clause.

Procedures regulating tribute payment by the allies to the Athenians, additionally, were entrenched and even had a penalty attached to their modification. In the case of the decree relating to the appointment of tribute collectors (423 B.C.E.) (Fornara 133), the person conspiring to invalidate the decree (or to thwart the payment of tribute) was charged with treason. The decree relating to the reassessment of the tribute of the Athenian empire (425/424 B.C.E.) (Fornara 136) prescribed the loss of citizen rights (*atimia*) and the confiscation of property for those raising a motion to nullify the decree. Given that the allies were aware of Athenian inconsistency (based both on the simple-majority decision procedure itself and the unstable composition of the assembly), it is possible that they might have hoped to evade their tribute payments either by the nullification of the decree by a later majority or by failure to enforce the decree. On this reading, the penalty provision is perhaps best read as emphatic – pay the tribute or else – but the purpose of entrenchment itself was to signal commitment to the allies.

Some financial decrees were also entrenched and even prescribed the penalty within the decree itself – with the penalty for proposing a change of the law often taking the form of the death penalty. One is the famous Athenian coinage decree (Fornara 97), which barred the use of foreign coins, weights, or measures; entrenched a section stipulating that surplus from a minting operation was to go into a special fund; and one who proposed to do otherwise was subject to the death penalty.[28] This might suggest a legislative check; given that demagogues performed the bulk of detailed financial work,[29] entrenchment here could have served to thwart efforts at siphoning from the fund. Entrenchment, then, arises in a case of informational asymmetry that may easily lead to exploitation: The demagogues have access to resources and to information that may be inaccessible to the people as a whole, and the use of entrenchment emphasizes the consequences of taking undue advantage of this position.

Another source, Kallias's second financial decree (Fornara 119), is somewhat less fraught with textual ambiguity and lends itself more readily to interpretation. The decree addressed the completion of portions of the Acropolis and specified that no other use of Athena's money was permitted and proposals to do so would be penalized, unless an immunity vote (*adeia*) was passed. Moreover, the decree said that both the need for an immunity vote and the penalty were identical to those governing the proposal of a property tax. So it appears that matters related to the collection and usage of funds were governed by a delaying procedure, indicating some general concern about risks of abuse in financial matters. The argument, common in precommitment models, that time delays permit cooling off could explain the entrenchment in these provisions, especially given the risks associated with financial matters, as the next example, relating to the case of the one thousand talents, shall demonstrate. (Note, however, that time delays may

---

[28] Traditionally, the decree has been understood as stating that those who propose to use foreign coins are liable to the death penalty. However, Lewis repeatedly argued that the death penalty instead applied to proposals against the fund (most notably, in Lewis 1997: 116–30); his reading is probably to be trusted. The dating is also controversial because of the use of the three-bar sigma, but the later dates (425/424 or before 414, instead of 450–446) seem to have found adherents recently.

[29] Hornblower (1992: 122).

permit publicity, which may have the perverse effect of heating up debate.) The use of entrenchment to regulate matters relating to property was not restricted to Athens: In Halicarnassus (Fornara 70) and Locris (Fornara 33), also, provisions relating to disputed property and to the settlement of new territory, respectively, were entrenched.

The final case of financial entrenchment is one that was actually abrogated. At the beginning of the Peloponnesian War, around 431, the Athenians enacted a decree preserving a special fund of one thousand talents from the money in the Acropolis and one hundred superior triremes, which were to be used only in case of an enemy attack by sea on Athens. The decree prescribed the death penalty for anyone who suggested, or put to a vote, a proposal to spend the money for any other purpose (Thucydides, 2.24.1). This appears to be a reasonably straightforward case of precommitment; that is, the Athenians recognized that in the heat of war they might be inclined to spend recklessly, and therefore they decided to create an emergency fund for a genuine threat on their land, with a penalty of death for those suggesting to touch it. However, not even the threat of capital punishment could dissuade the Athenians from modifying the law in a moment of crisis, and, as a consequence, the extent to which we should believe that the Athenians engaged in self-binding is in question.

After the failure of the Sicilian expedition in 413, the Athenians saw that their enemies were prepared to redouble their efforts against them and, perhaps worse, that their allies were becoming restless. When Chios, the best among the allies, revolted and it seemed clear that the other allies were likely to follow, the Athenians panicked: "In the consternation of the moment they at once canceled the penalty imposed on whoever proposed or put to the vote for using the thousand talents which they had jealousy avoided touching throughout the whole world, and voted to employ them to man a large number of ships..." (Thucydides, 8.15.1). The entrenchment of this provision could, in fact, have exacerbated their fearfulness: The lack of immediate access to the funds sharpened their hysteria. Had the money been readily available, they might have engaged in a more rational, less anxious deliberative process (if they had not already spent the talents, an admitted risk). Although the threat of revolution would in any event have elicited a highly emotional response, the feeling of being constrained, perhaps even trapped, might have heightened the response.

Given the Athenian commitment to legal change, some strong motivation must have been present for entrenchment clauses to appear. Athens wanted to be capable – and to be regarded as capable – of making binding agreements with allies. The belief that democracies were incapable of committing themselves inhibited their treaty-making ability, and so the Athenians had to send a signal to potential allies that they would not abrogate their agreements via the use of entrenchment clauses. Although Athens' allies must have known that the possibility of abrogation remained – that entrenchment was "only words," given the absence of penalties – the presence of entrenchment clauses in certain key cases suggests that they were meaningful to both Athenians and their allies as an emphasis on their intention, given the Athenian tendency toward inconstancy. The Athenians also may have feared abuse by demagogues, and entrenching the punishment enabled them to affirm the severity of the crime. Great ease of legislation could render them vulnerable by permitting the depletion of necessary resources, especially in the face of foreign threats.

Although Athenians believed that their strength derived in no small part from their ability to confront contingency with innovative solutions, their tendency to change law could have lethal consequences. The capacity to reverse course took a famously tragic form in 406 B.C.E., at the trial of the generals for the battle at Arginusae. The Athenians had amassed what remained of their resources, 10 generals and 150 ships, to rescue their fleet at Samos, which had been captured in the harbor of Mytilene. However, the rescuers, having stopped at the Arginusae islands for dinner, were met by the Peloponnesian fleet, and the Athenians were heroically victorious in the ensuing battle. Despite the victory, some ships had been lost, and so two generals and 47 ships had been left behind to collect the shipwrecked sailors, while the remaining generals and ships headed to Mytilene to rescue the fleet. A storm derailed both missions: The eight generals informed the Council and the Assembly that they had been unsuccessful, and the two generals left at Arginusae returned to Athens. The eight generals were immediately recalled to Athens for the process of *euthynai*.

A *probouleuma* was called for an immediate vote on the guilt of the generals, in violation of decrees governing due process, specifying that each accused person was to defend himself separately and that a trial before a jury court was required. Despite the presence of these laws, "the masses shouted that it was monstrous for anyone not to let the people do whatever they wanted," which was to summarily execute the generals (Xenophon, *Hellenica*, 1.7.12, trans. in Ostwald (1986: 444)). Although the Assembly was temporarily persuaded to try the generals separately, after one member raised an objection they changed their minds and executed the generals. In part, it was this tension on the part of the Athenians – on the one hand, to enact whatever they wished whenever they chose, and on the other, to restrain themselves from their worst impulses – that the revision of laws at Colonus was intended to resolve.

Revision of the Laws

The series of revisions began in 411, following the decision (under compulsion) by the Assembly to turn the democracy over to oligarchs, which Aristotle claimed was intended to win the support of Persia (Arist., *Ath. Pol.*, 29.2). Despite the pressures that the Athenians were under, it is unsurprising that they might wish to stabilize the laws, given the turbulence of the late fifth century. The reason for the choice to inscribe the centuries-old laws of Dracon and Solon, rather than drafting new laws, is less obvious, although, again, both oligarchs and democrats were in agreement that their rules constituted the ancient constitution.[30] Inasmuch as there was debate between the democrats and the oligarchs over the content of these laws, for both informational and ideological reasons it is reasonably clear that the motivation for the use of these laws was less their prescriptions than the legitimizing force that references to the "ancient constitution" provided. For the oligarchs, the ancient constitution was an explicitly conservative institution, designed to return Athens to its state before the "populism" of the late fifth century.

The 30 men[31] known as *syngrapheis*[32] were elected at least in part to draw up proposals derived from the laws of Solon – demonstrating the force of the appeal to the ancient constitution (*patrios politeia*) – which was perceived as the true form of Athenian government prior to its corruption by fifth-century legislation.[33] The proposals were presented to the Assembly, which had been gathered in Colonus, about an hour and a half outside of Athens and surrounded by armed guards. The distance from the turbulence of Athens could have served to insulate the assembly from pressure of the people as a whole or to allow secrecy; in any case, the lower classes would have been unlikely to travel this far.[34] However, the

---

[30] Hansen (1991: 162).

[31] Although Thucydides writes of only 10 syngrapheis (8.67), which Meier (1993: 557) follows, Aristotle's account of the 30 men is considered to be more reliable, as by Ostwald (1986: 369).

[32] *Syngrapheis* is derived from the verb *syngraphein*, which means "to compose in writing." Ostwald writes: "We should, therefore, expect a *syngrapheus* to collect facts and materials from various quarters and then weld them into a coherent whole in his written report, and what little we know of the activities of *syngrapheis* confirms this" (1986: 415–16).

[33] Ibid., 371.   [34] Ibid., 374; Meier (1993: 557).

presence of the guards could have served both to protect the assembly and to ensure the performance of their duties, the latter thereby constituting an implicit threat. The remote location also freed them from having to address the pragmatic concerns of an unstable city. Toward that end, perhaps, the *graphe paranomon*, the charge that one had proposed an illegal decree, was immediately suspended for the duration of the meeting at Colonus (Thucydides, 8.67.2). The rationale for the suspension was a return to the ideology of innovation or perhaps an appeal to deliberation for informational purposes – in contrast, perhaps, to the political wrangling of the late fifth century.

The Assembly ratified all of the proposals, which were generally oligarchic. They included the abolition of payment for public service, the election of archons with an appointed Council of 400, and the limitation of the franchise to five thousand citizens (Thucydides, 8.67.3). After a final proposal for the appointment of one hundred *anagrapheis* (publishers of laws) (Arist., *Ath. Pol.,* 30.1),[35] the Assembly was then dissolved. After the support of the proposals at Colonus, mercenary foreign hoplites policed the streets of Athens, and the Council of 400 needed weapons to evict the democratic Council; thus, it appears that the measures did not enjoy popular support, but whether that was either a cause or an effect, or neither, of the remote location of the meeting is unknown.

After the overthrow of the oligarchy and the return of democracy in the spring of 410, the Athenians embarked upon a comprehensive restoration of the laws, conducted by appointed *anagrapheis*. Given the latitude that this board would have in

---

[35] *Anagrapheis* is derived from *anagraphein*, or "to write up for display in public," and Ostwald suggests that their responsibility was to prepare the final texts of laws and publish them; moreover, it appears they had considerable discretion (1986: 416–18). Harrison notes that although *anagraphein* means "to publish," it does not necessarily mean "to engrave on stone" (1955: 30).

determining the content of these laws and the subsequent importance of these laws, the accountability of the *anagrapheis* was
essential, and, as a result, they were subject to the retrospective
review of *euthyna*.[36] The job of the *anagrapheis* was originally
intended to take only four months, but the project quickly expanded
from the republication of the Solonic laws still in force and Dracon's homicide law to a broader investigation of laws in force that
were perceived as part of the "ancient constitution." As a result, the
revision and the inscription of the laws on the Stoa Basileios ("the
portico of the king archon" in the Agora)[37] took until 404, when a
second oligarchic interlude took them out of force.

In 403, a final revision specified that the laws were again to be
in accordance with Solon and Dracon, but it noted that "anyone
who wishes" might suggest revisions; this may remind us of the
suspension of *graphe paranomon* prior to the meeting at Colonus.
Both the generally oligarchic Assembly in the earlier revision and
the democrats engaged in the later process feared that the institution of *graphe paranomon* quashed the ability to improve one's
institutions, although even the apparently conservative institution
of the *graphe paranomon* enabled the democracy – as embodied in
the jury courts – to reconsider the decisions that the democracy –
as embodied in the Assembly – had enacted.[38] Innovation had an
ambiguous position during this period, because the rhetoric of the
ancient constitution and the desire to preserve the laws of Solon
and Dracon were conservative in the restorative sense. However, a
call for "good suggestions" in the decree enabling the revision had
the clear purpose of introducing new institutional alternatives into
the pool of available mechanisms.

---

[36] Harrison seems to imply this is yearly (1955: 30), but Ostwald argues that the
yearly *euthyna* was suspended for *anagrapheis* and were reviewed only when
their job was finished (1986: 417).

[37] Hansen (1991: 163).   [38] Ober (1996: 119).

Two elected bodies were in charge of the revision; the Assembly had no role whatsoever in the creation of the law that was to be in force subsequently in Athens.[39] The laws were to be inscribed, and an uninscribed law had no force, as the decree cited in Andocides' *On the Mysteries*, makes clear: "A law which has not been inscribed shall not be employed by officials on any matter whatsoever" (Andocides, I.87). But after Andocides, there are no more references to the Stoa Basileios; instead, when a source for a law is cited, it is either a *stele* or a state archive. Hansen (1991: 164) writes: "The explanation is no doubt that the new revised corpus of laws did not stay unchanged for many years after 400, and corrections became so extensive that the Athenians had to give up continually republishing them on stone. The original laws were, thereafter, written on papyrus and kept in the archive; some were also copied and published on stone, but the idea of a law-code stable enough to be worth engraving in marble was abandoned."

Although the process became more complicated, the ability to change law was retained. Given the arduousness of the revision process that the Athenians had just undertaken, one might have expected that the Athenians would have permanently entrenched their inscribed laws. But they did not, and the commitment to pragmatic innovation again provides the reason.

Fourth-Century Institutions

A distinction between *nomoi* and *psephismata* shaped the fourth-century legislative process, called *nomothesia*, by which laws were both enacted and amended. Andocides reported a law separating *nomoi*, or general and time-unlimited laws, from *psephismata*, decrees that were specific and/or of limited

---

[39] Ostwald (1986: 512–13); Hansen (1991: 163).

duration: "No decree of the Council or Assembly shall prevail over a law" (Andocides, I.87). *Nomoi* were higher norms in hierarchical relation to decrees. A *psephisma* could never contradict an existing *nomos*, and in fact a *psephisma* was automatically repealed if it conflicted with a new *nomos*;[40] the proposer of a new *psephisma*, if it contradicted a *nomos*, would be subject to *graphe paranomon*.

The procedures for creating and changing *nomoi* were distinct from those governing *psephismata*. A potential *psephisma* was put forward by *probouleuma* by the Council (as seen in the fifth century), and the Assembly had the choice of altering, rejecting, or accepting the *psephisma*.[41] *Nomoi* were subject to a more cumbersome procedure, in which the Assembly had, in essence, only an originating role. Moreover, the creation of *nomoi* always took the form of amending the existing code. The modification of a given law, then, was not considered a piecemeal adjustment, but a change to the body of legislation as a whole, with an implication that even a small amendment altered in a way the nature of the corpus.

First, a proposal was made by *ho boulomenos* – that is, anyone who wished to modify the code – and the Assembly decided whether a revision might be necessary. If so, five defenders of the law, who would argue that the law was adequate as written, would be selected. The institutional bias was conservative, with a strong aversion to novelty in legislation; this is reflected both in the epigraphical evidence and in the political thought of the time. However, the conservatism was tempered by the progressiveness of the mechanism; a law mandated that one who proposed amending an existing law was required to simultaneously suggest an

---

[40] Hansen (1978: 324).

[41] Comprehensive discussions of these procedures can be found in Sealey (1982), *passim*, and in Hansen (1991: 165–77). Good primary sources include Demosthenes' *Against Timocrates* (24.21 and 24.33) and Aeschines' *Against Ctesiphon* (3.38–9).

alternative proposal (Demosthenes, 24.44).[42] Although the preference was against change, the mechanism encouraged the introduction of competing solutions.

Once accepted by the Assembly, the proposal was posted before the statues of the heroes in the Agora, publicizing the measure and allowing *ho boulomenos* to say what he wished. The Council exercised its agenda-setting power to fix the program at the Assembly, including the submission of a *probouleuma*, at which a decision to set up *nomothetai* (lawmakers), including their number and salary, was made. On the day of the hearing, the *nomothetai* were selected by lot from among the six thousand who had taken the oath of jurors for that year (the "Heliastic Oath," as it is known by classicists, in which the jurors promised to render verdicts in keeping with *nomoi* and *psephismata*, or, if none existed, with their own sense of justice).[43] The number of *nomothetai* appears to have varied with the importance of the matter: either 501, 1,001, or 1,501, at least.[44]

At a trial-like meeting chaired by a nine-person board (*proedroi* and a foreman, known as *epistates ton proedron*), the law was interrogated. The proposer spoke first, followed by the five defenders, and the *nomothetai* voted on the measure. Thus, whereas *psephismata* began with the phrase, "It was decided by the people," or "It was decided by the council and the people,"[45] *nomoi* had instead, "It was decided [resolved] by the *nomothetai*."

With the new distinction between law and decree in the fourth century came a separation of the procedures for the charges of "unconstitutionality." The *graphe paranomon* was used exclusively

---

[42] In the classical literature, this is known as the "repeal law"; see MacDowell (1975: 64); Hansen (1991: 166).

[43] MacDowell (1975: 64); Hansen (1991: 357).

[44] Hansen (1991: 168).

[45] Ibid., 167. The formulation in Harding is "Resolved by...."

for proposers of decrees, in the case that a decree contradicted a law or its enactment was procedurally invalid; the *graphe nomon me epitedeion theinai* addressed proposers of laws, in case the law violated substantive legislative principles or its enactment violated proper procedures. Both sorts of accusations could also address concerns about the broader democratic character of the law. The punishment for *graphe paranomon* for those convicted was a fine, which could lead to *atimia*, or loss of citizen-rights. The punishment for conviction of *graphe nomon me epitedeion theinai* was even more severe; in one case from Demosthenes, the penalty was death (Demosthenes, 24.138).

The rectitude and continued validity of the laws were affirmed at regular intervals by two laws, known as the "inspection law" and the "review law." The inspection law, cited by Aeschines in *Against Ctesiphon* (Aeschines, 3.38–3.40l)[46] requires that the *thesmothetai*, a board of six archons, review the law annually to determine whether there are inconsistencies, duplications, or invalid laws in force and, if so, to post them for the people, who may call *nomothetai* to rectify the situation. Under the review law, at the first Assembly meeting of the year, the entire law code was put forward for evaluation. If the people chose to reject any section, any citizen could propose a change, and the mechanism for *nomothesia*, with the appointment of *nomothetai*, operated as above. The review law, in contrast to the institution of the defenders of the law, is strikingly progressive. By opening the laws to wholesale revision on a yearly basis and piecemeal revision as needed, the Athenians reaffirmed their commitment to legal flexibility.

MacDowell (1978: 48) notes, "Presumably it was felt that the old method, by which a simple majority vote at one meeting of the Boule and one meeting of the Ekklesia was enough to abolish any

---

[46] Ibid., 166.

existing law, however fundamental, or to make a new one, however drastic, was one of the things that had made revolution easy in 404. What was needed was a more careful check on legal changes before they took effect." Although too-frequent changes were certainly destabilizing, not even Plato argued that legislation ought to remain unchanged. Given the comprehensive revision of laws that had just been completed, the Athenians might well have wished to forbid their laws to be amended. The process was turbulent, begun by oligarchs and interrupted via another coup, and the Athenians must have relished its conclusion. Nevertheless, they chose to preserve the ability to modify their laws, and the commitment to flexibility in the fourth century again derives from the concern that law ought to be able to contend with changing circumstances.

The belief that law ought to be flexible on the grounds of improvability (and overgenerality) is not simply implicit institutionally, but is addressed explicitly in the philosophical accounts of law in this period. Although Plato and Aristotle both rejected regular modifications on "legitimacy" grounds, each defended the capacity to change law, although in general Plato was far more skeptical than Aristotle about the advantages of law. Ideally, for Plato, as argued in *Statesman*, the true statesman rules without a need for law, but given the difficulty of finding such a person, the second-best option is rule by good laws in the form either of a written code or by "laws that are unwritten but embody ancestral customs" (*Statesman*, 295a, 297e). The dissatisfaction with law derives from its necessarily wide scope and its consequent inability to properly specify what is best for each member of the community (*Statesman*, 294a–b). Moreover, the unstable nature of human existence is at odds with permanent rules (*Statesman*, 294b). This does not mean, however, that the laws should keep pace with these changes, nor that anyone who wishes ought to be able to persuade the city to adopt new laws: The penalty for acts contrary to the laws or for modification of these laws ought to be death or other severe penalties (*Statesman*,

297e). The change of the laws weakens the force of the laws as a whole and as such is a step toward vice.

The Eleatic Stranger offered a scathing satire of decision making under the Athenian Assembly, in which a rule was made permitting anyone who wished to could advise the Assembly on navigation and medicine, two typical Platonic examples of spheres in which expertise is crucial. The decrees that the Assembly enacted with respect to these matters were to be inscribed, "[A]nd some of the rules so resolved are ordained as unwritten ancestral customs"(*Statesman,* 298e), perhaps a jibe at the efforts by democrats and oligarchs alike to highlight certain preferred provisions as part of the ancient constitution. Further, each year magistrates were chosen by lot to navigate and tend to the ill and were at the end of the term subject to *euthyna,* or the obligation to render accounts (*Statesman,* 299a). Young Socrates was properly horrified at the picture before him, and as a result the Stranger suggested that instead laws against inquiring into the legislator's laws and influencing people against the laws ought to be established with strict penalties.[47]

This is not to say that changes could not be introduced. However, they could only be enacted by the legislator, or by a similarly enlightened small group (because no large group was capable of acquiring any art) (*Statesman,* 300d–e). The laws were improvable, as the legislator took into account new information or "changing winds" (*Statesman,* 295d), but only the enlightened would be able to discern the correct legislative response. To rule a mass of people, then, the second-best course of action was rigid law, modifiable when necessary only by a legislator; ideally, though, flexible and specific guidance by a true statesman was the preferred solution.

---

[47] As noted above, in the discussion of Sparta, the Athenian Stranger in *Laws* praised the Spartans for the laws forbidding the young from inquiring into the relative merits of the law (Plato, *Laws,* 634d–e).

In *Laws*, the Athenian Stranger refined the argument, reiterating that the generality of legislation would leave certain gaps in the law, which the administrators of the law ought to repair, with the assistance of the original legislator, if he was alive (*Laws*, 772b–c). Experience would demonstrate where these holes existed, and the administrators would settle these matters yearly, until they were satisfied. (For matters of sacrifices and dances, the Athenian Stranger suggested that this period of experimentation – the tinkering with law to ensure a good fit – might be 10 years (*Laws* 772b–c).) After this point, the law ought to be considered immutable, but the Athenian Stranger could not entirely eliminate the possibility for change. If the "force of circumstances" was compelling enough, the administrators had to consult the officials, the citizens, and the oracles of the gods; and if the verdict was unanimous, then amendment was permitted (*Laws*, 772d). Thus, specification of the laws ought to take place and is in fact encouraged to occur by the regularity of the process, but only in the first few years. After that time, if the state of the world changes profoundly, laws may be modified, albeit by a cumbersome process, to keep up with circumstances.

In *Politics*, Aristotle emphasized his concern that laws not be changed too regularly. Weighing the advantages of small improvements over the risks of habitual modification, which may lead to disobedience, he argued that small errors should probably be left alone. The strength of the law, Aristotle argued, is in the habit of obedience supporting it; whereas a particular art, like medicine or navigation, may be improved without risks – other than a potentially harmful outcome if enacted by the unenlightened, as the Athenian Stranger claimed – regular innovation in law serves only to weaken law itself (*Politics*, II.8, 1269a12–20). As Bernard Yack (1993: 184) explains, "The acceptance of legal limitations rests more on habit than on instrumental rationality."

However, Aristotle echoed the Athenian Stranger's concerns about the generality of law, as in the famous passage on equity in *Nicomachean Ethics* (*NE*, V.10, 1137b12–23). The problem with law is that it is overly broad and therefore likely to err in its application to specific cases. This is not a default of law, nor does it imply the fallibility of the legislator, but it is rather a problem due to the disjunction between the particularity of practical matters and the universality of rules. As a result, where correction is needed for the sake of equity, a modification of the law is required, by reference to the legislator's intention, if he would have known of the particular case.[48] In *Politics*, Aristotle offered a similar point, noting that it is inadvisable to leave written laws unchanged, because whereas law is concerned with generality, "actions are concerned with particulars"(*Politics*, II.8, 1269a5).

In the fifth century, the Athenians ruled mostly by particular decrees, rather than general laws, which Aristotle described as the worst kind of democracy (*Politics*, IV.4, 1292a). Moreover, these decrees were in some cases entrenched and then abrogated, in what might be viewed as Aristotle's worst-case scenario, as in the case of the one thousand talents. Yet neither Plato nor Aristotle ruled out the modification of laws. In *Statesman*, although there was a strong preference to leave laws by an enlightened legislator untouched, modifications were ultimately permitted. Although the legal institutions of the fourth century also reflect a commitment on the part of the Athenians to stable law, by permitting modifications to occur, the Athenians reaffirmed their preference for flexibility, although in a fashion distinct from the simple-majority changes of the fifth century. This point is often neglected in favor of the "sovereignty of law" conception of the fourth century. Sealey (1986: 146–48), in particular, argues that *demokratia* meant "rule

---

[48] This nod toward intentionalism is echoed in Aristotle's *Rhetoric* at 1374b10. The distinction between changes made by judges and legislative amendment is certainly contested, as we shall see in Chapter 3. Judicial lawmaking is in this context read as amendment.

of law," rather than "popular sovereignty."[49] Yet as Josiah Ober argues, the concept of sovereignty is anachronistic in the ancient world and in any case ought not to be viewed simply as the institutional locus of legal power. Instead, Ober (1996: 121) argues, "[T]he concept of sovereignty can usefully be applied to democracy only by replacing the idea of 'sovereignty as located in institutions' with 'sovereignty as the ability to change institutions.'" Drawing on Ober's insight, the logic of pragmatic innovation is able to provide a foundation for democratic agency as directed toward the modification of laws in light of new technical knowledge or circumstantial change. The Greek world's relationship to Athens in the fourth century, as demonstrated in the use of entrenchment, reflected both the institutional changes in Athens and its enduring commitment to mutable law.

Entrenchment in the Fourth Century

As in the fifth century, the epigraphic record is somewhat spotty, and it is therefore difficult to make general claims as a result: Whereas there are 488 extant *psephismata* – although many are so fragmented as to make interpretation difficult – there are only eight *nomoi*. This is likely in part due to the infrequent publication of laws on stone, but Hansen (1991: 176) argues that the creation of *nomoi* was substantially less common.[50] This does not make analysis impossible, but it does suggest that great care is needed

---

[49] Josiah Ober points out this "constitutional law trap" into which those seeking an exterior rule of law in Athens tend to fall (1989: 22). The argument here is not designed to capture the understanding of law on the part of the Athenians in the fourth century, but only to point out that the institutions of the Athenians in the fourth century and the criticisms offered of legal institutions by elites may have permitted more flexibility than is ordinarily believed.

[50] The bulk of the evidence provided in Harding is overwhelmingly in the form of decrees, and the general claims derived from decrees are more reliable.

in drawing conclusions. This is not solely a problem of nonspecialists; classicists tend to assume that fourth-century provisions included entrenchment clauses while citing very few cases in which they actually appear and identify only one entrenched *nomos* at most.[51]

Alliances continued to be entrenched, in general, until the middle of the fourth century, and the cases in which they do not appear to be entrenched were decrees that are in generally poor condition (e.g., Harding 43) and thus inconclusive. Again, this is a somewhat weaker form of entrenchment, a "for all time" clause, analogous to the "forever" provision seen in the fifth century. But classicists tend to take seriously both "forever" requirements and specifications that the alliance should endure for a particular period; given this, the inclusion of decrees specifying that alliances ought to endure "for all time" should count as entrenched. The fact that alliances continued to be entrenched is likely attributable to the perception that because alliances were still made by the Assembly and Council, the ability for them to commit themselves continued to be rather shaky. The most famous case of entrenchment in a fourth-century alliance is certainly that of the Second Athenian Confederacy (Harding 35), which enabled Athens to become leader of the Greeks. The decree provided a penalty for one who proposed a contrary decree in the form of *atimia* (loss of civil rights), loss of property, death, and burial neither in Athens nor in allied lands. The remarkably severe form of entrenchment provided in this decree may emphasize the extent to which Athens was perceived as likely to deviate.

As in the fifth century, honorary decrees remained unentrenched, but the fourth century does offer a non-Athenian case, from Iasos, of an entrenched honor (Harding 114). Gorgos and Minnion,

---

[51] Lewis (1974: 88); Hansen (1991: 165).

sons of Theodotus, apparently did good deeds for the city, not the least of which was the recovery of an inland lake, and they were rewarded with an exemption from taxation and the front seat at public festivals for all time. The presence of such an entrenched honor suggests that the decision to leave honors without entrenchment clauses in Athens was intentional. By leaving honors flexible, it recognized that the recipient of an honor might later injure the city, and the honors should provide a special recognition at a given time (often in the form of a golden crown).

Laws, in general, do not appear to have been entrenched. A particular good example of this phenomenon was a law specifying the procedures for silver coinage (Harding 45), roughly analogous to the coinage decree in the fifth century. Unlike the fifth-century coinage decree, which was entrenched, the coinage law was flexible. Note also that it was elevated to the status of a *nomos* and was therefore not subject to the potential abuses of the Assembly. Additionally, the law provided, in accordance with the notion of *nomoi* as hierarchically superior to *psephismata*: "If there is any decree that has been inscribed anywhere on a stele [that is] contrary to this law, let it be destroyed by the secretary of the *Boule*" (Harding 45). Even Eukrates' law against tyranny of 337/336, which held that revolutionaries against the people could be murdered with impunity and prescribed disenfranchisement (*atimia*) for magistrates who deliberated during a tyranny – perhaps thereby lending legitimacy to the tyrants – refrained from entrenching the democracy.

It may be argued that Demosthenes, in *Against Aristocrates*, offered evidence of an entrenched law, because it prescribed *atimia* for modification of an aforementioned homicide statute.[52] However, Lewis (1974: 88) notes that this is actually Drakon's homicide law (cited differently, and incompletely, in the Fornara volume) and

---

[52] Hansen (1991: 165).

as such perhaps ought not properly to be considered within the scope of fourth-century legislation, per se. Moreover, Demosthenes was extremely supportive of unamendable law: Note, for example, Demosthenes' praise for the Locrians, who heard arguments for changes of law with a noose around the proposer's neck (which was tightened if the proposal was defeated), and who thus only changed one law in two hundred years, is another indicator of his tendency to reject modification (Demosthenes, 24.139–43).[53]

Despite the sparseness of the evidence, what can we make of the possibility that laws in the fourth century did not include entrenchment clauses and, moreover, that only a single category of decrees – alliances – tended to use them? The comparatively deliberate procedure of the fourth century might well lend itself to a diminished usage of these provisions, at least for domestic matters. After all, the procedure for enactment of legislation, and for its revision, was lengthy and cumbersome, as shown above. Moreover, the enactment of *nomoi* was a relatively infrequent act. As such, if entrenchment clauses once served to flag provisions that were especially crucial, in the context of a single, simple-majority procedure covering all legislation, the need for this sort of identification could be replaced by the use of *nomoi*. The need for a cooling-off process, similarly, was diminished when a slower law-making process was developed, as was any possible desire for precommitment. Externally, though, the Athenians were still perceived as untrustworthy democrats, and as such the entrenchment clause continued to serve as a means by which they could signal their commitment to potential allies.

Although the legislative procedure became more complicated in the fourth century, it is essential to keep in mind the enduring

---

[53] For example, as seen above, Hansen argues that Demosthenes wrongly characterized the propensity of the Athenians to enact *nomoi* and marvels at scholars' willingness to "put uncritical trust" in Demosthenes (1991: 176).

commitment to flexibility, which could easily have been jettisoned after the disasters of the late fifth century and the subsequent revision of the laws. The reason why they did not may be found in the enduring Athenian commitment to pragmatic innovation. In the cases in which entrenchment appears, it likely derived from the concern that the Athenian tendency to adjust its institutions in light of new information may leave both Athens and its allies vulnerable.

Conclusion

The Greeks, we have seen, both envied and feared the Athenian ability to innovate. Although, as Thucydides suggests, this quality enabled Athens to succeed in the military arena, it nevertheless undermined Athens' ability to create alliances with other city-states and ensure that its choices could be sustained in even the short term. Yet by the time of the revision at Colonus, the Athenians were well aware of the pernicious potential of flexible law and nevertheless decided to reaffirm the use of mutable law, if with some procedural checks. Here, I have offered an account of Athens as motivated by the ideology of pragmatic innovation, which may have initially appeared to contradict my findings from an analysis of entrenched decrees in fifth- and fourth-century Athens. However, I have suggested that the effort at entrenchment should not be viewed generally as an attempt at precommitment, but as a check on a body with the potential to exploit informational asymmetries and the fifth-century demagogues and as a sign of seriousness to prospective allies who had little confidence that Athens would be faithful.

The ideology of pragmatic innovation, the promise of ongoing learning, and the challenge to an account of precommitment constitutes the first set of arguments in defense of legal change. Two key insights about democracy emerge from the foregoing reflections upon Athens. The first is the fact that although at least some institutional commitments are certainly necessary for democratic agency, the ability to modify any institutions has long been viewed as the prerogative and as even a defining characteristic of democracy. Because this capacity leaves prospective allies nervous, however, democracies may occasionally have recourse to hyperconstraining devices, such as entrenchment, to signal that they at least intend to take seriously a particular commitment. Yet the faith that allies ought to have in a democracy that views change as fundamental is, of course, limited, and as a result a prospective ally's decision to embark on a particular alliance may be decided on grounds other than trustworthiness, such as the relative power of the partner.

The concern that Athens would amend ostensibly entrenched clauses was not restricted to prospective allies: The Athenians understood that the law would be unable to restrain a determined *demos*. The Athenians' prescription of death, in certain cases, for proposing an entrenched law's amendment suggests that they knew well that an effort to change the law might succeed, so that an additional, individualized barrier to modification was necessary. Yet even this constraint could be overcome, as the discussion of the thousand talents suggests, in light of changed circumstances. As a consequence, Athens could not have reasonably anticipated that entrenchment would prove an infallible barrier to efforts at change; in fact, they could not have believed that any such barrier could possibly exist. Entrenchment constituted a concerted effort on the part of the Athenians to signal both to themselves and to others the importance of a particular norm or treaty, but it could not credibly have been regarded as an effective means of self-binding.

The Athenians drew on the ideology of pragmatic innovation each time they enacted legislation, creating law without appeal to constitutionalism or revelation, and their prior decisions had little normative weight over their current judgments. Improvability and novelty, especially with respect to institutions, exemplified the

69

democratic character of Athens, and the belief that democrats were innovators endured. We shall return to this insight, and the epistemic promise that such an attitude suggests, in the conclusion of this book. Yet at a time, centuries later, when both democracy and innovation were viewed as suspect, the argument that democrats sought to destroy the "body of the laws" through their reforms emerged as a weapon against those who sought legal change, notably the Levellers of seventeenth-century England. The efforts at law reform during the Commonwealth period, against the backdrop of an ideology of ancient constitutionalism, highlight another dimension of the relationship between democracy and legal change: the distinctions between customary change relying on interpretation and the legal reforms attempted by deliberative assemblies.

Chapter Three

Legislation and Law Reform in
Seventeenth-Century England

In ancient Athens, as we have seen, legal change and innovation more generally were considered democratic traits. Yet despite the pride that the Athenians took in their capacity to confront contingency through legislative means, they occasionally had recourse to immutability, primarily as a means of reassuring anxious allies. The link between democracy and legal change through an ongoing process of legislation coexisted with an awareness of the costs associated with flexible law: The Athenians were neither naïve nor irrational in their decision to preserve a deliberate and deliberative mechanism of changing law in the fourth century. In fact, the commitment to legal change proved to be one of Athens' enduring legacies. In particular, James Harrington highlighted the Athenian activity of enacting and modifying law, conducted in the assembly via *chirotonia* (counting of hands), as a fundamental act of popular government.[1] In Harrington's words: "The legislative assembly or representative of the people, called the *nomothetae*, upon occasion of repealing an old law and enacting a new one, gave the *chirotonia* of the people."[2] Harrington, as Pocock has shown, used this claim to

[1] Harrington, *Prerogative of Popular Government* II.3 (1977: 94, 517–518); Pocock (1975: 397–398).
[2] Harrington (1977: 517).

demonstrate the civil nature of the choice of clergy and that, "[T]he primitive ecclesiae had been assemblies of citizens in the Athenian sense of the noun *ekklesia*."[3] Although Harrington's focus was on election rather than legal change *per se*, the distinctively legislative function of the Athenian assembly nevertheless constituted fertile ground for the development of republican thought.

To be sure, Athens was not widely embraced, not even by Harrington, who in the Preliminaries to *Oceana* identified the "ruin of it" as the "church or assembly of the people resolving and too often debating."[4] Democracy and innovation were both terms of abuse in seventeenth-century England, because both suggested a patricidal hubris in the belief in the ability of human reason to improve upon the past. As such, the question of who possessed the power to interpret – and thereby change – the law was disputed. Although few Englishmen believed that their common law and fundamental institutions had existed in the same, unaltered state from time immemorial – that is, prior to the Norman Conquest – nevertheless the rhetoric of an immutable ancient constitution served as a key political weapon.

As J. G. A. Pocock and many scholars since have noted, although the English characterized the ancient constitution as an unalterable body of law, they simultaneously regarded the constitution as a body of customary law undergoing constant and imperceptible change through interpretation and adaptation by trained judges and secondarily through parliamentary means via statute. Yet they did not regard statutes as either positive legislation or a mechanism for legal change, except in this customary sense of "fining and refining": Parliament could only address ambiguities in the fabric of the ancient constitution, and any efforts to enact legislation would be engaging in impermissible and doomed efforts at innovation. To

---

[3] Pocock (1975: 397).   [4] Harrington (1977: 177).

create or to modify laws through deliberate acts would be destructive and even anarchic.

As this chapter will demonstrate, only after the two houses of Parliament and the king had gone to war, accusing each other of seeking to alter the ancient constitution, did the concept of deliberate legal change slowly emerge, and with it the rise of a democratic and republican movement. The protodemocratic Leveller movement led the first major effort, which, though occasionally lapsing into restorative language, nevertheless called for reforms that could not be intelligibly viewed as part of the ancient constitution. Legal reform remained at the forefront throughout Commonwealth period, through the efforts of the Rump Parliament's Hale Commission, and of the law reform committee of "Barebone's Parliament." Although lawyers sat on these committees, particularly on the Hale Commission, lawyers also attempted to block change at key moments, resisting the encroachments of parliamentary agency in what had traditionally been their sphere of political influence. Moreover, as we shall see, the turn from Commonwealth to Protectorate was accompanied by a corresponding change in the logic of legal change, the power of which was exercisable by Parliament only within constitutional limits prescribed by the Protector. As the Protectorate waned, the language of ancient constitutionalism reemerged.

Despite the fact that throughout this period democracy remained a term of derision, the status of legal change in England in the mid-seventeenth century remains of significance for the discussion here for two primary reasons. As the historical account I have sketched very briefly already, and detail below, suggests, the view of law as changeable through deliberate, legislative means emerged in tandem with the rise of democratic movements and took its fullest expression in the deliberative bodies of the Commonwealth. Note that this is not tautological. The understanding of legal change as intentional (i.e., as not simply adaptive/interpretive) could have emerged earlier; there was little reason that statutory change could not have been conceptualized as deliberate change under the monarchy,[5] were it not for struggles over political authority in the first half of the century that encouraged opponents to charge each other with subverting the laws of the realm. In addition, although it is unsurprising that the calls for a return to ancient constitutionalism accompanied the move toward restoration, the need to do so suggests that both republicans and their opponents recognized that a key feature of the republican parliaments of the Interregnum was the effort at deliberate legal reform by laymen.

Second, at important moments common lawyers sought to preserve their dominance over legitimate legal change through appeals both to immutability and to the capacity of judges to discern the bounds of the law through artificial reason. The parallels between the efforts of the common lawyers and the power of judges today to determine the scope of legitimate constitutional change are striking. Because even immutable laws require ongoing interpretation – a mechanism, as I have suggested, of legal change – the power to interpret the "ancient constitution," or to determine the content of entrenched constitutional provisions, is the power to modify the law. Here, as in later cases, the move toward immutability is not one of restrictions on legal change per se; rather, entrenchment constitutes a shift of the locus of legitimate legal change away from parliaments to judges. As we shall see, the concept of ancient constitutionalism – of an "immutable" yet constantly changing body of laws – had political force precisely for this reason: The struggle to defend the ancient constitution was in fact a battle to define its contours and thereby to determine what constituted legitimate change.

---

[5] Shapiro (1980: 333) also makes this point.

Ancient Constitutionalism and the Nature
of Customary Change

The rhetoric of ancient constitutionalism included as a key claim that the common law had originated in time immemorial – that is, without a known origin – and had remained substantially unaltered. Although it is true that this claim coexisted – paradoxically, to use the language of Pocock (1987) – with the belief that the common law, as custom, was subject to ongoing and imperceptible modifications over time, the argument that the common law had not been, and could not be, altered retained considerable force and served a variety of political ends. The story of the development of a "common-law mind" and the doctrine of ancient constitutionalism is both fascinating and complicated. Here, I can only highlight a few elements of the way in which the debate over the unchangeableness of the common law and the power to interpret – and thereby change – the common law manifested itself during the period leading up to the Civil War.[6]

The classic defense of the inalterability of the common law is Sir John Fortescue's *De Laudibus Legum Angliae* (*In Praise of the Laws of England*). In this work, the Chancellor (Fortescue himself), instructed the Prince (Edward, son of Henry VI) as to the best conception of English law and government, holding that the customs of the realm had remained unaltered since the ancient Britons. The Chancellor demonstrated for the Prince the difference

---

[6] J. G. A. Pocock offered the classic statement of ancient constitutionalism in his classic work, *The Ancient Constitution and the Feudal Law* (1987), to which all subsequent analyses are indebted. Pocock's work has generated a vast literature of revisionists and defenders. In addition to Pocock, the discussion of ancient constitutionalism that follows in this section is greatly indebted to Johann Sommerville's *Politics and Ideology in England 1603–1640* (1986: 86–111); Glenn Burgess's *The Politics of the Ancient Constitution* (1992: 3–105); Janelle Greenberg's *The Radical Face of the Ancient Constitution* (2001); and Corinne Weston's "England: Ancient Constitution and Common Law," in *The Cambridge History of Political Thought 1450–1700*, ed. J. H. Burns, with Mark Goldie (1996: 374–411).

between royal rule, in which a monarch could change the law at whim, and the constitutional monarchy of England, in which the consent of the realm was necessary for modifications. The absence of changes affirmed the goodness of the law, the Chancellor emphasized: Not even the Romans sought to modify these ancient laws, judging the customs of England as the best possible. Their goodness did not derive from their age; rather, their antiquity simply reflected their superiority and the absence of any reason to modify them in light of their extraordinary justice.[7] Fortescue, therefore, linked arguments about the immemoriality of the law to its quality and drew on these theoretical and historical arguments to suggest that the king was limited in his capacity to legislate.

Sir Edward Coke drew on Fortescue's claim that the common law was unknowably old and therefore exceptionally good – and ought not to be changed – for antiabsolutist ends.[8] Though Coke concurred with Fortescue that the fact that the law had not been changed was indicative of its goodness and rationality, he also appealed to the compatibility of the common law with the natural law as additional evidence: The common law was founded on God's law. Although one may hold that Coke was idiosyncratic, no less a theorist of customary change than John Selden acknowledged a "meerely immutable part of nature" at the base of English law.[9] As Johann Sommerville has demonstrated, because all human laws had to conform to natural law, common law's goodness was in part its godliness, and therefore theorists who disagreed both on the origins and the evolution of the common law could concur that its core – whatever that was – was immutable.

The boundaries of the common law, the custom of the realm, were indefinite, and by definition the only way in which they could

---

[7] Fortescue (1997: 26–27).
[8] Sommerville (1986: 88, 92); Tuck (1979: 83–84).
[9] Selden, *Opera*, III, cols. 189, quoted in Tuck (1979: 84).

be clarified was through the interpretive judgments of lawyers. As commentators since Pocock have regularly noted, Coke argued that customary law was constantly undergoing a process of "fining and refining" through interpretation, and its goodness in part derived from the fact that it had been worked through by generations of legal minds. The argument that the common law ought not to be subject to deliberate alteration served as a key element in Coke's opposition to the King's prerogative.

> [F]or of all laws (I speak of human) [the common laws of England] are the most equal and most certain, of greatest antiquity and least delay, and most beneficial and easy to be observed.... If the ancient laws of this noble island had not excelled all others, it could not be, that some of the several conquerors and governors thereof, that is to say, the Romans, Saxons, Danes or Normans, and especially the Romans, who (as they justly may) do boast of their civil laws, would (as every of them might) have altered or changed the same.[10]

Judges were not bound by *stare decisis*; instead, they sought to "recognize distant relationships and subtle coherences in the law's fabric" to determine the implicit rules underlying the common law.[11] The faculty by which they did so was "artificial reason," the technique of drawing on evidence from cases and other legal documents, using logic to draw connections while engaging their moral judgment. Coke offered the classic presentation of the doctrine of artificial reason in *Calvin's Case*: "For reason is the life of the law, nay the common law itselfe is nothing but reason, which is to be understood of an artificiall perfection of reason, gotten by long study, observation, and experience, and not of every man's naturall reason." Customary change, then, was to occur through the process of ongoing specification by trained judges and lawyers: "[T]he lawes have beene by the wisdom of the most excellent men,

---

[10] Reports, preface to vol. 2.   [11] Gray (1992: 157–64).

in many successions of ages, by long and continual experience (the triall of right and truth) fined and refined, which no one man (beeing of so short a time) albeit hee had in his head the wisedome of all the men in the world, in any one age could never have effected or attained unto."[12]

The doctrine of artificial reason – the expertise possessed by common lawyers – was invoked against those who would seek to interpret or change the law. Because of his lack of this training, the king was unqualified to interpret the law: In his 12th report, Coke wrote of how he had said just this to James I, praising his natural gifts, but suggesting that only those possessing the artificial reason that came through prolonged study ought to embark upon this effort.[13] (He lost his judicial post in 1616, in no small part as a consequence of this slight.) Yet Coke also fretted about the ability of parliaments to enact the law: They "ought to have a care when they drafted measures that altered the common law because such statutes could wreak havoc" – for example, the statute *De Donis*, which harmed English land law.[14]

The concept of artificial reason – the defense of the exclusive power of trained legal minds to discern the common law – would also shape considerations of the relative power of judges and Parliament to interpret or change the law. Sir John Davies held that the common law could not be modified by Parliament and that customary laws were superior to statutory laws on epistemological grounds. Davies defended the goodness of the common law on the grounds that, as custom, it had not emerged from the deliberate will of a sovereign – that is, statutes, lacking the goodness that would result from a process of gradual customary development (made

---

[12] La Sept Part Des Reports Sr. Edw. Coke Chiualer, Chief Justice del Common Banke, Anno 1608.
[13] Twelfth Report; Sommerville (1986: 93).
[14] Greenberg (2001: 33).

without a prior determination of whether it was "fit and agreeable to the nature and disposition of the people") would always be inferior to the common law. "[When Parliaments] have altered or changed any fundamentall points of the Common Law, those alterations have been found by experience to be so inconvenient for the commonwealth, as that the common law hath in effect been restored again, in the same points, by other acts of parliament in succeeding ages."[15] Yet the question of whether the judges or Parliament was the supreme authority in determining the content of the common law was, and remains, an open question.[16] Coke, in Bonham's Case, held that judges were able to invalidate a statute that they determined to be contrary to the common law when the statute was "against common right or reason, or repugnant, or impossible to be performed." As Sommerville has suggested, though, the latitude this gave judges alarmed James I, who feared that the judges "may easily make of the law shipmens hose" and interfere with the capacity of the king-in-parliament, as well as parliamentarians, who worried that the royal influence on the judges would be excessive. In Edward Alford's words to the Parliament of 1621, "[I]t is dangerous that the judges, a fewe persons, dependant and timorous some of them, should judge betweene the king and the state of their liberties.... If this should be suffered, what will become of us?"[17]

Though the extent to which Parliament was viewed as sovereign in matters of interpretation remains controversial, it now seems clear, against Charles H. McIlwain, that Parliament was acknowledged to legislate, if exclusively within the boundaries of the common law.[18] Indeed, Thomas Hedley, speaking to the House of Commons in 1610, recognized the potential of the Parliament to enact

---

[15] Davies, *Le Primer Report des Cases et Matters en Ley Resolues et Adiudges en les Courts del Roy en Ireland*, in Wootton, 1986: 131–32.

[16] Gray (1992: 190); Sommerville (1986: 96–97).

[17] Sommerville (1986: 97).   [18] McIlwain (1910); Gray (1992: 182).

statutes that would amend the body of the law: It could not eliminate the constitution itself, although it could enact statutory changes that could improve upon the law in narrow, specific ways. In Hedley's words, "The parliament may find some defects in the common law and amend them (for what is perfect under the sun) yet the wisest parliament that ever was could never have made such an excellent law as the common law is. But that the parliament may abrogate the whole law, I deny, for that were includedly to take away the power of parliament itself, which power it hath by the common law."[19] Some common lawyers were willing to offer a great deal of latitude to the legislative power of Parliament – Selden famously argued that Parliament, if it chose to, could make a law that anyone getting out of bed prior to 9 A.M. could be put to death.[20] But that the purpose of statute was generally viewed as a means of giving the common law shape through specification and clarification also seems clear. Moreover, because Parliament, particularly the lower house, included a fair number of common lawyers who were highly influential, the quality of statutory law could not have hinged wholly on the competence of parliamentarians.[21] The argument for the superiority of custom to statute, then, was epistemic insofar as it prioritized the wisdom of generations over the enactments of a Parliament at an identifiable point in time, but it was also deeply political.

The political nature of the debate over the capacity to interpret the common law – which had become a struggle over the capacity to change the law – manifested itself in the belief that the authority to interpret the common law was viewed as a real power worth fighting over. Whereas judges sought interpretive authority over common law and to ensure that the statutes created by Parliament

---

[19] Quoted in Pocock (1987: 270–71).
[20] Burgess (1992: 23); Sommerville (1986: 99).
[21] Greenberg (2001: 18).

cohered with common law, parliamentarians feared that this would give the judges excessive power to interpret – and thereby change – the law. (Moreover, because the king appointed judges, they were considered to be excessively subject to royal influence and therefore unlikely to be good guardians of the liberties of the subject.)[22] It is clear that neither the king, nor Parliament, nor the common lawyers as a whole accepted that the common law had truly existed unchanged from time immemorial. Yet invoking the ancient constitution of the realm retained rhetorical force. If no one actually believed that the ancient constitution was in fact immune from change – if everyone tacitly acknowledged that as customary law it was undergoing constant modification – why was the charge of altering the ancient liberties of the realm taken seriously? Some have suggested that the opposing sides sought to play on the popular antipathy toward innovation. Charles Gray has argued that "any traditional society," in which change occurs slowly, will revere the past and hold that "innovation and '*ex nihilo*' legislation should be avoided." England, Gray holds, was unique in the extent to which its legal system embodied this perspective and placed "formal legal obstacles in the way of innovation – simply by requiring communal consent to it through Parliament."[23] Similarly, Sommerville has proposed that the ideological assumption that "innovation is evil" was held by almost everyone – but he also notes: "Englishmen were far from united on what constituted innovation, since they held radically divergent ideas on the past and present constitution of the realm."[24] That innovation was a "political malignancy" was widely argued, certainly, but was this belief sincere?

The idea that innovations had occurred – and that they might not be altogether destructive – was also in the air. Sir Francis Bacon, a supporter of law reform in his own right, concurred that change was

---

[22] Sommerville (1986: 96–97). [23] Gray (1992: 186).
[24] Sommerville (1986: 107).

endemic to customary law and regarded the effects of these changes to customary law as no more – and no less – vicious than other sorts of "innovations."[25] For Bacon, innovation was inevitable: The passage of time would demand that institutions be modified to keep apace. "Surely every *Medicine* is an *Innovation*; And he that will not apply New Remedies, must expect New Evils: For Time is the greatest *Innovatour*." An attractive feature of custom, for Bacon, was its flexibility in this regard: Even when it fell short, "at least it is fit" – at least it suited the society to which it applied and cohered with other customs. Were one to hold customary law as unchanging, then, disruptions would surely follow. Indeed, "a Frorward Retention of Custome, is as turbulent a Thing, as an *Innovation*."[26]

Bacon did not shy away from using the language of innovation, which suggests that there were resources available for a critical perspective on immutability and a positive account of innovation from within common-law reasoning. Bacon's deployment of the term in this context, a tweak at those who would deny the existence of change, suggests that actors knew well that all change – whatever the source – was essentially innovatory and that the aversion to the concept of legal change was almost disingenuous. Because Bacon took up the matter as a subject worthy of political theorizing, he must have sought to counter a set of beliefs; otherwise, he would not have attempted to speak seriously about the concept using the vilified language. By playing on the hostility to innovation in the

---

[25] Bacon (2000: 76), Essay XXIIII, "Of Innovations." The influence of Bacon on law reform movements in the 17th century is a complicated question; see in particular Barbara Shapiro (1980), who also traces the abortive efforts at reform during the late 16th and early 17th centuries, reaching, in her view, a peak in 1621. These earlier efforts – and perhaps the work of the Hale Commission – Shapiro suggests were strongly influenced by Bacon. However, as Shapiro notes, these early efforts at reform were focused primarily on questions of jurisdictional boundaries rather than the substance of law per se. (Shapiro 1980: 334–35)

[26] Bacon (2000: 75–76).

public realm – through characterizing one's opponents as seeking to subvert everything the public held dear – a struggle over the ability to enact legal change, and therefore determine the scope of political authority, was waged. The rhetoric of an immutable ancient constitution in mortal danger of being altered was a means by which the common lawyers, king, or Parliament could assert their rightful place in upholding – that is, in interpreting and therefore in changing – the law.

Through appealing to the immutability of the ancient constitution, then, a political actor could simultaneously genuflect to the wisdom of past generations, assert his interpretive authority (the ability to engage in customary change), and label his opponents sinister innovators aiming at the destruction of the body of the laws. By the time of the Civil War, of course, Parliament and the king were leveling this charge at each other. In one author's words, both John Pym and Charles I's chief minister, Thomas Wentworth, the Earl of Strafford, agreed "in an ideological rejection of change."[27]

Throughout the early part of the seventeenth century, the House of Commons defended the rights and liberties of Parliament as an immutable part of the ancient constitution, dating from time immemorial. James I had challenged this claim, asserting that these laws emerged from his and his ancestors' sovereignty. As the House of Commons faced the expansion of the king's prerogative, the authors of the Petition of Right, in the language of Pym, sought to restore the ancient constitution, "demanding their ancient and due liberties, not suing for anything new."[28] On the brink of Civil War, Charles I released the Answer to the Nineteen Propositions, in which he expressly repudiated his father's position and referred to the "ancient, equal, happy, well-poised and never enough commended Constitution of the Government of this Kingdom,"

---

[27] Russell, quoted in Zaret (2000: 41).
[28] Weston (1996: 383, 395).

emerging from the "experience and wisdom of your ancestors."[29] He charged the authors of the Nineteen Propositions with seeking the "total subversion of the fundamental laws" and seeking changes to the constitution that "will almost infallibly beget yet greater changes, which beget yet greater inconveniences." Most famously, the answer he provided was *nolumus leges Angliae mutari*" – "We do not wish that the laws of England be changed" – and thus he accused Parliament of seeking to alter the ancient constitution.

At the cusp of the Civil War, when the king and the two houses of Parliament accused each other of subverting the ancient constitution, the recognition that the constitution – whatever its borders or origin – had been sundered emerged. In this gap, the capacity to "restore" the fundamental laws was up for grabs. Although an unabashed attempt to enact legal change through Parliament would need to wait for the Commonwealth, calls for legal reform emerged during the Civil War, most notably through the democratic Leveller movement.

The Levellers and "Democratic" Legal Reform

The protodemocratic Leveller movement was committed not only to an assemblage of specific legal reforms, but also to the ability of representative assemblies to make and revise legislation. In part because of their defense of sweeping changes, they were tarred as "Levellers," as seeking the destruction of all law, and even as anarchists. As we shall see, the critics of the Levellers linked the democratic dimension of their platform to their commitment to legal change, but did the Levellers themselves?

First, one might note that to refer to the Levellers as "protodemocrats" is to evade a primary question about the Leveller movement: Was it democratic? The Levellers would not append

[29] Wootton (1986: 171).

this name to themselves, given the pejorative connotation of the term in the seventeenth century.[30] Yet it is difficult to view their major proposals for substantive changes – to freedom of conscience and expression, to an end to property qualifications for the franchise, to an end to conscription, to a dramatic reduction of legal fees, and to the simplification and translation into English of the law – in any way other than as distinctively democratic. Although as many, notably C. B. Macpherson, have long noted, the Levellers did not necessarily live up to their promise (particularly with respect to their compromises on the expansion of the franchise), terming them "protodemocratic" recognizes both their important role in the expansion of what we would regard today as major democratic ideals, while acknowledging the limited extent to which they could think of themselves as democratic and the incompletely democratic decisions they made.

Accepting that the term "democracy" is at best controversially applied to the Levellers, let us turn to the relationship between the Leveller democratic commitments and their concepts of legal change. This matter, too, is somewhat complicated: R. B. Seaberg, in particular, has argued against Pocock that the Levellers did not break with ancient constitutionalism and that their defenses of legal reform were often characterized in "restorative" language. Certainly, it is true that, as Seaberg holds, John Lilburne had called for an end to the Norman "innovation" and a return to "that part of the antient frame of government," the traditional Anglo-Saxon laws in force prior to the conquest in 1066.[31] We might take this to suggest that the Levellers regularly argued from continuity, for a return to fundamental laws and liberties disrupted by the Norman Yoke. However, just as the Levellers did not refer to themselves as "democrats," neither did they refer to themselves as "innovators,"

---

[30] See Wootton (1996: 426–428); Wootton (1986: 38–40); Sharp (1998: xii–xiii).
[31] Seaberg (1981: 795); Lilburne (1646).

because of the term's negative connotations. The Levellers some-times found it useful to portray themselves as upholders of the true English constitution, as no doubt Lilburne did during his trial for treason. Yet there is ample evidence that the Levellers vigorously defended the right of assemblies to make and alter legislation; even if this rhetoric occasionally took a restorative form, their proposals and procedures alike were undeniably progressive.

Let us now examine a few examples of the progressive – that is, forward-looking and "innovative" – accounts of legal change. *The Agreement of the People*, the first written constitution based on natural rights[32] and the fundamental statement of the Leveller movement, placed sovereignty in the hands of the people and gave political power to their representatives in the Commons (abolishing the "negative voices" of the king and lords).[33] The authors of the *Agreement* argued that such a statement was necessary, instead of a petition to Parliament for rights (which had already failed), because "No Act of parliament is or can be unalterable, and so cannot be sufficient security to save you or us harmless from what another parliament may determine if it should be corrupted."[34] Although it is true that the authors referred to the efforts of their ances-tors, "whose blood was often spent in vain for the recovery of their freedom," the more important dimension of the *Agreement* was precisely the effort at securing power through the consent of the people: Rather than appealing to Parliament, whose power derived from the people, "therefore the people are to declare what their power and trust is." Most importantly, the first power the *Agreement* identified as possessed by the representative government was that of "enacting, altering, and repealing of laws."

The "foundations of your freedoms," as identified in the Case of the Army, were to be "settled unalterably" by this *Agreement*,

---

[32] Wootton (1996: 412).   [33] Sharp (1998: xiv).
[34] Reprinted in Sharp (1998: 97).

suggesting that through the process of creating the *Agreement*, a new base for fundamental liberties was to be made immutable. We might also note, in passing, that the *Agreement* did seek to make indemnity in relation to the "late public differences" an unalterable provision; thus even in this early constitution entrenchment served a narrow, instrumental purpose, removing potentially disruptive matters from the table while locking in the interest of the framers. Although the Levellers were committed to the capacity of remaking the law and to providing a renewed foundation for it through popular consent, perhaps they nevertheless recognized the possibility that it might be disturbed yet again. (Indeed, in the text of the *Agreement*, they suggested the presence of opponents – including those who might cast aspersions upon them with "designs of 'anarchy' and 'community.'") On this reading, the natural liberties protected by the *Agreement* were to be considered unalterable (though perhaps not the *Agreement* itself); and although the products of the representative government would not be unalterable, the possibility of charging people with sedition for actions conducted during the war would be permanently excluded.

The capacity to engage in the ongoing process of legislation and revision was therefore secured by the *Agreement*, to which its authors expected opposition, in the form of anarchic or democratic slander. Again, although references to ancestors appeared in the *Agreement*, there is little reason to characterize this as in any way "restorative": A firm foundation for natural liberties was constituted through the process of legislation, which was to be both made by Parliament and revisable over time. Likewise, in *A Remonstrance of Many Thousand Citizens and Other Freeborn People of England to Their Own House of Commons*, written by Richard Overton and William Walwyn prior to the *Agreement*, the authors argued that "the laws of this nation are unworthy [of] a free people and deserve from first to last to be considered and seriously debated, and reduced to an agreement with common equity and right reason." Though the authors acknowledged the presence of Norman "bondage," the marks of such extended all the way to the Magna Charta, which itself was "but a beggarly thing containing many marks of intolerable bondage." In this way, though fundamental liberties might be traceable to a pre-Norman period, the laws were so profoundly corrupted that only through a process of "debate" – through serious deliberation – could they be made consonant with "right reason." (At Putney, Thomas Rainsborough argued that "since all good laws that were now enjoyed were once innovations, the army should without delay proceed to secure the liberties of the people."[35])

One of the most important Leveller pamphlets advocating legal reform, as historians have noted, was John Warr's *The Corruption and Deficiency of the Lawes of England Soberly Discovered* (June 11, 1649). Warr used the Norman Yoke to show that the issue of conquest was totally irrelevant and challenged the entire notion of appealing to the historical past to determine legislation: The "original" of British law prior to the Romans is utterly lost.[36] He suggested that in fact the British might have "borrowed some laws from the Greeks, the refiners of human spirits, and the ancientest inventors of laws," perhaps along with the Phoenicians, and pointed out that the etymology of many British words "seems to be Greekish," noting parenthetically that this claim could be developed "if it were material to this purpose." But it was not: Instead, Warr's

---

[35] Gooch (1959: 129).

[36] Veall held that Warr, along with Lilburne, defended a restorative account (pre-Norman) of legal reform, though he noted that "in later Leveller manifesto this theory was abandoned." Although as suggested, Lilburne used restorative language, the extent to which any Leveller actually wished to commit himself to a pre-Norman doctrine is questionable; it's more likely that such language was occasionally viewed as necessary for rhetorical purposes to counter the charge of anarchy or destructiveness.

point was that law had undergone constant alteration since literally prehistory, and so the matter of origins was both incapable of resolution and, even if discernable, irrelevant. On these grounds, he challenged the entire notion of "fundamental law," arguing forcefully that the concept served to reify unjust customs and did not signify some special status that ought to offer such laws immunity from change.

> By this it appears that the notion of fundamental law is no such idol as men make it. For what, I pray you, is fundamental law, but such customs as are of the eldest date and longest continuance? Now freedom being the proper rule of custom, 'tis more fit that unjust customs should be reduced, that they may continue no longer than that they should keep up their arms because they have continued so long. The more fundamental a law is, the more difficult, not the less necessary, to be reformed.[37]

From this theoretical foundation, Warr called for many of the Levellers' most important proposals – clarity of legislation, proportionality of punishment, and accessible (local) courts – and urged the senate to "clear the channel of the law."[38]

Similarly, other pamphleteers of the period argued that piecemeal legal reform should be conducted by a committee, such as *The Representative of Divers Well-Affected Persons in and about the City of London*, who called for a complete English translation and overhaul of the body of the laws by Parliament while acknowledging that the matter would take time to avoid a period of abject legal uncertainty.[39] Nicholson called for a representative body, selected

---

[37] *Corruption and Deficiency*, contained in Wootton (1986: 153).
[38] Ibid., at 163.
[39] Feb. 6, 1659, E 541 (16), p. 13. Veall took this pamphlet as a compromise between "traditional Leveller demands and the proposals of the moderate reformers." (1970: 104).

by King and Parliament, to "to extract, invent, and find out, new, good, equall, just and necessary, Lawes, plaine, easy and free from all dilemmas and ambiguities, according as they in their wise-dome shall think fit and convenient, all the rest of the Lawes, together with all old names and distinctions as of Common, Civill and Statute Lawes, being repealed and taken away forever...."[40] Yet even more moderate reformers, such as Henry Robinson, suggested that although it was inconceivable that a "new body of Lawes can be prepared on a sudden," more moderate reforms to the court system ought to be implemented in the short term.[41]

It should now be clear that the Levellers did not always defend their proposed changes in the language of restoration, but frequently appealed either to natural reason or to the public reason of a deliberative assembly as basis for legal change. The democratic nature of Leveller legal reform – both in the substance of these changes and the proposed procedures – has also been illuminated. In part, the Leveller movement constituted an epistemological challenge to the lawyers: Not only did the Levellers seek to simplify and anglicize the law, to reduce legal fees, and to try cases in localities,

---

[40] *The Lawyers Bane or the Laws Reformation and New Model*, Aug. 13, 1647, E401 (36), p. 3.

[41] *Certain Proposals in Order to a New Modelling of the Lawes and Law-Proceedings*, 1653, p. 24. The sources for these reforms could be simple, untrained human reason, worked through in assemblies, or it could be natural law. As suggested by "An Impartial Well-willer to the Peace and Well-beeing of All," in *An Experimental Essay Touching the Reformation of the Lawes of England* [Aug. 17, 1648, E 541 (16)], one could even learn from consulting the laws of other commonwealths. Though, citing Bacon, the author also called for a reduction to first principles, he advocated drawing on the laws of other countries as a means of gaining insight into the best foundation of law. "The way to make the best Platforme for a Common-wealth, were to send Letters into All Countries of the world, and have a short draught from thence, of all the Excellencies and Inconveniences of their Governments, & some appointed, to compare all those draughts with our Common-wealth, and then it might easily be mended, and made a better Common-wealth, than ever was in the world, by any humane appointment." (p. 6)

but they also offered an explicit challenge to the artificial reason of judges.

Consider briefly the following passage from the *Large Petition* in the context of the Leveller commitments to freedom of conscience: "That no man for preaching or publishing his opinion in Religion in a peaceable way, may be punished or persecuted as hereticall, by Judges that are not infallible, but may be mistaken (as well as other men in their judgements, least upon pretence of suppressing Errors, Sects, or Schisms, the most necessary truths, and sincere professors thereof may be suppressed, as upon the like pretence it hath been in all ages."[42] The judges purported to possess infallibility – a point on which later critics of the common law, notably Jeremy Bentham, would focus – yet the knowledge they possessed about divinity was accessible by laypeople as well as lawyers. Likewise, the lack of clarity of the common law "benefited only lawyers, a profession unknown before the conquestion, and the king."[43]

The Levellers, then, advanced a substantively egalitarian platform from a progressive rather than restorative position, and they sought parliamentary supremacy at the same time as they defended a body of law grounded on right reason and equity against the interests of lawyers. Moreover, they were committed to what we have here recognized as a quintessential democratic trait: a body of law, created and revisable by a parliament. Yet opponents, including Cromwell and the army officers, would caricature the substantively democratic dimension of the Leveller platform. Law reform under the Commonwealth and the Protectorate, as we shall see, was to take a form distinct from the sweeping changes proposed by the Levellers: Republican law reform would be narrow, instrumental, and pragmatic.

---

[42] *Large Petition*, March 1647; reprinted in Sharp (1998: 82) in the text of William Walwyn's *Gold Tried in the Fire* (4 June 1647).
[43] Wootton (1996: 427).

Law Reform under the Commonwealth

In the wake of the execution of Charles I and the abolition of the monarchy and the House of Lords, the fabric of the law had been unmistakably torn. Half the judges of the common-law courts refused to serve in the Commonwealth, and some lawyers regarded all efforts by the "Rump Parliament," as it was to be derisively termed, to enact law reform as illegitimate, even laughable; nor, for that matter, did the Levellers warmly embrace the efforts of the new government.[44] Although the lawyers who would comprise the law reformers of the Commonwealth typically regarded themselves as serving to repair the law, rather than engaged in a novel legislative process, the view that the republic was sphere in which a deliberative process of legal change could occur was also present. (Note, though, that the term "republican," like the term "democrat," was one of derision.)[45] Whereas in the past, men were guided solely by tradition (and artificial reason) rather than by "principles in reason and knowledge," a newspaper happily proclaimed, "to the contrary in these our days, the meanest sort of people are not only able to write, &c., but to argue and discourse on matters of highest concernment."[46]

The link between republicanism and the capacity to enact, to alter, and to repeal legislation was suggested during this period by Marchamont Nedham. In a series of editorials for the newspaper *Mercurius Politicus* in 1651–52, Nedham famously argued that the Romans had no liberty until the people possessed supreme power. In particular, Nedham claimed, the Roman people lacked liberty, not only until they possessed the power of calling and dissolving

---

[44] Skinner (2002: 229–30).
[45] Worden, in van Gelderen and Skinner (2002: 307).
[46] Hirst (1999: 255).

the assemblies and of altering their form of government, but of "enacting and repealing laws."[47] Nedham, notably, was far more inclined than other republicans to praise Athenian democracy as well.[48] In particular, Nedham cited approvingly the work of Solon in establishing the Areopagus' power in the "managing of state transactions," but leaving the legislative authority in "a successive course of the Peoples Assemblies," and thus he "is celebrated by all Posterity, as the man that hath left the only Pattern of a free state, for all the world to follow."[49]

Though Hobbes was far less supportive of the Rump than was Nedham, the publication of *Leviathan* nevertheless provided additional support for the capacity of the Rump to deliberately alter the law. As Quentin Skinner has argued, *Leviathan* was published in the late stages of the "Engagement Controversy," in which the question of whether to "engage" (to accept the oath of "engagement" to the new Commonwealth's authority) was contested; the argument that the obligation to obey the new government depended upon its capacity to protect its subjects targeted those who would challenge the legitimacy of the Commonwealth. In this context, one might also suggest that his argument that the sovereign possessed the power to create and to alter law had particular force as a defense of the Rump's activities with respect to law reform: "The Soveraign of a Common-wealth, be it an Assembly, or one Man, is not Subject to the Civill Lawes. For having power to make, and repeale, Lawes, he may when he pleaseth free himselfe from that subjection, by repealing those Lawes that trouble him, and making of new; and consequently he was free before."[50] Further, Hobbes specifically

---

[47] *Mercurius Politicus* 73 (23–30 Oct. 1651), p. 1157.
[48] Harrington (1977: 35).
[49] *Mercurius Politicus* 73 (23–30 Oct. 1651), p. 1158.
[50] Hobbes (1991: 184).

targeted Coke and defenders of customary law and artificial reason, as he would later develop in the *Dialogue concerning the Common Laws*. Law is never against reason, Hobbes acknowledged, but not "(as Sr. *Ed. Coke* makes it,) an *Artificiall perfection of Reason, gotten by long study, observation, and experience.* (as his was.) For it is possible long study may encrease, and confirm erroneous Sentences..: and therefore it is not that *Juris prudential,* or wisedome of subordinate judges; but the Reason of this our Artificiall Man the Common-wealth, and his command, that maketh law."[51]

The Rump Parliament took up the matter of law reform openly and seriously, drawing on some of the criticisms of the common law suggested by the Levellers. The lawyers, termed "verminous caterpillars,"[52] were widely held responsible for the worst abuses, due to their professional interest in making the law more opaque in its language, and therefore less comprehensible by and accessible to laymen. Both the fees and the absence of local justice were regular sources of complaints, particularly the need to travel to London for judgments. Yet the Rump Parliament is perhaps best known for the failure of its efforts at law reform than for its sweeping innovations. Though members of the New Model Army viewed the cause of law reform as a primary justification, if not the main reason, for the Civil War, the Rump's efforts at enacting legal change were relatively unsuccessful. Discussions of law reform often occupied the Rump from 1649 through 1651, but with few noteworthy accomplishments; the major reform was that all court proceedings should be conducted in English.[53] In 1652, the Rump appointed a commission on law reform, chaired by the lawyer Sir Matthew Hale; and though the Hale Commission comprised a serious, deliberative effort at legal change through legislative means, it, too, had only

---

[51] Hobbes (1991: 187).   [52] Worden (1974: 106).
[53] Worden (1974: 107); Woolrych (1982: 7).

limited success and partially for this reason is still considered a hallmark of the republican Commonwealth.[54]

Did lawyers enable or hinder law reform? On the one hand, because lawyers comprised much of the Hale Commission, as first noted by Mary Cotterell (1968), they could not all have resisted the project of reform. Yet it is certainly true that the cause of law reform was not widely supported by lawyers, and indeed, the Hale Commission's inability to see its reforms enacted was substantially due to the opposition of the lawyers in the Rump. In Blair Worden's words, it was the case "not only that lawyers provided the main opposition to law reform, but that such reform as was achieved came only when fear, or an instinct for self-preservation, drove them to make concessions to reforming sentiment."[55] Moreover, while failed lawyers had a taste for reform,[56] successful members of the "legal dynasty," notably Bulstrode Whitelocke, were far from supportive of the cause of reform. Unsurprisingly, Whitelocke sought to characterize the reformers as uneducated zealots and as Levellers, bent on the destruction of English law and their ancient freedoms. Pamphleteers likewise mocked the intellectual pretences of lawyers and accused them of abusing their positions for their own benefit:

> Now Gentlemen Lawyers where are you; you that have for so long a time strutted it up and down the Temple and other Courts of Iniquity, with your longsided Gownes, and your flat bottom Caps, like so many Rooks waiting for your prey, daily contriving how to inrich your selves, and to impoverish the Commonwealths, or like Water Pots which only refresh your own ground, when alas you ought to be like showers of Raine which inrich their Neighbours

---

[54] I focus here primarily in the logic of legal change rather than the substance of the modifications; see Shapiro (1975: 292–97).

[55] Worden (1974: 110).

[56] Worden (1974: 109); *Law's Discovery*, June 27, 1653, E 702 (18).

as well as themselves (*Lawyers Last Farewell: or The Poor Mans Freedom Enlarged*).

Perhaps most importantly, the lawyers were not only interested in retaining their own authority over the law, but had a "strong fancy of a single necessary governor."[57] As the resistance of judges to sit under the Commonwealth suggested, there was a sharp difference in the reception of republicanism by lawyer and nonlawyer MPs. The lawyers' reluctance to concede the realm of legal change to the assembly as a whole, whom they regarded as ignorant on legal matters, and the assembly's suspicions of the lawyers and their efforts to consolidate interests, may be viewed as the primary hindrance to the cause of legal reform in the Rump Parliament.

The Hale Commission itself was composed of 21 members, many of whom, as suggested, were lawyers, but radicals were also represented on the Commission, perhaps most famously Major William Packer, Colonel Thomas Blount, and Hugh Peters. Deliberations were sophisticated and even the nonlawyers were fairly well educated about legal matters.[58] The Commission met from January to July 1652 on 71 occasions and prepared 16 bills. As Cotterell claimed, it is clear that although the Commission was committed to "practical, piecemeal reform," nevertheless it did accept some of the proposals of the Levellers and other radical groups: The Commission adopted a proposal for new county courts and abolished debt imprisonment.[59] Other subjects of legislation included criminal law and procedure, matrimonial law, mercantile law, and the regulation of the legal profession.

Sir Matthew Hale's leadership of a program to reform the law through deliberate legislative means was perfectly consistent with his commitments in his jurisprudential writings on the topic. Hale

---

[57] Worden (1974: 117).
[58] Veall (1970: 83); Cotterell (1968: 694–95).
[59] Cotterell (1968: 697).

was committed to the cause of legal reform, both as a reformer himself and in his theoretical work, in which he supported the change of the common law through legislation. Although Hale is perhaps most famous for his Seldenian metaphor of the Argonaut ship – which, like the common law, had been on so long a voyage that each part had been replaced though the ship remained the same – his views on legal reform were in fact more subtle than often appreciated. Though he did not call for full-scale constitutional change, he was committed to substantive legislative reform and parliamentary sovereignty in the form of legal change.

Rather than arguing for progress via judicial interpretation, Hale argued for intentional and deliberate modification of the law by Parliament and viewed the source of the English law as essentially irrelevant. In his work "Considerations Touching the Amendment or Alteration of Lawes," Hale held that a reformer ought not to be either "over-busy and hasty and violent" in one's zeal for amendment or "wilfull and over-strict adhering in every particular to the continuance of the lawes in the state we find them." Although the call for a "happy medium" may at first glimpse appear banal, Hale in fact offered a rich theoretical account of the mechanisms of legal change. Mutability could interfere with the desired goals of publicity, experience, and predictability, and any resulting inconveniences might generate a disposition against innovation. Though people accustomed to their laws and believing in the goodness of their customs might accept some minor changes introduced subtly, Hale argued, the moment that a change appears to be for the worse, "then presently the mouths of people are opened against innovation, and the higher their expectation is raised upon the pretence and promise of benefit, the more they are enraged by any though inconsiderable disappointment therein."[60]

---

[60] Hale (1787: 255).

The dispositional argument reappears in the discussion of those who hunger after amendment. Some people just have a preference for new things, Hale claimed: "The very same itch of novelty and innovation, that carries some dispositions to novelty in garbs and gestures, or to new fashions in cloathes, carries such when they happen to be in place to innovations and new fashions in lawes."[61] Others might wish to eradicate any law that they perceive to be even slightly opposed to their interest. Still others hankered after perfection, believing that they will create a "faultless" system. Notably, though some had a taste for innovation and sought perfection in legislation, Hale remarked upon the futility of this search because of human fallibility: "[I]t is most certain, that when all the wisdom and prudence in the world is used, all human things will still be imperfect."[62] Only God can create a perfect law. Yet even He is unable to create a law suited to every society at every point in time, Hale argued: "Let any man but consider the judicials given to the Hebrews, he will find them in a special manner accommodated and attempered to the state of that people, which would not be apposite to the state of another people."[63] Even divine law requires "supplementals" to permit it to accommodate new exigencies and emergencies. Note that for Hale human fallibility became the justification for and against change. One should not hasten to modify the laws in the hope of achieving perfection; this is futile, given the limitations of our reason. Nor should one resist change out of reverence for one's ancestors and the relative imperfection of our wisdom; even good laws may become antiquated.

Hale's moderate approach to deliberate legal change was a hallmark of the commission that bore his name, but its outcome was to prove largely unsuccessful. Though the Parliamentary Law Committee had in general been in agreement with the bills submitted by

---

[61] Ibid., 256–57. [62] Ibid., 257.
[63] Ibid., 259.

the Commission, and though the Parliament committed two days to reading the bills and then set aside a day a week for their consideration, by the time the Rump was dissolved in April 1653 no legislation had been passed. Cromwell mocked the law committees and criticized the Parliament for failing to enact any law reform. Cromwell's nominated Parliament, referred to pejoratively as "Barebone's Parliament," thus took up the challenge, beginning with the draft bills of the Hale Commission; seven of the MPs had in fact been on the Hale Commission.

Barebone's Parliament itself appointed a committee for law reform, which examined in detail the text of the Hale Commission drafts. Once again, the drafts had only limited success; only two of the Hale Commission's draft bills were successfully passed: one eliminating payment of fines for bills and writs initiating actions at law, and the second the Act Touching Marriages.[64] In part because of the length of debates on the latter, the radical members of Parliament became eager for real progress on the matter of law reform, and a new committee was proposed. The distinction between the real proposed motion to appoint a committee to consider "a new Model of the Law" and the Parliamentary Clerk's misheard motion for "a new Body of the Law" – which seemed to jeopardize the entire corpus of law – meant that the committee was controversial from its very inception. As Austin Woolrych has written, "[C]ommon report had it that the committee's purpose was to destroy the whole venerable fabric of the known law of the land." Conservatives, such as the author of *Confusion Confounded*, held that the effort was truly to destroy the whole law, whereas the author of *Exact Relation* suggested instead that the effort was in fact simply to codify and "rationalize" the law – that is, assess their compatibility with "right reason." The efforts of this parliamentary

---

[64] Woolrych (1982: 268).

committee were wide-ranging; in all, 26 acts were passed, including the Leveller proposal of an Act for the Relief of Creditors and Poor Prisoners.[65]

As Barebone's Parliament broke down, Nedham wrote *A True State of the Case of the Commonwealth*, to which Cromwell would be substantially indebted. Nedham criticized standing parliaments (i.e., the Rump), in part on the grounds that they would generate a "multitude of unnecessary laws (many of which were made upon occasion of, and to serve and suit with the Concernment and Interests of particular Members)."[66] Yet simultaneously, he reaffirmed that the "first great Act of Sovereignty lies in the Enacting, and the altering or annulling of Laws: which is expressly to be in Parliament" – that is, in a "succession of parliaments."[67] The dual character of the defense of legal change – the acknowledgment that the first act of sovereignty of a commonwealth (recall that Nedham was not hostile to democratic republics) was in altering laws and the simultaneous concern that this inclination be checked (here through time-limited parliaments) – is, as we have already seen, characteristic of democrats.[68] Cromwell would draw heavily on Nedham in his speeches in the years to come;[69] the intuition that Parliament's ability to modify law should be constrained, however, was also implicit in the Instrument of Government.

At the point of the collapse of Barebone's Parliament – perhaps in part because of the call for a "new Body," but likely more

---

[65] Veall (1970: 86); Woolrych (1982: 292).

[66] Nedham, *True State of the Case of the Commonwealth* (1654: 11). There is some dispute over authorship, though most scholars today accept that Nedham almost certainly wrote the text.

[67] Ibid., 30.

[68] And perhaps of Nedham himself, of whom Pocock has written, "shuffled the dominant concepts of the Civil War and the Rump years with a brilliance if anything enhanced by what seems to have been a signal lack of sincerity or consistency." (Pocock 1975: 381)

[69] Woolrych (1982: 96).

immediately due to religious disputes that emerged in the late fall of 1653 – Major-General John Lambert, a chief army officer under Cromwell, submitted a written constitution, the Instrument of Government, to his colleagues and to Cromwell, who was named Lord Protector. The dimension of constitutionalism offered a new wrinkle in the cause of law reform, as parliamentary efforts at legislation now became stymied by a substantially unamendable constitution. The cause of law reform, though far from dead, became similarly complicated.

Entrenchment of the Instrument of Government

The Instrument of Government, which brought about an end to the Commonwealth, is salient both inasmuch as it is among the earliest written constitutions and, for our analysis here, because of its formal entrenchment. As is often noted, the Instrument had no formal mechanism for amendment. However, the authors of the Instrument took care to make certain provisions entrenched; and although these were primarily contentious matters, Cromwell explicitly declared that he regarded some of the "fundamental" constitutive provisions to be unalterable.

Although, again, no amendment procedure was specified, Article VI did read: "[T]he laws shall not be altered, suspended, abrogated, or repealed, nor any new law made, nor any tax, charge, or imposition laid upon the people, but by common consent in Parliament, save only as is expressed in the thirtieth article." That article declared only that while the Parliament should ordinarily have responsibility for raising funds for the military, the Protector and Council should have this authority, along with the power to enact legislation, where necessary for "peace and welfare" prior to the first Parliament. Though this would seem to give Parliament substantial latitude to amend the Instrument as it saw fit, in fact, as Heath demonstrated, Lambert shrewdly gave Cromwell remarkable authority to entrench the Instrument.[70] Article XXIV, for example, seemed not to grant the executive a negative on legislation, giving the Protector instead merely a 20-day suspensive veto, but in fact gave him sweeping authority to determine what constituted legislation in compliance with the Instrument. The Parliament had the authority to enact whatever it liked, "provided such Bills contain[ed] nothing in them contrary to the matters contained in these presents." Who could determine the compatibility of parliamentary legislation with the Instrument? In the absence of a judge, the Protector could arrogate this authority to himself, and indeed pamphleteers recognized this possibility.[71]

Although there was no specific entrenchment clause, certain provisions were textually identified as unalterable. The protected provisions, however – as, recall, in Athens – did not extend to the most salient or salutary dimensions of the Instrument – for example, the situating of legislative authority with the Parliament and Protector. Instead, a number of controversial clauses supported primarily by the army, as represented by Lambert, were entrenched. The first provision protected religious freedom for Christian sects, though explicitly not "Popery" or "Prelacy" (Article XXXVII), and Article XXXVIII provided that "all laws and clauses in any law, statute or ordinance to the contrary of the aforesaid liberty, shall be esteemed as null and void." The use of tithes, until another means of maintenance was found, was also protected. Second, the law regulating revenues from the sale of the crown lands, and the securities for the sale of these lands, was to be held "good and firm" and "not be made void and invalid upon any pretence whatsoever" (Article XXXIX). Third, as Heath suggested, the army's interest in protecting articles of capitulation – which the army believed had been violated by Barebone's Parliament when it confirmed the sale of the

---

[70] Heath (1967: 13 and passim).   [71] Ibid., 29.

lands of the royalist commander Sir John Stawell – was reflected in Article XL.[72]

In addition to the textually irrevocable provisions, Cromwell, in a speech to Parliament on September 12, 1654, argued, "In every government there must be somewhat fundamental, somewhat like [the] *Magna Charta*, that should be standing and be unalterable." He suggested that fundamental provisions such as "government by a single person and parliament" is "the *esse*, it is constitutive." Cromwell termed the laws that "parliaments should not make themselves perpetual"; "liberty of conscience," which "is a natural right"; and the control over the "militia" by Protector and Parliament (and, in the absence of a seated Parliament, of the Protector and Council), fundamental and unalterable. Although there were "circumstantial things, which are not like the laws of the Medes and the Persians" – that is, they should be alterable – "the things which shall be necessary to deliver over to posterity, these should be unalterable, else every succeeding parliament will be disputing to change and alter the government, and we shall be as often brought into confusion as we have parliaments."[73]

Nevertheless, Parliament sought to alter the Instrument, and, as Woolrych has written, "One way of discovering what...was most contentious in this constitution is to examine how the parliaments attempted to change it."[74] The most significant efforts at amendment surrounded religion, Protector-Parliament distribution of power, and the control (including financing) of the armed forces.[75] The first Parliament immediately offered proposals that ran counter to the entrenched provisions, from the rejection of the very concept of a Protectorate (for which Hale offered a compromise position of checks and balances), control over the army, and the matter of religious tolerance; partially in response to the efforts

---

[72] Ibid., 31.
[74] Woolrych (1982: 375).

[73] Abbott (1937–47: III, 451–62).
[75] Ibid.

of MPs to amend the Instrument, Cromwell dissolved the Parliament in January 1655. The second Protectorate Parliament, called in September 1656, also attempted to alter the Instrument, in part by calling Cromwell to accept the throne. Though he rejected the crown, on May 25, 1657, he accepted a revised constitution (which now included, most saliently, a bicameral legislature), The Humble Petition and Advice. The Humble Petition likewise lacked an amendment clause, and it reiterated that "no laws be altered, suspended, abrogated, or repealed, or new law made, but by act of Parliament"; continuity with the Instrument was provided in Articles XV and XVI (misnumbered as XVI and XVII) so that any provisions not explicitly contrary could be maintained.

It is worth noting that Cromwell himself continued in some fashion to advocate law reform, primarily through commissioning the work of the reformer William Sheppard. Sheppard's careful work was to be largely in vain, though, as Cromwell never seriously took up his proposals, perhaps because of ambivalence, and perhaps because of time constraints.[76] Moreover, Cromwell claimed that he was ill informed about the matter, despite the presence of Sheppard's work. In Cromwell's own words, "[S]urely the laws need to be regulated. . . . I confess, if any man would ask me, why, how would you have it done? I confess I do not know how. But I think verily at least, the delays in suits and the excessiveness in fees, and the costliness of suits, and those various things. . . . The people are greatly suffering in this respect; they are so."[77] Reforms were even less successfully implemented under the Protectorate than they had been under the Commonwealth.[78] Instead, with the decline of the Protectorate came calls for a return to ancient constitutionalism. Though individual, piecemeal legal changes would be enacted in the late seventeenth and entire eighteenth centuries,

---

[76] Hirst (1990: 127–31). [77] Hirst (1990: 144–45).
[78] Sommerville (1990: 257); Hirst (1999: 307).

substantive reform would not occur until well into the nineteenth century.

Conclusion: Judicial and Legislative Authority

Efforts at defining the scope of legitimate legal change characterized much of the seventeenth century, as we have seen, and theoretical accounts of the mutability of law intersected with pressing political concerns about the locus of political authority. Under the Commonwealth, Parliament was free to take up the matter of legal change, to appoint committees to study the matter of law reform, and then to debate these matters publicly, whereas the capacity to modify the law under the monarchy and the Protectorate was somewhat constrained, in the former by the ideology of ancient constitutionalism and in the latter by a nascent form of constitutional entrenchment. That is, the doctrine of ancient constitutionalism – its simultaneously unchanged yet constantly adapting body of law, evolving primarily through interpretation of the common law – gave way during the Civil War and in the Commonwealth to deliberate legislative efforts to reform the body of the law. What can we make of such a story?

We can place efforts at parliamentary legal change against two opposing perspectives. The first is a vision of a common law that ought to be changed only through the imperceptible workings of interpretation (to which we shall return momentarily), and the second is the nascent form of constitutional entrenchment that we see in the Instrument. Taking up the latter only briefly, note that as in entrenchment efforts that precede and follow it, the Instrument attempted to secure narrow, contentious matters against revision. Entrenchment clauses typically reflect the degree to which framers regard attempts to modify the constitution as likely. The Protectorate's use of entrenchment reflected the republican legislative efforts that preceded it. The prescribed ability of the Parliament to alter or revise the law solely by The Protector's consent suggested that the authors were certainly aware that the legislature would attempt to do just that. The entrenchment of particular provisions, and Cromwell's speech defending a more expansive concept of fundamental law, emerged in response to this possibility.

Let us step away from the seventeenth century and turn to the second set of arguments. Of course, today the question of the appropriate scope and locus of legal change, particularly constitutional change, continues to challenge us. Our debates over judicial review, in particular, reflect the importance of this question: We readily find ourselves struggling over the familiar distinction between majoritarianism – caricatured, perhaps, by the words of the Athenians, "the masses shouted that it was monstrous for anyone not to let the people do whatever they wanted" – and constitutional adjudication, granting power to judiciary to strike down legislation, ensuring that the masses do not get their way, and thereby enable the democracy to live to see another day. On this view, whereas democratic assemblies, left to their own devices, would spend their time changing their laws until the very concept of law became utterly meaningless, judges provide an indispensable check on the legislature's power to modify law and thereby secure, rather than subvert, real self-government.[79]

Yet, it may be readily acknowledged, judges do more than simply serve as a barrier to change: They themselves, as countless scholars have noted,[80] play a key role in constitutional change through the process of constitutional interpretation. It may be held that the mechanism of interpretation is importantly different from the process of legislation. As we have seen, certainly this was the belief in seventeenth-century England prior to the Civil War: Although

---

[79] This is a somewhat reductive account of many theorists, notably Eisgruber (2001), who develops this point with considerable subtlety and elegance.

[80] Recent defenders of this concept include Levinson (1995) and Knight (2001), among many others.

both judges and Parliament could interpret the law and make law that specified the common law, to deliberately alter the common law by legislative means was to court charges of anarchic innovation. How does the capacity of judges to modify the law differ from legislators' ability to do so? I wish to suggest three possibilities, which, while not exhaustive, nevertheless seem both salient and plausible: (1) intent, that is, legislative change is "intentional" and judicial change is "unintentional"; (2) interest, that is, legislators seek to advance the interest of their constituents or of pressure groups, whereas judges are relatively immune from such pressure; and (3) expertise, wherein judges have a body of knowledge that they bring to bear when they engage in interpretation, that legislators, or at least the people as a whole, lack when they seek to amend the constitution. I shall suggest that these three arguments distinguishing between the capacity of judges and of legislators to change the law are themselves disputable. Insofar as these arguments serve to ground the assertion that judges may offer a safer home for constitutional development than legislators, that assertion also becomes dubious.

Intent

Friedrich Hayek, famously, posited a distinction between the "spontaneous" order of customary law, on one hand, and legislation as the "deliberate making of law," on the other.[81] Hayek, in fact, lauded the "deeply entrenched tradition of a common law that was not conceived as the product of anyone's will but rather as a barrier to all power, including that of the king – a tradition which Edward Coke was to defend against King James I and Francis Bacon, and which Matthew Hale at the end of the seventeenth century masterly restated in opposition to Thomas Hobbes."[82] Indeed, Hayek

---

[81] Hayek (1973: 72).   [82] Ibid., 85.

located the "freedom of the British" in the fact that the common law "exist[ed] independently of anyone's will." The role of the common-law judge, Hayek wrote, was to simply articulate and clarify the customs that would have generated the expectations that should, at least, have guided disputants' actions.

In contrast, Hayek argued that legislation "gave into the hands of men an instrument of great power which they needed to achieve some good, but which they have not yet learned so to control that it may not produce great evil." He urged us to shed the myth of "constructive rationalism," taught to us by theorists such as Hobbes, Rousseau, and Bentham, the belief that laws emerging from an "intentional" process[83] of human design ought to guide us, and which in turn will "necessarily lead[. . .] to a gradual transformation of the spontaneous order of a free society into a totalitarian system conducted in the service of some coalition of organized interests."[84] Notably, Hayek thought that the concept of law as the product of a deliberate will originated in Athens and was, regrettably, exemplified by contemporary representative governments. Yet Hayek also acknowledged that by virtue of the fact that the "judicial development of law is of necessity gradual," modification may require legislation, because the judge "cannot really alter" the law, even if he finds that he is disappointing expectations or that a law is producing manifestly unjust consequences.[85]

Even if we accept Hayek's distinction in principle between the deliberate legislation of an assembly and the unintentional, purely spontaneous, evolutionary development of a customary law – if not the rest of the argument – we may yet challenge the concept of "spontaneity." Surely, one might argue, this depends upon an exceptionally strict account of legal formalism; any less restrictive conception of judicial agency will not accommodate Hayek's distinction.

---

[83] Ibid., 27.

[84] Ibid., 2.

[85] Ibid., 88–89.

What is significant, though, is the extent to which Hayek did link up deliberate enactment with the development of democratic legislatures, capable of creating and altering whatever legislation they chose. We may well agree with Hayek on this point, even if we think that this is not a matter of grave regret. Democracy may require that we be capable of engaging in collective decision making in enacting legislation, subject to reconsideration and revision. As we have seen – and as Hayek would largely concur[86] – the Athenians drew on the ideology of pragmatic innovation each time they enacted legislation, creating law without appeal to constitutionalism or revelation, and their prior decisions had little normative weight over their current judgments. We may believe that intent does matter, but as an attractive element of a democracy that enables itself to change course, rather than as a regrettable feature of assemblies that makes judicial decision making more attractive.

Interest

I will say relatively little about the role of interest, as the logic is fairly straightforward, as, I believe, is the challenge. But one might readily believe that judges are insulated from the pressures of election – life tenure will exclude concerns about "personal interest and political ambition" with which most other people, legislators and ordinary citizens alike, must reckon.[87] Moreover, judges are obligated to recuse themselves if they have a stake in a case, and they are forced to give a "public account": to provide reasons for their decisions and to issue an opinion outlining these reasons.[88]

---

[86] Hayek implied that Athens was still attached to earlier conceptions of customary law during the fourth century, as his example of the use of the *graphe paranomon* suggests (1973: 82).

[87] Eisgruber (2001: 57–59).

[88] Ibid. (2001: 60).

Legislators are certainly not subject to the same reason-giving requirement, although their constituents or the media may call upon them to explain their votes, particularly if they choose to run for higher office. As a result, we may believe that where legal change must occur, we are better off having it occur through interpretive procedures than through the contentious process of legislators.

The challenge, however, is simple and obvious; indeed, some readers may view this as a dirty trick. The challenge rests in *Bush v. Gore*, in which a majority of the Supreme Court justices found that Florida's vote recount violated the equal protection clause of the Fourteenth Amendment, thereby effectively handing the presidency to George W. Bush. We may believe that the case was exceptional; we may even believe, like Judge Richard A. Posner, that the decision was required for the stability of our republic, lest the acting presidency be handed over to Lawrence Summers, Secretary of the Treasury. Yet as Judge Posner himself has written, the justices had a clear interest in the outcome of the decision of "who would be making, though subject of course to Senate confirmation, appointments to the Supreme Court if any vacancies occurred."[89] Although *Bush v. Gore* may not portray the court at its finest, it does indicate that where the personal interests of judges are particularly acute, they are no less likely to adjudicate on the basis of these interests than legislators, or the people as a whole, would. Life tenure may insulate judges from the presence of some external pressures,[90] but as human beings they cannot be insulated from internal ones. Indeed, as we have seen, a major challenge issued by opponents of the common law and common-law judges, as we have seen, was the concern that lawyers and judges

---

[89] Posner (2003: 330, 332).

[90] Note that elected judges may face many of the same "external pressures" that legislators do. For a discussion of this matter with respect to the death penalty, see Huber and Gordon (2004).

were ultimately interested in preserving their own sphere of influence and, in the words of Bentham, in protecting their "sinister interests."

Expertise and Epistemic Considerations

The democratic challenge to the common law was in part economic – the costs of fees and of travel to London were prohibitive – but it was also motivated by the concern that the class of the legal cognoscenti were inclined to protect themselves and, by failing to make the laws explicable, to enable them to preserve their sphere of esoteric knowledge. Today, the special knowledge of judges – their superior wisdom, as a function both of advanced legal training and, as Ronald Dworkin has suggested, their capacity to engage in moral reasoning – is offered as a justification for granting judges authority to make some of the most important decisions affecting the community: not the selection of the president, perhaps, but certainly the limits of our rights pertaining to controversial issues such as abortion, capital punishment, affirmative action, and euthanasia, and thus to change the substance of the laws of the land in exceptionally important ways. Dworkin is the most familiar proponent of the epistemic defense of judicial agency. He argues, famously, that "matters of principle," in particular questions of rights, ought therefore to be determined by the body most likely to get the right answer; there is at least no reason to resist the claim the Supreme Court may be that body in the United States and in his view good reason to affirm it.[91]

Recall that at the inception of the Commonwealth, a newspaper proclaimed that the scope of deliberation was no longer restricted to those possessing artificial reason, "to the contrary in these our

---

[91] Dworkin (1990: 331); Dworkin (1996).

days, the meanest sort of people are not only able to write, &c., but to argue and discourse on matters of highest concernment."[92] What citizens of democracies know, what they are capable of learning, has been a matter of real importance to political theory from Athens, but it has taken on a new life in the past two decades with the rise of deliberative accounts of democracy. Through life under the Commonwealth, people indeed acquired the capacity to think seriously about profound political questions, "matters of highest concernment," and, I suggest, we democrats would do well to believe that the public is capable of this, even if for a variety of reasons they may fail to take up the challenge. Notably, recent scholarship on deliberation – particularly the experimental work done by James Fishkin – provides us with reasons to be optimistic about the capacity for serious discussions and the rapidity of learning. Though, as Dworkin has suggested, attention to Supreme Court cases may have an educative purpose that enriches deliberation,[93] the case of abortion – which, whatever the merits of *Roe v. Wade* – suggests that the public is not inclined to discuss this from the perspective of substantive due process, but from overt and morally serious perspectives on the nature of life. As Jeremy Waldron has suggested, moreover, there is a certain tension – perhaps even a poignant contradiction – in arguing that we require decisions about the nature of rights to be taken out of the hands of legislators or of the people as a whole, by virtue of the fact that we cannot trust them to act responsibly – that is, with the gravity and concern for humanity that provided the justification for considering people to possess rights in the first place.[94]

I have strayed far from my discussion of the seventeenth century, but permit me to suggest one final point. As we have already seen, if constitutional interpretation may extend to amendment – as I have

---

[92] Hirst (1990: 255).
[93] Dworkin (1996: 30–31).
[94] Waldron (1999b: 295–96).

already suggested that it might – then entrenchment importantly does not exclude the possibility of constitutional change. Instead, it takes the power of legal change out of the hands of assemblies and grants it to judges. Judicial interpretation of the entrenched provision may not veer into the realm of amendment – as Levinson suggests, the boundaries are not entirely porous – but it may. And if it does, given the entrenched nature of the provision, neither the legislators, nor the people whom they represent, may have any recourse. Entrenchment clauses are indeed, in this sense, entrenched against the public, but perhaps not against judges. We shall return to this point in the chapters that follow. But let us now turn to the United States, whose framing was shaped in many ways by the common-law tradition and to the concept of reason that guided its debates over the scope and locus of legal change.

Chapter Four

Fallibility and Foundations
in the U.S. Constitution

The great privilege of the Americans is therefore not only to be more enlightened than others, but to have the ability to make repairable mistakes.

– Tocqueville

As the previous chapters have suggested, debates over legal change often hinge upon the relative competence of various bodies to enact modifications. What sort of expertise should political authorities vested with the power of legal change possess? For example, should "artificial reason" trump the outcome of legislative deliberations? The creation of the U.S. Constitution is, in this regard, no exception. Yet in the United States, these arguments took a distinctive form: The language of amendment during the debates over the Constitution was that of fallibility, both individual and collective. By emphasizing the boundaries of their own reason and the fundamentally experimental nature of their lawmaking, Americans developed a process by which future generations could learn from, and correct, the errors that the new Constitution would inevitably contain.

The framers' concepts of legal change were shaped, of course, both by the unanimity requirement for amendment of the Articles of Confederation and by the state constitutions' amendment procedures. This gave them considerable practical experience with respect to the mechanisms of amendment, yet they turned nevertheless to strikingly abstract discussions of the nature of amendment. In so doing, the language of fallibility served as a touchstone. Such an argument may seem counterintuitive, calling to mind the improbable image of framers struck by insecurity during their deliberations. It may well be the case that fallibility constituted a rhetorical device, masking particular interests over the mechanisms and scope of legal change. Yet the choice of "fallibility" as a trope is nonetheless surprising and provocative. Explaining why the framers may have had recourse to such language – why fallibility emerged as a focal concept and the purposes such an appeal served – is a key aim of this chapter. As we shall see, however, the logic of fallibility, however, was insufficient to thwart efforts at limiting amendment.

After specifying the mechanism governing amendments, Article V of the Constitution reads as follows: "Provided that no amendment which may be made prior to the year one thousand eight hundred and eight shall in any manner affect the first and fourth clauses in the ninth section of the first article; and that no state, without its consent, shall be deprived of its equal suffrage in the Senate." That is, Article V restricts the possibility of amending the Constitution on the two central debates in the Federal Convention: participation in the slave trade, and representation of states in the Senate. The first, governing the slave trade, is an example of time-limited entrenchment; the second, on representation, is an example of what has here been termed "*de facto* entrenchment*," because no state would willingly surrender equal suffrage. Of course, these articles do not embody infallible principles, and the framers did not claim that they did. Entrenchment emerged, transparently, as the product of bargains.

It is sometimes argued that entrenchment was the only means by which the constitutional project could have "gotten off the ground." Such an argument holds that the use of entrenchment, particularly as a gag rule, will resolve debates, enabling ordinary politics to

116

ensue without divisive topics reemerging to destabilize nascent societies. Here, however, I hope to demonstrate that a commitment to the possibility of legal change is more likely to induce consensus than even a short-term use of entrenchment is likely to be. Drawing on recent work by historians, I suggest that the logic of the "gag rule" is, at best, incoherent, requiring asymmetric beliefs about demographics. Likewise, what I have termed the *de facto* entrenchment of the equal suffrage of states in the Senate – because no state would willingly deprive itself of equality – does not seem to have been demanded by the small states. The restriction of Article V seems to have been an unnecessary, and regrettable, feature of the American constitutional project. In conclusion, I suggest that contemporary efforts to establish limits to constitutional change betray the framers' attractive intuition that the principle of fallibility ought to encourage us to abandon the search for limits to constitutional change.

Debates over Amendment at the Federal and Ratifying Conventions

The framers, Jack Rakove reminds us, were empirically minded and had a wealth of constitutional experience on which to draw in the form of the state constitutions.[1] Eight constitutions included procedurally difficult mechanisms for change, attributable, according to Gordon Wood, to a newly emergent conception of constitutional or fundamental law as hierarchically superior to statutory law.[2] As Wood has demonstrated, by the time of the Convention

---

[1] Rakove (1997: xv, 30–31, 97).

[2] Wood (1998: 306–10). For the texts of early constitutions, the Avalon Project at the Yale Law School's "Documents on Law, History and Diplomacy" is an excellent on-line resource. http://www.yale.edu/lawweb/avalon/avalon.htm. See also Walter Dodd's 1910 work, *Revision and Amendment of State Constitutions*. Maryland, Delaware, and South Carolina put the authority to enact

117

the ability of the people to modify their constitution was generally accepted, although the form that constitutional change should take was contested.[3] Perhaps as a result, few discussions on amendment took place in the Federal Convention (and even those were brief), although the possibility of amendment – and the logic underlying

change in the hands of the legislature, albeit via more complicated procedures: Maryland (1776) required the approval of two successive legislatures; Delaware (1776) called for a supermajority of the legislature; and South Carolina (1778) included a waiting period of 90 days and a majority vote of both houses. Pennsylvania (1776) prescribed that a Council of Censors was to be elected every seven years to scrutinize the constitution and guard against encroachments, an institution which was copied by Vermont (1777) except for its mode of election (Dodd, 1910: 28, 34; Wood, 1998: 308). Georgia (1777) required a constitutional convention after receiving petitions from voters in a majority of the states' counties. Rhode Island, whose colonial charter served as a constitution, was initially subject to legislative review, although case law rendered that action suspect (Dodd, 1910: 32). New York's constitution of 1777 addressed amendment in a similarly implicit fashion. (It also provided for a Council of Revision, but this seems to have had the form of an ex ante check on legislation at odds with the constitution.) While North Carolina's 1776 constitution lacked an amendment clause, in directing the provincial congress to draw up a constitution, the Council of Safety argued on August 9, 1776, that "as it is the Corner Stone of all Law, so it ought to be fixed and permanent" (Dodd, 1910: 13). The Constitution of Virginia of 1776 is, perhaps notoriously, silent on the matter of amendment. In *Notes on Virginia*, Jefferson argued for the capacity of the legislature to amend the constitution: "to render a form of government unalterable by ordinary acts of assembly, the people must delegate persons with special powers. [The other states] have accordingly chosen special conventions to form and fix their governments" (Koch and Peden, 1993: 226). Further, Massachusetts (1780) and New Hampshire (1784) each tabled the question of amendment, entrenching the constitution for a period: Massachusetts entrenched the constitution until 1795, at which point a vote of two-thirds would compel the General Court to call a convention, and New Hampshire delayed seven years, at which point a constitutional convention would convene and the changes would require ratification by a two-thirds majority. Delaware, moreover, made totally unamendable the Declaration of Rights, the state's county structure, the bicameral legislature and its internal rules, the importation of slaves from Africa and the sale of "negro, Indian, or mulatto slave[s]," and the clause forbidding the establishment of religion. New Jersey's 1777 constitution entrenched trial by jury.

[3] Wood (1998: 306–10).

118

such an option – had substantial consequences for the shape of the debates.

The first resolution on amendment, on June 5, 1787, held that "provision ought to be made for the amendment of the Articles of Union whensoever it shall seem necessary, and that the assent of the National Legislature ought not to be required thereto."[4] In the first sustained discussion of the proposal, General Charles Pinckney of South Carolina initially disputed the "propriety or necessity" of the resolution.[5] Elbridge Gerry of Massachusetts responded that the "novelty [and] difficulty of the experiment requires periodical revision. The prospect of such a revision would also give intermediate stability to the Govt. Nothing had yet happened in the States where this provision existed to prove its impropriety."[6] From early in the debates (June 5), Gerry suggested that the Constitution ought to be regarded as improvable and as the product of an innovative and likely imperfect process and that the possibility of enacting amendments would induce the states to compromise. This perspective was to have considerable influence.

The second discussion of amendment, six days later, found many states resistant to amendment, holding with Pinckney that amendment was unnecessary (though Pinckney would later change his mind, arguing, "It is difficult to form a Government so perfect as to render alterations unnecessary; we must expect and provide for them").[7] Virginian George Mason supported the resolution on the grounds that the "plan now to be formed will certainly be defective, as the Confederation has been found on trial to be." In perhaps the most famous words on this topic from the Convention, Mason argued that "amendments therefore will be necessary, and it will be

---

[4] Farrand, ed., *The Records of the Federal Convention of 1787*, vols. I–III (1966) [hereafter, *Records*], I, 22.

[5] *Records*, I, 121.   [6] Ibid., I, 122.

[7] Ibid., III, 121, "Observations on the Plan of Government."

better to provide for them, in an easy, regular, and Constitutional way than to trust to chance and violence."[8] Mason's language was Machiavellian: Fortune will inevitably turn, the laws will be found wanting, and so the legislator must keep an eye toward taming the "chance and violence" by institutional means.[9]

Mason advocated relatively easy amendment because of the defects of the Articles of Confederation, in part with respect to the unanimity requirement. But in Madison's account of his remarks, Mason then turned to the specific procedure of amendment: "[I]t would be improper to require the consent of the Natl. Legislature, because they may abuse their power, and refuse their consent on that very account."[10] (Mason reiterated his concern about the power of Congress once the final formulation of the amendment procedure had been developed, calling the role of Congress in the amendment procedure "exceptionable & dangerous."[11])

The second draft of the amendment clause, Article XIX, read, "On the application of the Legislatures of two thirds of the States in the Union, for an amendment of this Constitution, the Legislature of the United States shall call a Convention for that Purpose."[12] In addressing Gerry's concerns about the possibility for two-thirds of the states to "subvert the State-Constitutions altogether,"[13] Alexander Hamilton responded by highlighting the utility of amendment in general on the grounds that the Constitution would be found to be imperfect, before turning to the particular formulation of the clause.

> It had been wished by many and was much to have been desired that an easier mode for introducing amendments had been provided by the articles of Confederation. It was equally desirable

---

[8] Ibid., I, 202–3.
[9] I am indebted to Bernard Manin for this observation.
[10] *Records*, I, 203.   [11] Ibid., II, 629.
[12] Ibid., II, 159.   [13] Ibid., II, 557–58.

now that *an easy mode should be established for supplying defects which will probably appear in the new System*. The mode proposed was not adequate. The State Legislatures will not apply for alterations but with a view to increase their own powers – The National Legislature will be the first to perceive and will be most sensible to the necessity of amendments, and ought also to be empowered, whenever two thirds of each branch should concur to call a Convention – There could be no danger in giving this power, as the people would finally decide in the case.[14]

One might argue that Hamilton's remarks about the amendment procedure were simply one manifestation of his general concerns about the risks of state sovereignty. Although this is certainly correct, the way in which Hamilton chose to frame his point at this particular point in the Convention – September 10, long after the representation debates had concluded – is noteworthy on different grounds. Prior to advancing his preferred amendment procedure, Hamilton reiterated the need for an amendment clause more generally on the grounds of the likelihood of *defect* and the necessity of a means of remedying these imperfections. This claim was repeated throughout the ratification debates, where it came to have force as a means of inducing reluctant actors to accept irksome provisions without rejecting the Constitution as a whole.

Discussions of amendment in the ratifying conventions and in the Federalist Papers regularly appealed, in a variety of modes, to the limitations of human reason and foresight in designing political institutions. One such argument, which will here be termed "epistemological fallibility," was deployed most visibly in the Federalist Papers – as shall be seen shortly – but also appeared in debates in the federal and ratifying conventions. Epistemological fallibilist arguments suggested that a key cause of defects, corrigible through amendment, is the inevitability of human error. In the

---

[14] Ibid., II, 558 (italics added).

Massachusetts ratifying convention, Bowdoin argued that the Constitution would necessarily fall short. "Like all other human productions, it may be imperfect, but most of the imperfections imputed to it are ideal and unfounded, and the rest are of such a nature that they cannot certainly be known but by the operations of the Constitution; and if, in its operation, it should in any respect be essentially bad, it will be amended in one of the modes prescribed by it."[15]

A slight variant on epistemological fallibilist arguments consisted in the argument that humans could not anticipate every possible exigency and that their foresight was necessarily limited; here, this shall be termed the "circumstantial fallibilist" argument. A claim along these lines was advanced by James Iredell at the North Carolina ratifying convention, in which he argued that the inclusion of an amendment clause (which he took as a novelty) emerged from the framers' humility in recognizing these limitations.

> The misfortune attending most constitutions which have been deliberately formed, has been, that those who formed them thought their wisdom equal to all possible contingencies, and that there could be no error in what they did. The gentlemen who framed this Constitution thought with much more diffidence of their capacities; and, undoubtedly, without a provision for amendment it would have been more justly liable to objection, and the characters of its framers would have appeared much less meritorious.... [I]t is a most happy circumstance, that there is a remedy in the system itself for its own fallibility, so that alterations can without difficulty be made, agreeable to the general sense of the people.[16]

A third form, "progressive fallibility," is compatible with both epistemological and circumstantial fallibility: Amendments may be necessary not only because of the imperfection of man or the passage of time, but because advancements in human knowledge have occurred. Progressive fallibility entails the pragmatic claim that

---

[15] Elliot, ed. (1836: II, 83).   [16] Ibid., III, 176–77.

learning will enable improvement, regardless of the quality of the deliberations or their outcomes – which may have been the best achievable by human beings at that point – and it is incumbent upon the current generation to recognize that their laws may be superseded as a function of these innovations. In this fashion, Rev. Samuel Stillman at the Massachusetts convention noted that the Constitution is not "like the laws of the Medes and Persians, immutable" – note the echo of Cromwell here – and "experience will teach us what amendments are necessary."[17]

Overall, the language of fallibility had the appealing attribute of inducing compromise on the part of delegates and, more regularly, as a means of concluding debates. Fallibility possessed unique strategic value as a rhetorical device, because once a proposal had been defended through an appeal to human imperfection, to reject the argument would be tantamount to asserting one's own infallibility. Indeed, to be accused of asserting one's own infallibility was utterly shameful. In Iredell's words from the North Carolina convention, "Those gentlemen who are so self-sufficient that they believe that they are never in the wrong, may arrogate infallibility to themselves, and conclude deliberation to be useless. . . . No gentlemen will say that his [judgment] is not fallible."[18] This language could have induced reluctant delegates to deliberate, as Iredell, in encouraging the North Carolinians not to reject the Constitution out of hand, intended it to do. More frequently, however, the language was used to suggest that a *true* gentleman would not implicitly assert his own infallibility by refusing to set aside his view on what was optimal.

In this vein, the appeal to fallibility served as a means of eliciting support for adopting the Constitution. In a rich defense of the

---

[17] Ibid., II, 169.
[18] Ibid., III, 14. See also the Virginia Convention, in which Randolph insisted, "Infallibility was not arrogated by the convention" (Elliot, 1836.: III, 122).

proposed Constitution from this perspective at the Federal Convention, Benjamin Franklin argued that the Assembly could not be expected to create a "perfect production," though it had done quite a good job. In this context, he suggested that those who wished to prolong deliberations in the hopes of getting their own way tacitly advanced their own infallibility.

> Steele, a Protestant in a Dedication tells the Pope, that the only difference between our Churches in their opinions of the certainty of their doctrines is, the Church of Rome is infallible and the Church of England is never in the wrong. But though many private persons think almost as highly of their own infallibility as that of their sect, few express it so naturally as a certain french lady, who in a dispute with her sister, said "I don't know how it happens, Sister but I meet with no body but myself, that's always in the right" – *Il n'y a que moi qui a toujours raison.* . . . On the whole, Sir, I cannot help expressing a wish that every member of the Convention who may still have objections to it, would with me, on this occasion doubt a little of his own infallibility – and to make manifest our unanimity, put his name to this instrument.[19]

For Calvinist framers, such as Madison, the appeal to fallibility would have had particular resonance.[20] Contemporary scholarship by Richard K. Matthews and Garrett Ward Sheldon emphasizes that Madison's political theory was founded on his Calvinism, particularly on his view of human frailty and the sin and weakness at the core of human nature.[21] The constitutional project, like all human endeavors, was doomed; the best that could be done was to

---

[19] *Records*, II, 641–43.

[20] Fallibility also arose in the context of political corruption, as in this passage from Patrick Henry on the risk that the president would promote his own interests against that of the people: "Man is a fallen creature, a fallible being, and cannot be depended on without self-love." (Elliot, 1836: IV, 388).

[21] Sheldon (2001: 20–26); Matthews (1995: 32).

construct a temporary bulwark.[22] In defending the proposed Constitution against fault-finders in Federalist 37, Madison argued that perfection was unattainable, as a product of the defective nature of human judgment.[23]

> Persons of this character will proceed to an examination of the plan submitted by the convention, not only without a disposition to find or to magnify faults; but will see the propriety of reflecting, that a faultless plan was not to be expected. Nor will they barely make allowances for the errors which may be chargeable on the fallibility to which the convention, as a body of men, were liable; but will keep in mind, that they themselves also are but men, and ought not to assume an infallibility in rejudging the fallible opinions of others.

Throughout the ratifying conventions, the challenge to resisters was their unrealistic – and perhaps even ungodly – expectation that perfection could be achieved. In the Massachusetts convention, Ames argued, "Do they expect a perfect constitution? Do they expect to find that perfection in government which is not to be found in nature?"[24] In the New York ratification debates, likewise, calls for adoption of the Constitution took the form of a lament that the search for an ideal constitution might derail the process: "[A]bove all things, I dread lest the chimerical ideas of perfection in government, which gentlemen may have formed, should induce them to reject this, as falling short of their standard. Perfection, sir, is not the lot of humanity. . . . Nay, such is the weakness of our judgment, that if a perfect plan were offered to our choice, we should conceive it defective, and condemn it."[25] Similarly, in the

---

[22] Matthews (1995: 244). Sheldon, for example, argues the Calvinist strain is evident in Madison's concerns about faction, the causes of which are "sown in the nature of man" (Federalist 10) (Sheldon, 2001: 25).

[23] As in a letter to Archibald Stuart dated Oct. 30, 1787, in *Letters of Delegates to Congress* (vol. 24: 533).

[24] Elliot, ed. (1836: II, 155).

[25] Robert Livingston, June 19, 1788 (Elliot, ed., 1836: II, 210).

Connecticut convention, Gov. Huntington argued that because of the limited nature of human foresight, continuing the convention's efforts to anticipate problems down the road would be of little value. "The Author of nature has given mankind a certain degree of insight into futurity. As far as we can see a probability that certain events will happen, so far we do well to provide and guard. But we may attempt to go too far. It is in vain to think of providing against every possible contingency."[26]

As a means of securing compromise and concluding debate, the language of fallibility and infallibility proved invaluable. It had the attractive feature of bolstering the speaker's humility while calling his opponent's into question and as a means of securing acquiescence while avoiding the charge of stifling deliberation. After all, because the amendment clause would serve, in Iredell's words, as a "remedy in the system itself for its own fallibility," it would certainly enable debate to be reopened at a later point, should it turn out that the decision made was incorrect. But to threaten to delay or to derail conclusion of a debate on the grounds of assuredness in one's own point of view would be hubristic in the extreme.

The fallibility of deliberations among a plural body had particular resonance as a means of securing agreement, particularly for delegates steeped in the republican and even democratic merits of legislative assemblies.[27] A delegate who clung to his own preferences – given the difficulty of securing agreement through deliberation

---

[26] Elliot, ed. (1836: II, 199).

[27] See Wood (1998: 162–64), for the account of legislatures as the most important part of any government and their embodiment of the democratic element of the society. A "well-regulated" democracy had acquired some positive connotations by this point, as John Marshall's words at the Virginia convention suggest: "What are the favorite maxims of democracy? A strict observance of justice and public faith, and a steady adherence to virtue" (Elliot, ed., 1836: III, 223–24). However, democracy still retained some of its negative connotations from the seventeenth century as turbulent and imprudent (see, for example, Hamilton's words at *Records*, I, 299).

among such disparate elements and the necessarily imperfect outcome of such a process – would be implicitly at odds with the principles animating the entire constitution-making endeavor. In arguing that the North Carolina convention ought to seriously consider adopting the Constitution, in light of the fact that it had been debated by "many of the best and greatest men upon the continent," Iredell asked, "Is it probable that we are less fallible than they are? Do we suppose our knowledge and wisdom to be superior to their aggregate wisdom and information?"[28] The plural nature of the assembly provided an additional justification for accepting the outcome as necessarily imperfect, aggregating the fallible knowledge of the individual actors: The best that could be hoped for was a wiser, if still defective, outcome. In Federalist 85, Hamilton wrote,

> The result of the deliberations of all collective bodies must necessarily be a compound, as well of the errors and prejudices, as of the good sense and wisdom, of the individuals of whom they are composed. The compacts which are to embrace thirteen distinct States in a common bond of amity and union, must as necessarily be a compromise of as many dissimilar interests and inclinations. How can perfection spring from such materials?[29]

Note that although the language of fallibility and the prospect of future amendment were most often used by Federalists as a means of advocating adoption of the Constitution as written, anti-Federalists could also use them as a means of advancing amendments at the moment. In the Virginia Ratifying Convention, Patrick Henry concurred with the general approach, proclaiming, "This, sir, is the language of democracy – that a majority of the community have a right to alter government when found to be oppressive." Henry, though, quibbled with the power of a minority to

---

[28] Elliot, ed. (1836: III, 14).   [29] Hamilton et al. (1961: 523–24).

thwart amendments; after all, "in such numerous bodies, there must necessarily be some designing, bad men," inclined to obstructionism. The Federal Farmer argued, further, that the amendment clause was in fact a conservative device: The "few" were likely to conspire against the "many" to block amendments, and to accept the Constitution on the condition of later amendment indicated "servility of character."

The language of fallibility was therefore deployed in two distinct fashions as a means of bringing about an end to debate and the adoption of the Constitution. One was a direct method: Because the outcome of the deliberative process would be necessarily defective (as a product of the aggregation of fallible individual minds), there was no need to strive for perfection. The second, and perhaps more important, was an indirect mechanism: The amendment procedure, reflecting the framers' acknowledgment of their own fallibility, would enable any defects to be corrected in an "easy and regular" fashion later on.

The capability of the Constitution to be amended, derived from a belief in human fallibility, was a key rhetorical tool used by the framers as a cloture device. In an apparent paradox, however, two provisions of the Constitution were exempted from the amendment power, ostensibly because to fail to entrench these clauses would have resulted in the demise of the Constitution: The slave trade was protected through 1808, and the equal suffrage of states in the Senate was permanently entrenched.[30] Does this suggest that these two provisions were viewed as infallible? It is clear that they were not. But was entrenchment necessary, and should we infer that a

---

[30] It is true that neither of these cases is a perfectly straightforward case of entrenchment, because the slave trade had a sunset clause on its unalterability and the equal-suffrage provision (i.e., a state's abandoning its equal status) could be altered unanimously. They are, however, conventionally regarded as limits to Article V; among the many authors who do so, see Ackerman (1991: 13) and Vile (1994: 1).

primary value of entrenchment is as a means of bringing debate to a close?

Temporary Entrenchment of the Slave Trade

In his speech to the North Carolina convention defending amendment on fallibility grounds that we have already considered, James Iredell addressed the decision to secure the slave trade against amendment until 1808.

> The subject of this article was regulated with great difficulty, and by a spirit of concession, which it would not be prudent to disturb for a good many years. In twenty years, there will probably be a great alteration, and then the subject may be reconsidered with less difficulty and greater coolness. In the mean time, the compromise was upon the best footing that could be obtained. A compromise likewise took place in regard to the importation of slaves. It is probable that all the members reprobated this inhuman traffic; but those of South Carolina and Georgia would not consent to an immediate prohibition of it – one reason of which was, that, during the last war, they lost a vast number of negroes, which loss they wish to supply. In the mean time, it is left to the states to admit or prohibit the importation, and Congress may impose a limited duty upon it.[31]

For Iredell, although the compromise was regrettable, to insist upon an end to slavery at the Convention would have resulted in the collapse of the entire constitutional process. This was the best possible outcome, in his view, particularly in light of the passions excited by the matter, and one that reflected a "spirit of concession." Did the debate over entrenchment in fact exemplify this spirit of compromise? The debate in the Convention of September 10, 1787, substantially reshaped the amendment procedure of the U.S. Constitution. A primary concern throughout the day had

---

[31] Elliot, ed. (1836: II, 177–78).

been the possibility that a majority of states could use the amendment process as a weapon and "introduce innovations that may subvert the State-Constitutions altogether," as Elbridge Gerry of Massachusetts put it.[32] It was in this context that a representative raised the concern that three-fourths of the states could modify the Constitution against the interests of a particular state. The interest prompting John Rutledge of South Carolina to raise the matter was slavery. Rutledge said he "could never agree to give a power by which the articles relating to slavery might be altered by the States not interested in that property and prejudiced against it."[33] According to Madison, "In order to obviate this objection, these words were added to the proposition: 'provided that no amendment which may be made prior to the year 1808. shall in any manner affect the 4&5 sections of the VII article,'"[34] and the postponement was "agreed to."[35] In the Constitution, the relevant sections are located in the first and fourth clauses in Article I, Section 9, and read as follows:

> The Migration or Importation of such Persons as any of the States now existing shall think proper to admit, shall not be prohibited by the Congress prior to the Year one thousand eight hundred and eight, but a Tax or duty may be imposed on such importation, not exceeding ten dollars for each person.
>
> No Capitation, or other direct, Tax shall be laid, unless in Proportion to the Census or Enumeration herein before directed to be taken.

Rutledge's rationale for selecting 1808 as the date, Rakove has told us, was that the force of an additional 20 years of slave importation and the southwestern movement of population would assure the security of the slave trade by amassing a critical percentage of

---

[32] *Records*, II, 557.
[34] Ibid.

[33] *Records*, II, 559.
[35] Ibid.

the populace in slave states;[36] the logic read that from the sheer fact of slavery's prominence and moral support in the population, its legal exclusion would rob the Constitution of its legitimacy. One must infer from this story that Rutledge believed that an indefinite ban on modification would be more difficult to gain, because otherwise he would have proposed unlimited entrenchment – yet because he thought the clause would have the force of entrenchment, he did not fear modification.

Indeed, it was widely expected that the southwesterly migration was likely to increase the population and the political might of the South: Madison had written Washington on April 16, 1787, that he expected proportional representation to be relatively easy to enact, because "[a] majority of the States, and those of greatest influence, will regard it as favorable to them. To the Northern States it will be recommended by their present populousness; to the Southern by their expected advantage in this respect."[37] Yet the North had symmetrical access to information about demographic trends, and so the story must be more complicated: The sunset clause did not emerge from naïveté on the part of the North about the likely expiration date of the slave trade.[38] To untangle the logic, we must examine the debates over apportionment in the House and the slave trade. As we shall learn, the selection of 1808 as the end date for the sunset clause appeared earlier, and the clause's inclusion in the amendment procedure specified in Article V was at a minimum redundant and at a maximum merely emphatic. The sunset clause in the amendment clause reflects a bargain struck some weeks earlier, in which a

---

[36] Rakove (1997: 72, 91).

[37] Madison to Washington, April 16, 1787, in Hutchison et al., ed. *Papers of James Madison* (9: 382–85). I am grateful to Jon Elster for drawing my attention to this quotation.

[38] The historical account that follows – especially the migration story – has been greatly influenced by Rakove's masterful work, *Original Meanings* (1997).

decision was made to include a sunset clause on a slave importation provision.[39]

Concerns about legislative flexibility given the possibility of demographic shifts were at the forefront of the lower-house apportionment debate. The entrenchment of representation was an option, and, as suggested above, migration information was readily available. Gouverneur Morris of Pennsylvania advocated "irrevocably fixing the number of representatives which the Atlantic States should respectively have, and which each new State will have," so as to "secure to the Atlantic States a prevalence in the National Councils."[40] In particular, Morris worried about the western states, as Madison noted: "He dwelt much on the danger of throwing such a preponderancy into the Western Scale suggesting that in time the Western people wd. outnumber the Atlantic States."[41] According to Rakove, Morris's motivation was neither abolitionism nor racism, but fear that a population-based rule for apportionment would result in the marginalization of Pennsylvania and the commercial/maritime states of the Northeast to the "interior & landed interest" of the South and West.[42] A wealth-based rule for apportionment, under which slaves were considered property, would have been acceptable, and while serving together on a committee on apportionment, John Rutledge and Morris concurred on this point.[43] The committee, on which four large-state delegates and two Massachusetts delegates sat, proposed on July 9 that the national "[l]egislature be authorized from time to time to augment

---

[39] For clarity, I have chosen to emphasize the first half of the clause regulating the importation of slaves, today included in Article I, Section 9, clause 1, but will not address to any great extent its related provision, Article I, Section 9, clause 4, also governed by the sunset clause ("No Capitation, or other direct, Tax shall be laid, unless in Proportion to the Census or Enumeration herein before directed to be taken"). This provision addresses the ability to levy taxes by any rule other than the three-fifths clause.

[40] *Records*, I, 533; Rakove (1997: 71).   [41] *Records*, I, 571; Rakove (1997: 71).

[42] Rakove (1997: 73).   [43] Ibid., 71.

ye. number of representatives" at their discretion on the basis of both wealth and population.[44]

The method of apportionment supported by the committee would be governed by legislative discretion, which would take account of slaves as property. Morris argued that constitutional reference to slavery was therefore unnecessary (a controversial point throughout the Convention). Moreover, Morris claimed that Pennsylvanians would chafe at having slaves counted alongside freemen; aggregating the groups for demographic purposes would imply that slaves had an equal right to representation. Yet Morris's point was more threatening: The inclusion of a reference to slavery in the Constitution would imply its perpetuity and prompt the rejection of the Constitution.[45] If the Southerners insisted upon counting slaves, Morris and Rufus King (of Massachusetts) said, the Union could not last. General Charles Pinckney of South Carolina similarly threatened the collapse of the constitutional process over slavery: "Genl. Pinckney reminded the Convention that if the Committee should fail to insert some security to the Southern States agst. an emancipation of slaves, and taxes on exports, he shd. be bound by duty to his State to vote agst. their Report."[46]

The initial suggestion to include a sunset clause seems to have been made by King. On August 8, he railed against the fact that "in two great points the hands of the Legislature were absolutely tied. The importation of slaves could not be prohibited – exports could not be taxed. Is this reasonable? . . . Shall one part of the U.S. be bound to defend another part, and that other part be at liberty not only to increase its own danger, but to withhold the compensation for the burden? . . . There was so much inequality & unreasonableness in all this, that the people of the Northern States could never be reconciled to it." Moreover, and most importantly here, "he had

[44] *Records*, I, 559.
[45] *Records*, I, 604.   [46] *Records*, II, 95.

133

hoped that some accommodation wd. have taken place on this subject; that at least a time wd. have been limited for the importation of slaves."[47]

On August 21, Luther Martin of Maryland proposed a measure to permit taxation on the importation of slaves. The debate that followed the proposal, on August 22, set the initial terms for the bargain. Pinckney accepted the taxation on slaves as a compromise measure.[48] Morris seized upon the possibility for a compromise, suggesting that additional clauses related to taxes on exports and a navigation act "may form a bargain among the Northern & Southern States."[49] Martin, a member of the committee that brokered the deal, offered a detailed account of the decision to limit the importation of slaves. According to Martin, the eastern states exchanged the temporary importation of slaves for the elimination of restrictions on the creation of navigation acts; a simple majority decision rule would leave the southern states financially vulnerable to the commercial states.

> I found the *eastern* States, not withstanding their *aversion to slavery*, were very willing to indulge the southern States, at least with a temporary liberty to prosecute the *slave trade*, provided the southern States would in their turn gratify them, by laying no *restriction* on *navigation acts*; and after a very little time, the committee by a great majority, agreed on a report, by which the general government was to be prohibited from preventing the importation of slaves for a limited time, and the restrictive clause relative to navigation acts was to be omitted.[50]

Thus, the committee's report of August 24 placed a time limit at 1800, the importation of slaves could be taxed (the requirement that the tax could not exceed $10 per person was not introduced

---

[47] *Records*, II, 220.   [48] *Records*, II, 373.
[49] *Records*, II, 474.
[50] Luther Martin, "Genuine Information," in *Records*, III, 158.

until the end of debate on August 25), and navigation acts were no longer subject to a two-thirds majority for enactment.[51] Rufus King's compromise suggestion to subject slavery to a time limit had succeeded.

On August 25, General Pinckney moved to push the expiration date to 1808, to which Madison responded, "Twenty years will produce all the mischief that can be apprehended from the liberty to import slaves. So long a term will be more dishonorable to the National character than to say nothing about it in the Constitution."[52] Madison was overruled; the clause was approved by a vote of seven states (New Hampshire, Massachusetts, Connecticut, Maryland, North Carolina, South Carolina, and Georgia) to four (New Jersey, Pennsylvania, Delaware, and Virginia). But Rutledge was not yet satisfied; he pushed for the reiteration of the 1808 rule in the amendment clause. "The earnestness of S. Carolina & Georgia was farther manifested by their insisting on the security in the V article, against any amendment to the Constitution affecting the right reserved to them." More than three decades later, Madison described the conflict over the importation of slaves as potentially devastating and the resolution of the sunset clause as the only solution to the impasse.

> In the convention the former States [those opposed to the continued importation of slaves] were anxious, in framing a new constitution, to insert a provision for an immediate and absolute stop to the trade. The latter were not only averse to any interference on the subject; but solemnly declared that their constituents would never accede to a Constitution containing such an article. Out of this conflict grew the middle measure providing that Congress should not interfere until the year 1808; with an implication, that after that date, they might prohibit the importation of slaves into the States then existing, & previous thereto, into the States not then existing.[53]

---

[51] Rakove (1997: 88). [52] *Records*, II, 415.
[53] Ibid.

Madison attributed the willingness of the eastern states (Connecticut, Massachusetts, and New Hampshire) to push the date to 1808 to both "the tone of opposition in the States of S. Carolina & Georgia, & such the desire to gain their acquiescence in a prohibitory power...influenced however by the collateral motive of reconciling those particular States to the power of commerce & navigation; against which they felt, as did some other States, a very strong repugnance."[54] Although Connecticut, Massachusetts, and New Hampshire were aware of the possibility that slavery might continue to "produce mischief" even after the time period elapsed, the possibility that South Carolina and Georgia might withdraw or that the navigation acts would be restricted was sufficiently high that they acceded to the 1808 date – or so it has been argued.[55]

Yet it is not clear that South Carolina and Georgia would have actually refused to join the Constitution if the right to import slaves had not been preserved. This is a difficult counterfactual to assess, but a key piece of evidence provided by historian Paul Finkelman suggests that the constitutional enterprise did not hinge on the sunset clause: Neither of the states was actively importing slaves from Africa at the time of the Convention. In fact, South Carolina did not import slaves from Africa from 1787 until 1803; but from 1803 to 1808, eighty thousand new slaves were imported. In Finkelman's words, to argue that the sunset clause was necessary would entail

---

[54] Letter, James Madison to Robert Walsh, Nov. 27, 1819, in Kurland and Lerner, ed. (1987: Vol. 3, Article 1, Section 9, Clause 1, Document 20).

[55] Freehling (1972); Maltz (1992); Fleming (2001: 94). In addition, Russell Hardin seems to claim this, arguing that the threat of an amendment against slavery was sufficient to "[break] the initial coordination," and only after settling the matter "more or less irrevocably" could the constitution serve its coordinative purpose (Hardin, 1999: 99). The presence of a sunset clause, rather than an entrenchment clause, makes this story somewhat complicated, as shown. If the purpose of the clause was simply to delay debate until 1808, the coordination of interests might also have been in flux.

the claim that the Deep South would have "rejected the constitution over the right to import slaves in the future when they in fact were not currently importing them."[56]

In addition, if importation truly was the issue that could have broken the Convention, it is not clear why a sunset clause would have resolved the matter. Either the framers must have believed that in 1808 they would have been less passionate and a reasonable compromise could be secured then that could not be achieved at the Convention; or they must have thought that in 1808 they would be able to get an outcome preferable to the one that they were now forced to accept. Now, the former may be the case: As we have seen, given the framers' language of fallibility elsewhere, they may have viewed themselves as gripped by passion and incapable of achieving an optimal outcome at this point. But why they might have expected themselves to be less passionate about the matter 20 years later is less clear: Presumably, the issue was likely to generate a similarly heated response if it remained sufficiently contentious to demand a reconsideration. Moreover, if the framers were so passionate that they could not find a resolution, it is difficult to argue that they were simultaneously sufficiently rational to put aside their passions temporarily.

That is, the matter would have been heated if it were still unresolved. But perhaps both sides imagined that the matter would have been essentially decided on one side or another by that point. The argument that each side anticipated that at a later date they would be in a better position to achieve their preferred outcome seems to accord with the historical evidence, but explaining the asymmetry between the forecasts of each is more challenging. Understanding the incentives of the slave states is less complicated: If they anticipated, with Rutledge, that 20 years would suffice for the *de facto*

---

[56] Finkelman (2001: 31–32).

entrenchment of slavery, then acquiescing to a later reconsideration would not have cost them much. However, why did the northern states not anticipate this as well? They would have had to believe that the legitimacy of slavery was in danger in spite of demography and that in 1808 they would be able to renegotiate the agreement on terms more favorable to them – particularly in light of the fact that the states were not currently engaging in the importation of slaves. Alternatively, they may have acquiesced in light of the benefits they stood to gain from the navigation acts agreement. Finally – and perhaps most plausibly, if regrettably – they may well have believed that the benefits of coordinating on a Constitution were sufficient to outweigh the long-term costs of accepting slavery, but accepted the 1808 rule to placate the ratification assemblies. It is hard to avoid concluding, with Paul Finkelman, that the Northern delegates could not have believed that this would render slavery temporary and that they simply capitulated on the matter.

Whatever the explanation, the representatives were left to justify the bargain to their constituents. In explaining the decision to the South Carolina House of Representatives, Pinckney argued that the representatives of the southern states had "endeavored to obviate the objections [of the northern states] that were made in the best manner we could, and assigned reasons for our insisting on the importation, which there is no occasion to repeat, as they must occur to every gentleman in the house: a committee of the states was appointed in order to accommodate this matter, and, after a great deal of difficulty, it was settled on the footing recited in the constitution."[57] James Wilson, in the Pennsylvania Ratifying Convention, provided a similar defense: "I consider this [time limit] as laying the foundation for banishing slavery out of this country; and though the period is more distant than I could wish, yet it

---

[57] Debate in South Carolina House of Representatives, Jan. 16–17, 1788 (Elliot, ed. 1836: IV, 272–73, 285–86).

will produce the same kind, gradual change, which was pursued in Pennsylvania."[58]

Note that this was not the final effort at entrenching slavery in the United States. The notorious "Corwin Amendment," proposed by Representative Thomas Corwin of Ohio, was among the proposals seeking to protect slavery as a means of preventing war; the final version of the proposed constitutional amendment was entrenched: "No amendment shall ever be made to the Constitution which will authorize or give to Congress power to abolish or interfere, within any state, with the domestic institutions thereof, including that of persons held to labor or service by the laws of the said state."[59] The House and the Senate both approved the Assembly, and it was signed by James Buchanan[60]; further, Lincoln supported the amendment, and in his first inaugural said, "Holding such a provision to now be implied constitutional law, I have no objection to its being made express and irrevocable."[61] Though approved by Illinois, Maryland, and Ohio, the amendment was insufficient to preserve the Union.

Entrenchment of the Equal Suffrage of States in the Senate

Although the debate over the inclusion of the sunset clause was brief, in comparison to the decision to protect the equal suffrage of the states in the Senate, it was positively protracted: The clause was accepted without any debate whatsoever in response to the "circulating murmurs" of the fretful small states.[62] In Madison's words, South Carolina and Georgia then united "with the small states, who insisted on a like security for their equality in the

---

[58] James Wilson, Pennsylvania Ratifying Convention, Dec. 3, 1787 (Elliot, ed. 1836: II, 451–53).

[59] Vile (2003: 118).

[60] Bernstein with Agel (1993: 91), cited in Vile (2003: 118).

[61] Vile (2003: 118).   [62] *Records*, II, 629.

Senate."[63] Certainly, the matter of specifying the amendment procedure had become thorny, and the reemergence of representation in the debates could not have been welcome.

Even prior to the Convention, representation was anticipated to be a sticking point. In fact, Delaware included in its instructions to delegates that the revisions to the Articles of Confederation were not permitted to "extend to that part of the Fifth Article of the Confederation of the said States ... which declares that 'In determining Questions in the United States in Congress Assembled each State shall have one Vote.'"[64] John Dickinson and George Reed had in fact requested these instructions as a commitment device securing them externally against pressure from other states on this point.[65] The small states, eager to preserve their status as equal legislative actors, argued that proportional representation, as provided for in the Virginia Plan, would threaten their interests, reduce their authority in the nation overall, and subvert their autonomy *qua* states. The large states, for their part, argued that they had little reason to act in concert against the small states – the major schism, Madison argued, would be Southern versus Northern interests – and that the national government would protect the interests of the citizens as a whole.[66] By July 2, the states were at stalemate: The vote on a motion for equal suffrage in the Senate, proposed by Oliver Ellsworth of Connecticut, was tied, and a committee composed of a member from each state was elected to try to resolve the deadlock. The deal brokered by the committee provided for an equal vote in the Senate and proportional representation in the lower house and specified that all appropriations bills would originate in the lower house and not be subject to amendment by the upper house.

---

[63] Letter, James Madison to Robert Walsh, Nov. 27, 1819, in Kurland and Lerner, ed. (1987: Vol. 3, Article 1, Section 9, Clause 1, Document 20).
[64] *Records*, III, 574–75. [65] Rakove (1997: 60)
[66] Ibid., 66–67.

The days that followed were largely taken up with apportionment in the lower house, and relatively little time was spent on the question of equal suffrage in the Senate. The debate that did occur on the question was increasingly polarized. The stakes were high, and the feeling was articulated that if compromise were reached, it would be untouchable. In James Wilson's words, "If equality in the second branch was an error that time would correct, he should be less anxious to exclude it being sensible that perfection was unattainable in any plan: but being a fundamental and a perpetual error, it ought by all means to be avoided."[67] The belief among the large states seems to have been that the small states would eventually concede, and it appears that they were surprised by the small states' narrow victory on July 16. The possibility of collapse loomed overnight, but in the morning, only Gouverneur Morris seems to have been willing to begin renegotiations. The decision "to yield to the smaller State, and to concur in such an Act however imperfect & exceptionable" prevailed.[68]

Although the Convention had finally settled the issue of the slave trade on September 10, when debate on Article V was reopened on September 15 the consequences of the amendment procedure for the integrity of the states was still unsettled. Sherman was the first to raise the point, arguing that a three-quarter majority vote could reduce a state's equal suffrage in the Senate or even abolish a state.[69] After all, the battle over representation had been nearly destructive to the Convention. A state, Sherman implied, would be foolish to risk the renegotiation of its status after ratification; without entrenchment, the bargain could be immediately reopened after ratification, with disruption the only certain outcome. At a minimum, the proposed amendment procedure should be modified to require a convention.

---

[67] Elliot, ed. (1845: V, 315).,   [68] *Records*, II, 20.
[69] *Records*, II, 629.

In response to Mason's concerns about the role of Congress, Morris and Gerry proposed that a convention would be called upon the request of two-thirds of the states; while Madison pointed out that Congress would be as bound to propose amendments requested by two-thirds of the states as to call a Convention, he had no substantive objection, and the new procedure was added. After a few unsuccessful efforts to further modify the status of conventions, the debate turned again to Sherman's concern about the vulnerability of states. Sherman first suggested an addendum to the procedure providing "that no State shall without its consent be affected in its internal police, or deprived of its equal suffrage in the Senate."[70] The phrases "internal police" and "equal suffrage" were sufficiently provocative that Madison immediately responded: "Begin with these special provisos, and every State will insist on them, for their boundaries, exports &c."[71] The proposal was rejected by all but Connecticut, Delaware, and New Jersey, in response to which Sherman moved that Article V should be struck altogether, seconded by David Brearley of New Jersey. This, too, only Connecticut, New Jersey, and a divided Delaware accepted. Gouverneur Morris then proposed as an alternative "that no State, without its consent shall be deprived of its equal suffrage in the Senate."[72] The "circulating murmurs of the small States" gave the suggestion additional force, as the threat of disruption grew, and the motion "was agreed to without debate, no one opposing it, or on the question, saying no."[73] Without dissent, Article V had again been constrained for the sake of the general constitutional bargains.

Although Sherman did praise the "easy and peaceable mode of making amendments" in a letter to William Floyd, his efforts against the use of the amendment clause continued after

[70] Ibid., 629–30.
[71] Ibid., 630.
[72] Ibid., 631.
[73] Ibid.

ratification.[74] Tellingly, he framed his objection to proposed amendments in the language of fallibilism: "I do not suppose the constitution to be perfect, nor do I imagine, if congress and all the legislatures on the continent were to revise it, that their united labours would make it perfect. I do not expect any perfection, on this side the grave, in the works of man, but my opinion is, that we are not, at present, in circumstances to make it better."[75]

Although Sherman's rejection of Madison's changes was formalistic, it had theoretical bite. Sherman interpreted Article V as permitting only supplemental amendments, not those that would repeal a portion of the text: "We might as well endeavor to mix brass, iron and clay, as to incorporate such heterogeneous articles, the one contradictory to the other.... When an alteration is made in an act, it is done by way of supplement: The latter act always repealing the former in every specified case of difference."[76] Sharply put: "All that is granted to us by the fifth article is, that whenever we think it necessary, we may propose amendments to the Constitution – not that we may propose to repeal the old, and substitute a new one."[77]

In contrast to the ubiquitous arguments from fallibilism in the discussions of amendment, the debates over the inclusion of the slavery clause and the equal-suffrage clause in Article V were characterized by appeal to undisguised self-interest. Although the decision to constrict Article V could conceivably have taken the form of an argument from infallibility – a hypothetical certainty in the immorality of slavery, for example – the provisions selected were not of this ilk. Indeed, the two most contentious debates of the convention found an uncomfortable home in the amendment clause.

---

[74] Collier (1971: 282).   [75] Sanderson (1823–27), II, 286–87.
[76] *Annals of Congress* 1790, 734–35; Boardman (1971: 293).
[77] *Annals of Congress* 1790, 742; Boardman (1971: 294).

Article V, Fallibility, and Infallibility

Turning to the third set of arguments defending legal change, we might note that a rich literature on amendment emerged in the early 1990s, partially as a function of the renewed interest in constitutional theory after 1989. This work was largely empirical, examining the exclusivity of the American Article V or prescribing a particular level of flexibility for a transitional democracy. Yet, as the title of the best compendium of this work implies (*Responding to Imperfection,* Levinson, ed., 1995), the theoretical potential of the topic is considerable. Although many have recognized that the notion of amendment presupposes the fallibility of a constitution – if constitutions were perfect, no amendment procedure would be necessary – the importance of fallibilism has not been fully appreciated by contemporary constitutional and democratic theorists. In particular, the implications of this claim in a negative sense (the decision to make certain laws unamendable is problematic, because it is suggestive of infallibility) have been almost entirely unexplored.

Beyond the framers, such an argument also has a distinguished pedigree in democratic theory through the writings of Jeremy Bentham and John Stuart Mill. The French Constitution of 1791 made constitutional change extraordinarily difficult: While affirming "*le droit imprescriptible*" to change its constitution, three successive legislatures had to approve a proposed amendment before it could be referred to an Assembly of Revision. Further, no changes were permitted for the first two legislatures, meeting every two years – thus resulting in a 10-year sunset-claused entrenchment of the whole constitution. In "Necessity of an Omnipotent Legislature," Bentham argued that the constituent assembly had asserted its own infallibility in creating immutable law. In comparison, Bentham wrote, "The infallibility of the Pope *rentre dans l'ordre de la nature.* Twelve hundred infallible persons deriving their infallibility like the Bramins from birth, like the Popes from election, or like the Grand

Lama from something between both, to all this I am ready to subscribe without difficulty."[78] Fallible men, "brought into the world without a miracle, subject to human infirmities and passions,"[79] composed the Assembly. As Iredell and Hamilton had argued, the idea that any product of the Assembly could be infallible was particularly outrageous insofar as every act of the Constitution emerged from a process of arguing and bargaining. The Assembly spent two and a half years "doubting, disputing, changing, struggling," and at some point, upon voting, "all of a sudden at a certain hour of a certain day have worked itself up into infallibility."[80]

Mill most famously adopted both the language of fallibility and of infallibility in his defense of the freedom of discussion in *On Liberty*. Elsewhere, in supporting a parliamentary reform bill that would expand working-class electoral power, Mill also argued in favor of invoking fallibility in asserting political authority: "There is a better way of persuading possessors of power to give up a part of it: not by telling them that they make a bad use of their power – which, if it were true, they could not be expected to be aware of – but by reminding them of what they are aware of – their own fallibility."[81] Continuing, Mill invoked Tocqueville's praise for the self-correcting nature of American legislatures (see the epigraph opening this chapter) and insisted that Parliament ought not to stop at simply "repealing bad laws which Parliament itself had made" – instead asking, rhetorically, "But is this all that the Legislature of a country like ours can offer to its people?"[82]

Arguing on behalf of mutable law from the perspective of fallibility – and against the implicit assertion of infallibility inherent in the creation of immutable law – thus has a rich history. Further, it is a

[78] Bentham, *Necessity of an Omnipotent Legislature* (Bentham 2002: 279).
[79] Ibid. [80] Ibid.
[81] Mill, John Stuart (1963–91: XXVIII, 64), cited in Urbinati (2002: 83).
[82] Ibid., 67 A fuller discussion of fallibility and infallibility in the works of Bentham and Mill appears in Schwartzberg (forthcoming).

remarkably attractive insight for democrats. This logic emphasizes the contingent nature of the outcomes of an assembly, reminding us that bargains and even good arguments ought to be subject to revision. This insight is especially valuable for outvoted minorities. The capacity to modify laws – to reopen debate at a later time – may induce minorities to accept the verdict of assemblies, rather than withdrawing or attempting to revolt. Yet fallibility goes further than simply giving the minority an institutional incentive to obey. The minority is told: Although this is the outcome of the majority decision (and, perhaps, on Condorcetian grounds possesses some special truth status), it is indeed fallible – we could, in principle, be wrong, and you could be correct. Such an argument grants the minority a certain epistemic dignity, further encouraging them to regard the outcome of a majority decision as rightly commanding their obedience but as genuinely revisable in the future. Jürgen Habermas has argued similarly. In his words, "[B]ecause of its internal connection with a deliberative practice, majority rule justifies the presumption that the fallible majority opinion may be considered a reasonable basis for a common practice until further notice, namely, until the minority convinces the majority that their (the minority's views) are correct."[83] The ability to deem the fallible outcome of majority votes legitimate, Habermas argues, depends in part on the capability of the minority to reopen debate and, through the force of the better argument, persuade the majority to reverse their decision. Thus, entrenchment is a risky strategy: "Doubts about the legitimacy of majority decisions on matters with irreversible consequences are revealing in this regard."[84]

Despite the framers' seminal arguments on behalf of constitutional change – grounded upon the appeal to fallibility – and the prominent political theorists who have defended such an approach,

---

[83] Habermas (1996: 306).   [84] Ibid., 179.

few today defend amendment on such grounds. Indeed, in the American context, even scholars generally supportive of extensive popular powers of amendment have reaffirmed the value of entrenchment.

Limits to Amendment and "Substantive Principles"

The contemporary literature on Article V has tended to focus on two questions: the exclusivity and scope of the amending power. The question of exclusivity – that is, whether or not constitutional change can occur outside of the method prescribed in Article V – is less important for our current discussion. If one construes amendment broadly – in Levinson's language, as any "legal invention not derivable from the existing body of accepted legal materials,"[85] – one may account for a wide array of fundamental changes to the legal order, only some of which occurred formally through the amendment procedure specified in Article V. Two salient changes that did not, Bruce Ackerman has argued, include Reconstruction and the New Deal. According to Ackerman, these cases demonstrate that Article V does not monopolize the mechanism of constitutional change. In Ackerman's view, this is fortunate because it bolsters the dualist, or two-track, nature of American democracy, wherein occasionally "constitutional moments" emerge, breaking through the passivity of ordinary politics to motivate the citizenry to reconsider the foundations of their democracy. Although these constitutional moments can generate constitutional amendments, more often they do not, in part because the mechanism of Article V is overly stringent (and should, in Ackerman's view, be replaced by a "Popular Sovereignty Initiative").[86] The argument that legitimate constitutional change may happen outside Article V via appeal to

[85] Levinson (1995: 16). [86] Ackerman (1998: 415).

a majority of the population, as Akhil Amar also claims, is salient insofar as it appears to emerge from something external to the constitution: an underlying conception of the right to change.

This argument – that there are substantive principles "beneath" the constitution, which may or may not be susceptible to change – brings us to the more important question of the scope of the amending process. The claim that there are implicit limitations on Article V date, as John R. Vile has demonstrated, to the early part of the 19th century, in which John C. Calhoun argued that states could secede in response to amendments that would radically alter the Constitution.[87] Scholars such as Thomas Cooley and William Marbury would develop the logic of implicit limits to constitutional amendment from the perspective of states' rights; Marbury identified women's suffrage in particular as among those alterations that were impermissible on the grounds that they constituted a violation of state legislative power.[88] Contemporary scholars have argued that the Constitution embodies certain "first principles," as Akhil Amar has suggested, or "substantive limits," beyond which the Constitution cannot be amended, or, if it did, would no longer be recognizably the American Constitution. Tellingly, however, scholars dispute what constitutes these substantive limits, which suggests the broader contestability of these sorts of claims. Efforts at restricting the boundaries of constitutional amendment are bound to be challengeable, and reasonable people are likely to disagree about what constitutes an unalterable principle. From Amar's perspective, there is an unalterable foundation of the Constitution in the form of popular sovereignty, derivable primarily from the many references in the Constitution to the "rights of the people" so constituted. Likewise, Walter Murphy argues forcefully for a contemporary defense of substantive limits, referring to the Basic Law of the

---

[87] Vile (1995: 193).   [88] Ibid., 193–194; Marbury (1919).

Federal Republic of Germany (to be taken up in the next chapter). Murphy's claim is that there are changes to the Constitution that would so subvert the democratic order that the Constitution would become illegitimate. As such, the Constitution should be understood as embodying principles such as the "democratic order" and "human dignity."[89] This, Murphy argues, is because both democracy and constitutionalism rely on consent, and the deprivation of human worth via a particularly appalling amendment would necessarily fail to command genuine consent of the whole realm. Given that these sorts of substantive limits must be given institutional meaning – "practical effect," in Murphy's language – in order for them to have teeth, and given that this meaning is bound to evolve over time, the declaration of substantive limits on change is, in essence, granting the judiciary the sole authority to enact change on fundamental questions.[90]

As Lester Orfield argued in 1942 in rejecting substantive limits on change, "support for the broad view of the power to amend is found in the fact that the framers of the Constitution regarded

---

[89] Barber (1984) echoes this claim, although Barber's appeal to the right-answers thesis is beyond the scope of this chapter.

[90] Brandon has offered four reasons to be skeptical of substantive limits to constitutional amendment. First, there are tensions in the constitution that would make a claim of unconstitutionality hard to substantiate. Second, constitutional meanings are dynamic over time, and as such it is difficult to argue that a particular amendment is at odds with a preexisting constitutional norm. Third, empirically, amendments receiving wide support would be difficult to challenge, and, fourth, the constitution will therefore prove to be a weak barrier to change. Yet Brandon argues that limits may be possible if the value is explicit, if it is part of a network of mutually supported values, if the amendment does not really reflect the public will, or if it is procedurally ambiguous. Brandon gives too much away: If he is correct that the Constitution is comprised of tensions over values and that the meaning of particular provisions is in constant motion, seeking limits to constitutional change is likely self-defeating. The explicitness of the value does not mitigate its capacity for shifting interpretation, and in the context of a link with existing values the need for specification may be even greater (Brandon, 1995: 215–36).

their work as far from perfect and consequently anticipated a wide use of the power to amend."[91] Yet those deploying arguments for substantive limits to change, like explicitly entrenched provisions, likely do not actually seek to reify "first principles." Few would deny that our conception of what constitutes a life worthy of dignity, for example, is constantly shifting: Ideally, perhaps, it occurs in the direction of ensuring that the treatment of prisoners, for example, is less rather than more cruel, or that the importance of granting the right of marriage to gay and lesbian Americans becomes widely recognized. To the extent that we accept the durability of change – and our fallibility, both in enacting and revising laws – we have a choice: We can permit amendments and locate this authority in the people and their representatives, or we can situate this authority with judges. Again, in restricting the possibility of amendment, we do not actually reify our laws; instead, we shift the power to determine what constitutes cruelty, for instance, to the courts. To the extent that constitutional laws are entrenched, we are unable to use the amendment procedure to counter judicial determinations of their scope. Instead, we must wait for a later court to revise these past decisions – if it is willing to do so.

The framers defended amendment as a solution to the problem of fallibility. These arguments took two distinct forms: an epistemological fallibilism about the product of human design and a circumstantial fallibilism about the effects of time on the institutions. Rather than offering an evolutionary approach to legal change, though, the framers chose to include an amendment clause. Yet the desire to resolve the two most contentious matters at the

---

[91] Orfield (1942: 116–17). Orfield also cites *"expressio unius est exclusio alterius,"* the danger of limiting the scope on revolutionary grounds, the Supreme Court's view that no such limitations exist, the empirical implausibility of abuse of the clause, and the sovereignty of the people of the United States (115–26).

Convention – slavery and apportionment – led them to retreat from this commitment: They chose to remove, in effect, the capacity to change each state's equal suffrage in the Senate and to exclude temporarily the ability to modify the slave trade. This was not on the grounds of moral or rational certainty, but on the grounds that without these self-interested provisions, the entire constitutional project would fail. This may or may not have been true, but in any case the logic through which these clauses were protected competed with the background belief in human frailty underlying the amendment procedure.

Today, as we shall see in the following two chapters, the use of unamendable clauses or highly inflexible laws may be epistemologically and morally serious: We may believe that the concept of human dignity, for example, ought to have the status of infallibility. But it may be purely instrumental, the result of constitution makers trying to lock in bargains. The language of fallibilism that grounded the creation of Article V reaffirms the experimental nature of the American constitutional project. Yet as successful as the experiment has been, Article V contains a perpetual reminder of its deficiencies in the form of the slavery provision. In disabling amendment, we may protect the reprehensible, instead of simply securing the precious.

Chapter Five

Protecting Democracy and Dignity in Postwar Germany

Since Athens, as we have seen, critics have targeted democracy for its tendency to change its laws. In the post–World War II world, such arguments have taken on new force: The flexibility of the Weimar Constitution is often taken to be a contributing cause of the rise of Nazism and the ensuing human tragedy. At the time, the risk that democracy could by democratic means, perhaps through established amendment procedures, turn itself into dictatorship seemed very grave indeed. In light of such an argument, to reject entrenchment may seem to be not only obtuse but perhaps even inhumane. As a result, in transitional societies – particularly in transitions from regimes marked by humanitarian disaster – entrenchment seems to be an obvious and wholly uncontroversial decision. Who would challenge the German desire to enact such a rule in the wake of atrocities? The German protection of human dignity, with federalism and the democratic order, thus represents the hardest case for an argument against entrenchment.

Predictably, scholars regularly regard the decision to entrench in Germany as the inevitable response by the framers to the deficiencies of Weimar and a *cri de coeur* against Nazism.[1] It is reasonable,

---

[1] The assumption that the human dignity clause simply reflects the exigencies of the end of Nazism is widespread, even among experts on German jurisprudence. See, for example, an article by the former president of the German

of course, that such a view would be widespread. It makes intuitive sense that the framers would have wished to respond to the deficiencies in the Weimar Constitution – including, arguably, its mutability – that aided Hitler's ascent to power. However, such a story is at best incomplete. It does not adequately take account of the jurisprudential context in which the choice was made – in particular, it neglects the rival theories of Carl Schmitt and Hans Kelsen and the possibility that the latter might have served as an intellectual resource for a rejection of entrenchment. It also fails to acknowledge the bargaining that surrounded the decision to entrench and the role that institutional and self-interest may have played in such choices. That is, both ideas and interests played fundamental roles in the decision to entrench in the German Basic Law, but alternative ideas and interests might have prevailed; there were ample grounds for rejecting entrenchment. Finally, the argument that the entrenchment of human dignity was the necessary response to Hitler may discourage us from probing more deeply into the consequences of the protection of such norms, lest we appear to treat "dignity" cavalierly. Here, I seek both to explain entrenchment in Germany as the non-obvious and even contingent outcome of a series of debates and bargains, and as a relatively undesirable one at that.[2]

Federal Constitutional Court, Ernst Benda (1999); Currie (1994: 9); Steinberger (1990: 214); Fox and Nolte (1995); Katz (1996); Kommers (1997).

[2] We should be careful on several counts: In particular, we ought not to elide the distinction between explanatory and normative analysis, that is, between analyzing the process of institutional emergence and assessing the desirability of the outcomes of such a process, as James Johnson cautions us (Johnson 2005). Simply because an institution emerges (as most do) from a bargaining process marked by power inequities does not mean that institutions cannot be justified normatively. However, it should lead us to scrutinize the consequences – particularly the non-obvious effects – of these institutions more carefully and to beware of imputing "moral motivations" to framers simply from the normative attractiveness of their outcomes. This is especially important when the outcomes of such choices are not subject to reversal without the potentially insurmountable costs of constitutional revolution.

The relevant provisions of the Basic Law read as follows[3]:

Article 79(3)

Amendments to this Basic Law affecting the division of the Federation into Länder, their participation on principle in the legislative process, or the principles laid down in Articles 1 and 20 shall be inadmissible.

Article 1 reads as follows:

(1) Human dignity shall be inviolable. To respect and protect it shall be the duty of all state authority.
(2) The German people therefore acknowledge inviolable and inalienable human rights as the basis of every community, of peace, and of justice in the world.
(3) The following basic rights shall bind the legislature, the executive, and the judiciary as directly enforceable law.

Article 20 provides that

(1) The Federal Republic of Germany is a democratic and social federal state.
(2) All state authority is derived from the people. It shall be exercised by the people though elections and other votes and through specific legislative, executive, and judicial bodies.
(3) The legislature shall be bound by the constitutional order, the executive and the judiciary by law and justice.
(4) All Germans shall have the right to resist any person seeking to abolish this constitutional order, if no other remedy is available.[4]

---

[3] Official translation from the Press and Information Office of the Federal Government, available at http://www.bundesregierung.de/Webs/Breg/EN/Federal-Government/FunctionAndConstitutionalBasis/BasicLaw/basic-law.html (accessed July 11, 2006).

[4] It is worth noting one central ambiguity here in the protection of Article 1. Articles 2–19, which specify basic rights, are not expressly protected, though they might readily have been. As such, we could think that the force of Article 1 is solely to protect "human dignity." Yet, because human dignity grounds

I shall focus on the decision to protect human dignity (and therefore basic rights) and, briefly, federalism in the German Basic Law; but in doing so, I adopt a slightly different methodology from that used in the preceding chapters. Analyzing the decision to entrench requires, in part, a historical reconstruction of the framing of the German Basic Law, comparable to the accounts offered in the previous chapters. Here, however, I examine different points at which the logic could have turned to demonstrate the contingent and even paradoxical nature of the decision to entrench; there was nothing inevitable about the outcome. The horrors of the recent past and the need for Allied approval did indeed constrain the framers' choices. But I hope to show that they had considerable latitude in terms of the formulation of the possible provisions protecting basic rights and federalism and the extent to which these norms would be subject to amendment. However, the Germans did not want to begin a formal process of constitution making, preferring to defer doing so until after the return of full sovereignty by the Allies. Thus, entrenchment was a counterintuitive decision, given their wish for a transitional document. Indeed, neither human dignity nor federalism was entrenched until the second reading of the Basic Law.

Given the paradoxical nature of the choice, what could have compelled the framers to entrench rather than opt for ordinary constitutionalism? Whereas the entrenchment of federalism emerged at the last minute as the outcome of a bargain (and Allied pressure), the protection of human dignity is a far more complicated story. Although the reason for entrenchment may have been the failure

"human rights" in the German constitution, and because the entrenchment clause also protects the democratic order, we might expect that amendments to such provisions as Article 2 (rights of liberty) and Article 3 (equality before the law) would also be unconstitutional. In particular, Article 2's provisions securing the right to the free development of personality, the right to life, and the inviolability of the person are very closely linked to Article 1, and so scholars tend to regard such provisions as similarly entrenched. See the discussion in Karpen (1988: 32–33).

of Weimar, few members of the constituent assembly would have pinned the rise of Hitler solely on the institutional form of the mechanism for constitutional change. Though the amendment of the Weimar Constitution to extend President Ebert's term in office and the unconstrained possibility of legislative departure from the Constitution (*Verfassungdurchbrechung*) surely would have shaped the framers' views,[5] Weimar had an additional and complicated effect on the decision. Unpacking the "response to Weimar" hypothesis more carefully, I suggest that the criticisms of Weimar by Carl Schmitt (along with the work of Richard Thoma and Arnold Brecht) considerably influenced the framers. But there was nothing inevitable about this: Hans Kelsen, whose theory of constitutional adjudication led to the decision to create a constitutional court, criticized the use of entrenchment – and Kelsen could have provided the framers with the intellectual grounding for an alternative decision not to entrench.

Even in the hard case of postwar Germany, then, the choice of entrenchment was not obvious, and the framers could have adopted ordinary constitutionalism without failing to take human dignity seriously. Yet the most salient objection is what I have called the "democratic autophagy" argument: There is a risk that democracies may, through democratic means such as constitutional amendment, subvert those principles and norms essential to democracy (thereby consuming itself). In this context, the argument holds that in the absence of entrenchment, Germany would have been vulnerable to dictatorial incursions, leading to the abrogation of human rights or of democratic principles more broadly. Obviously, this is a difficult counterfactual to assess, but we can try to analyze the situation in the following way. First, we can ask: Has entrenchment ever served as an effective constraint on a democracy bent on legal change? The answer is likely to be no. If entrenchment is the sole effective

---

[5] Currie (1994: 7).

bulwark against tyranny, as both Kelsen and later Rawls suggested, the state of the democracy must be extremely vulnerable, probably so much so that an entrenchment clause would have minimal effect. That said, entrenchment might well serve some purpose as a lingering reminder of the devastation in the recent past. Even if entrenchment is primarily hortatory, however, it is important to assess whether it reifies power asymmetries or leads to normatively unattractive consequences.[6] In this section, I will focus on the use of entrenchment as a means of shifting power away from the legislature and toward the judiciary. In Germany, this has meant that the constitutional court's power to interpret the human dignity clause is unchecked and irrevocable, except through subsequent decisions. In conclusion, I assess the broader legacy of the human dignity clause for contemporary constitution making.

The Allies and the Basic Law

First, how much autonomy did the Germans actually have in the design of their constitution? This is a familiar question but a necessary precursor to our discussion: If the Germans did not actually possess the power to determine whether or not to entrench, analyzing their decision making would be, at best, pointless. A short but incomplete answer is that the Allied Control Authority did indeed have the power to place conditions on constitution making, yet the risk that an "imposed" constitution would lack legitimacy served as a formidable constraint on its ability to dictate the constitution. Both the German ministers-president and the military governors recognized the importance of an "organic" constitution, one that did not emerge from the occupying forces, lest the constitution fail due to public perception that the constitution essentially

---

[6] See Knight (1992) for an account of power asymmetries and distributive conflict as the source of institutional emergence and change.

represented a continuation of occupation by legal means. Further, the members of the Allied Control Authority were not monolithic in their preferences for the German constitution, even on the most salient issues, such as federalism, and the variation in the design of the four administrative zones reflected these divisions. The constitution, then, could be at most only partially shaped by the Allies, given the need for the constitution to possess a German pedigree and the heterogeneity of their own views.

Concerns about legitimacy, in fact, had led to the decision to reject entrenchment in the Japanese constitution in 1946. Constitutional discussions had as their subtext the pervasive concern that as soon as the occupation ended, the Japanese would shed the constitution[7]; as in Germany, the Americans were preoccupied with the fear that the Japanese would view the constitution as inauthentic and externally imposed – yet they were also worried that in the absence of entrenchment, the Japanese would modify their laws, and thus the Government Section draft initially entrenched basic rights. However, when MacArthur received the final draft, he deleted only one provision: the entrenchment of basic rights, likely on the grounds that it would seem to bind the Japanese excessively.[8] Thus, there was some precedent to which the Allies could turn in Germany: If constitutional legitimacy was at stake, the Allies might not have preferred Germany to entrench. As we shall see, however, the American delegation did later pressure the Germans to protect the rights of the *Länder* and in so doing might have induced them to entrench federalism.

---

[7] See, for example, the discussions in "'Meeting of the Steering Committee with Committee on the Emperor,' original draft, Wednesday, 6th February 1946," included in Takayanagi et al. (1972: I, 134).

[8] *Foreign Relations of the United States 1946* (1971: VIII, 124–25); MacArthur, both publicly and in confidential memoranda on the constitution, repeatedly emphasized his concern that the Japanese would reject an imposed constitution.

The Germans, then, could have retained the authority not to entrench human dignity, at a minimum, but they could not have refused to engage in constitution making. Against the preferences of the ministers-president, the Allies insisted that the Germans create a constitution prior to the return of sovereignty on pain of delay in the transfer of authority. Again, the Germans wished to preserve as much decision-making power as possible in the creation of the constitution; they did not wish to take orders from the military governors on the design of the document. Yet in June 1948, at the conclusion of informal talks in London, representatives of the six powers (United States, Britain, France, Belgium, Netherlands, and Luxembourg) had decided to convene a meeting of the military governors and the ministers-president of the western zone in Germany to authorize the latter to form a constituent assembly. The representatives issued a communiqué in which they outlined their recommendations for the constitution, outlining the "general principles" that the constitution would need to contain to receive the military governors' approval.

The central paragraphs in this document read as follows:

> The constitution should be such as to enable the Germans to play their part in bringing to an end the present division of Germany not by the reconstitution of a centralized Reich but by means of a federal form of government which adequately protects the rights of the respective states, and which at the same time provides for adequate central authority and which guarantees the rights and freedoms of the individual.
>
> If the constitution as prepared by the Constituent Assembly does not conflict with these general principles the military governors will authorize its submission for ratification by the people in the respective states.[9]

[9] "Communique Issued by the London Six-Power Conference," June 7, 1948. Reprinted in Ruhm von Oppen (1955).

The ministers-president responded coolly to the communiqué; again, they had wished to defer the creation of the constitution until after full sovereignty had returned. After a brief effort on the part of Social Democratic and Christian Democratic leaders to decline the directive in the communiqué, the ministers-president instead reluctantly accepted the mandate to create a constituent assembly, but outlined certain proposed revisions in the "Coblenz Resolution." Some key requests were terminological: The ministers-president proposed to call the constituent assembly a "Parliamentary Council," designed to create not a constitution but a provisional "basic law" that could be converted into a constitution upon the transfer of sovereignty.[10] After some negotiations, particularly over the relationship of the Occupation Statute (which outlined the relative powers of the Allies and the German government) and the constitution, the military governors agreed to these changes.[11]

Note the significance of the reluctance on the part of the Germans to engage expressly in the act of constitution making. As Carl Friedrich argued, the distinction between *Verfassung* (constitution) and *Grundgesetz* (basic law) hinged in part on the dimension of sovereignty that the former was thought to possess and the latter did not. This point was of special importance to the Germans, who wished to keep sharp the distinction between a law created under occupation and one that emerged from a truly sovereign community and the permanence of the former and the provisional and transient dimension of the latter.[12] Bear in mind:

---

[10] Friedrich (1949: 469–70).

[11] Ibid., 473, also noted that the Occupation Statute, against the wishes of the ministers-president, did not recognize universal human rights or civil liberties, other than habeas corpus and immunity from arbitrary searches and seizures.

[12] Ibid., 477.

If the Germans did not want to confer even the status of constitutional law on the outcome of the so-called Parliamentary Council, why would they have wished to entrench the outcome of such an assembly?

Again, the Germans sought to maximize their own agency, both throughout the constitution-making process and after the return of sovereignty. At the first substantive discussion of the Parliamentary Council, held in Bonn on September 8, 1948, the Social Democrat and legal scholar Professor Dr. Carlo Schmid complained: "There are almost more limitations than grants of German powers in Document I." Document I, the authorizing document for the constituent assembly, had reiterated the communiqué's requirement that the constituent assembly draft "a democratic constitution which will establish for the participating states a governmental structure of federal type which is best adapted to the eventual re-establishment of German unity at present disrupted, and which protect the rights of the participating states, provide adequate authority, and contain guarantees of individual rights and freedoms."[13] Rather than entrenching, however, Document I prescribed an amendment procedure identical to the ratifying procedure: a two-thirds majority vote of the *Länder* (with a simple majority of the voters in each state).[14]

Schmid chafed both at the insistence that the Germans create a constitution and at the subsequent obligation to receive Allied approval. In his words, "A constitution which has to be approved by somebody else represents the policy of the one entitled to approve it, but does not represent a true result of the sovereignty of the

---

[13] "Document I, Constituent Assembly (Meetings of Military Governors and Ministers-President of the Western Zones on Future German Political Organization), (MGMP/P(48)1), 1 July 1948," reprinted in *Documents on the Creation of the German Federal Constitution* [hereinafter, *Documents*], at 44.

[14] Document I, in *Documents*, at 44.

people of the one who has to obtain approval."[15] Further, Schmid also rejected the idea that a future German constitution would need to develop via the amendment of the Basic Law; rather, he preferred that the Basic Law prescribe the conditions for its own replacement by a constitution emanating from a "free self-determination" by the German people.[16]

During the period August 10–25, 1948, prior to the plenary session of the constituent assembly (termed the Parliamentary Council), the military governors appointed an expert delegation to meet at Herrenchiemsee to create a draft constitution. This committee included representatives for each of the 11 *Länder* and 14 advisors, primarily high officials and constitutional scholars.[17] This first, comprehensive constitutional draft repeatedly characterized rights as "inviolable" (Articles 1, 3, 5) and specified that fundamental rights may not be set aside (Article 21(1)). However, the entrenchment provision in the Chiemsee draft differed both in content and in form from the one ultimately accepted by the Germans. The Chiemsee draft did entrench democracy, if in a very broad form. Article 108 read as follows: "Motions for amendments to the basic law, through which the free and democratic fundamental order is to

---

[15] "Excerpts from the Speech of Dr. Suesterhenn (CDU), Opening the Plenary Meeting of the Parliamentary Council held in Bonn on 8 September 1948," in Documents, at 78.

[16] In contrast, however, Prof. Dr. Adolf Suesterhenn of the Christian Democrats argued that in fact the Basic Law ought to be seen as an emanation of the sovereign will, rather than the product of the Allies: "[We] feel completely free in fulfilling our function and responsible only to the German people and the Lord....The CDU/CSU faction does not regard the principles and minimum requirements set forth by the Military Governors as restrictions of its political freedom of will; for these principles conform with what my faction demands from the future German constitution on its own accord, without regard to the existence of a Military Government, and to the demands of the Occupying Powers" (idem, in *Documents*, at 82).

[17] Kommers (2006).

be abolished, are not permissible."[18] The Chiemsee draft did not specifically entrench human dignity – though it did specify the inviolability of the "dignity of human personality" and the role of the public power in preserving such dignity – nor did it entrench federalism, although it did make amendments to the federal structure more difficult to enact than other alterations. Article 107 provided that a law incorporating a deviation from "the federal type of fundamental order" required unanimous approval of the Bundesrat, whereas the normal amendment procedure prescribed in Article 106 required two-thirds of both the Bundestag and the Bundesrat plus an affirmative vote in a referendum receiving at least 50 percent participation.[19] The experts then submitted the Chiemsee draft to the ministers-president, who accepted the report and referred it to the Parliamentary Council as a source of guidance during deliberations.

The first reading of the constitution rejected entrenchment entirely, favoring again a unanimous vote of the Bundesrat for modification of the federal order, and it omitted any special protection of basic rights. However, by the second reading, entrenchment had indeed emerged: The amendment clause protected Article 1 (human dignity clause and the inviolable character of basic rights) and Article 21 (the democratic and social federal character of the state; the emanation of state authority from the people; the exercise of power in accordance with the Basic Law via elections and governmental responsibility to the people; and the limitation of governmental action by the law). The third reading kept the

---

[18] "Chiemsee Proposal: Draft of a Basic Law (Appendix to the Report of the Constitutional Meeting at Herrenchiemsee from 10–25 August 1948. Translated and Summarized by Governmental Structures Branch, Civil Administration Division)," reprinted in *Documents*, at 73.

[19] That is, unless an alternative Senate proposal, contained in the Chiemsee draft, had been accepted, which would have required a majority of the Bundesrat for some modifications to the powers of the federal government. Chiemsee's referendum for amendment lasted through the second reading and was then eliminated.

entrenchment of the second reading and retained the malleability of the federal structure, adding only that "[a] law by which the organization of the Federation into Länder and the basic co-operation of the Länder in legislation and the administration (Article 65) are affected shall require the approval of a majority of four-fifths of the votes of the Bundesrat" (Article 106(3)). Only in the fourth reading did all four provisions – Articles 1 and 20 (the adapted Article 21), the organization of the Federation into *Länder*, and the role of the *Länder* in legislation/administration – acquire entrenchment.

Rights and the Response to Statutory Positivism

Despite his stated opposition to constitutional permanence, Carlo Schmid – the head of the Social Democratic Party (SPD) faction, chairman of the Main Committee, and a member of the Committee on Principles and Basic Rights – played an instrumental role in the decision to entrench. In Schmid's words:

> I am of the opinion that it does not allow the concept of democracy to set itself the conditions for its elimination. Only where one goes so far as to believe in democracy as something that is necessary with regard to the dignity of man, does democracy represent more than the product of a decision on mere practicability. But if one has that much courage, one must also have the courage to be intolerant toward men who want to use democratic methods to kill democracy.[20]

Schmid's argument from democratic autophagy, however, seems to be in tension with his prior rejection of constitution making and certainly of entrenchment. So how did he come to hold it? This is a complicated story. The explanation for the decision to

---

[20] "Excerpts from the Speech of Dr. Carlo Schmid (SPD), at the Plenary Meeting of the Parliamentary Council held in Bonn, 8 September 1948," in *Documents*, at 79.

entrench fundamental democratic principles – notably human dignity and thereby basic rights – lies primarily in the history of German jurisprudence. There are at least three possible jurisprudential sources for the "eternity clause," protecting human dignity and the fundamental principles of democracy: Richard Thoma, Carl Schmitt, and Arnold Brecht. Is a jurisprudential plausible? Scholarship on constitution making today tends – rightly, in my view – to focus on institutional interest and self-interest in constituent assemblies. Yet in this case, many, if not most, framers of the German Basic Law were familiar with these jurisprudential arguments: The members of the Parliamentary Council were disproportionately lawyers, many of whom had studied jurisprudence, and several were professors of law. Carlo Schmid himself was a law professor who in the postwar era would visit Carl Schmitt at his home in Plettenberg.[21] Thus, jurisprudence and constitutional theory likely shaped the framers' views of their available options, particularly because the issue of the limits to constitutional amendment had been debated vigorously in the recent past.

Briefly, statutory positivism, given its fullest expression by Paul Laband, dominated jurisprudence during the time of the German empire. Its central tenets included both the denial that natural law provided any limits to positive law and the argument that the will of the state was the source of all law, constitutional and "ordinary," including all rights. All law, therefore, had equal juridical status; and as the law was an emanation of the sovereign's will, it had no validity outside this will – all law was of human design. As such, there were no substantive – and ought to be no procedural – limitations on the capacity to modify any law.[22] At the turn of the century, scholars focused on the logical problems associated with the Labandian claim that amendment must follow formal rules. If all

---

[21] Müller (2003: 61).
[22] Caldwell (1997: 36); see also Kelly (2003: 87).

law is the emanation of the sovereign will and is therefore mutable, the procedures themselves regulating the creation and flexibility of the law must be similarly flexible, the critics argued; if not, then the amendment procedure is entrenched and therefore substantive limits to amendment, in fact, exist, which are prior to the sovereign's will.[23]

The question of whether there could be limits to constitutional change took its sharpest form after the collapse of the monarchy and the creation of the Weimar Constitution. Despite the continuing importance of statutory positivism, the Weimar Constitution did include a comprehensive set of basic rights. Such a view emerged – as the decision to entrench human dignity in the Bonn Constitution – through the influence of a combination of abstract ideas about the nature of rights and through straightforward political wrangling. In the first draft, Hugo Preuss, the drafter of the Constitution, did include a few fundamental rights – in particular, equality before the law, liberty of faith and conscience, and the protection of national minorities,[24] likely as a concession to Catholics, who continued to recognize the validity of natural law, desired the protection of religious freedom, and endorsed certain communal rights, such as marriage against "'certain communistic teachings.'"[25] By the second draft, the Weimar constitutional committee had been persuaded to include 12 rights, largely due to pressure from political parties across the spectrum. This effort included an attempt by social liberal Friedrich Naumann to update the concept of rights,

---

[23] Ibid., 38.

[24] Koch (1984: 266). Hucko argues that this should be read as a "somewhat empty gesture in order to honor the achievements of the movements for emancipation of earlier times" (1987: 58). However, given the dominant attitude toward rights of the period, the explanation that Preuss wished to honor past achievements seems peculiar. A more plausible explanation may be a desire to satisfy the Catholics, who he knew would demand a substantial list of rights in the assembly.

[25] Caldwell (1997: 75).

in the form of epigrams like "Green light for the fit and able" and "Order and liberty are siblings," which failed.[26] Ultimately, 56 articles of basic rights were included: The right-wing German National People's Party (DNVP) and the industry-backed National Liberal Centre (DVP) were largely responsible for them, although they were loosely based on the 1849 constitution and shaped by Professor Konrad Beyerle, a deputy of the Bavarian People's Party (BVP).[27] As Peter Caldwell has argued, "Much less than a coherent totality, the catalog of rights codified compromises protecting the basic interests of the groups that put the constitution together."[28] Likewise, the level of flexibility appended to these rights emerged from a compromise: The acceptance of a two-thirds majority for amendment reflected both the Catholic Center's desire to protect basic rights against encroachments and the positivists' wish to affirm that these laws were ultimately mutable.

Amendment of the Weimar Constitution, Article 76, required a two-thirds vote with a two-thirds quorum or a simple majority vote in a popular referendum. As Caldwell has noted, Richard Thoma and Gerhard Anschutz turned to the Labandian analysis of the 1871 constitution for their commentary, arguing that there were no substantive limits to amendment, as long as the people followed the proper formal procedure for change. Anschutz criticized Schmitt for his appeal to substantive limits to the constitution on theoretical grounds[29] and on practical (and ideological) grounds rejected the claim, in particular, that the federalist system was inviolable: The particular *Land* was subordinate to the federal state, and the formal ability of the federal state to amend any provision emphasized the superior status of the republic. For Thoma, the rejection

---

[26] Hucko (1987: 58–59).   [27] Koch (1984: 270); Hucko (1987: 59).
[28] Caldwell (1997: 74).
[29] Anschutz, "Die Verfassung des Deutschen Reichs," quoted in Jacobson and Schlink (2000: 29).

of substantive limits derived both from his view of the nature of parliamentary decision making and a commitment to democratic agency. The shifting coalitions and bargains endemic to parliamentarism stood in contrast to the Schmittian theory of the immanent and homogeneous will of the German people. In Thoma's words:

> Thus the Weimar Constitution is not only historically based on authorization by the majority of the nation, but also at present always based on its freely revocable sufferance. The opinion that the doubled *pouvoir constituant* regulated by Article 76 cannot be without limits, that one cannot have "really decided in Weimar for a system of apparently legalized coup d'état," fails to appreciate the idea – daring, perhaps, but sublime in its consistency – of free, democratic self-determination.[30]

Yet though Thoma had explicitly argued for the futility of establishing limits to change, he appears to have revised his view of the utility of these substantive limits by 1948, when he served as an advisor in drawing up the Basic Law: He proposed a "norm of inviolability," which may have served as the basis for the entrenchment clause.[31] Thus, Thoma constitutes one possible direct source of entrenchment, but there remain two other potential candidates: Carl Schmitt and Arnold Brecht.

Schmitt and the Eternity Clause

Carl Schmitt asserted that he was the author of the "eternity clause," as several authors have noted.[32] His claim to be the father of entrenchment is plausible in two respects: Such arguments are

---

[30] Thoma, "The Reich as a Democracy" (2000: 163).
[31] Thoma, "Über Wesen und Ersheinungsformen der Modernen Demokratie quoted in Jacobson and Schlink (2000: 286).
[32] Schmitt (1958: 345); Preuss (1999: 166); Jacobson and Schlink (2000: 286); Fox and Nolte (1995: 18–20).

indeed to be found in his constitutional writings, and his effect on the legal scholars who designed the constitution, in particular Carlo Schmid, was unquestionably strong. Yet, of course, Schmitt was *persona non grata* during the constitution-making process because of his Nazism; and despite the tantalizing and ironic twist such a pedigree of entrenchment would provide, we must examine this boast carefully if not skeptically.

Schmitt posited a substantive conception of constitutionalism, which theoretically grounds his endorsement of entrenchment. Schmitt's critique of statutory positivism and parliamentary sovereignty targeted precisely the question of limits to amendment. The mechanisms by which particularistic interests are translated into parliamentary majorities were, on Schmitt's reading, fundamentally undemocratic.[33] Without constraints on the ability of the Parliament or the people as a whole to modify the law, more broadly, the Constitution was reduced to abject contingency and to formalistic "quantitative majoritarianism." As Schmittian democracy depended on homogeneity – and the elimination of heterogeneous elements[34] – quashing factionalism and particularistic claims was a crucial precondition to the proper exercise of the monistic sovereign's power. Because of this, the counting of votes to determine the people's will negated the uniformity intrinsic to democracy. "The will of the people can be expressed just as well and perhaps better through acclamation, through something taken for granted, an obvious and unchallenged presence, than through the statistical apparatus that has been constructed with such meticulousness in the last fifty years."[35]

---

[33] The opposition to technology implicit in this rejection of mathematics and functionality is crucial, and it is thoughtfully analyzed in John McCormick's *Carl Schmitt's Critique of Liberalism: Against Politics as Technology* (1997: ch. 5).

[34] Schmitt (2000: 8–14); see also Cohen and Arato (1994: 232).

[35] Schmitt (2000: 16).

The rejection of the "statistical apparatus" took its sharpest form in addressing matters of constitutional change and limitation of that change. In the first place, Schmitt was disdainful of the content of contemporary constitutionalism, which protects the outcome of bargains by the representatives of particularistic interests via the hurdle of a two-thirds majority for amendment. Second, apart from the substance of the constitution, Schmitt did not accept that the presence of a supermajority in any sense shields a minority from abuse by the majority. The notion that there could be persistent minorities violates the presumption of homogeneity. Moreover, if there were in fact such a minority, "it would be a peculiar type of 'justice,' to declare a majority all the better and more just the more hard pressed it is, and to maintain abstractly that ninety-eight people abusing two persons is by far not so unjust as fifty-one people mistreating forty-nine."[36]

Schmitt argued further that if a particular provision requires protection because of "its special inner value," a protection of 67 percent, rather than entrenchment, "obviously constitutes a half measure and only emergency aid."[37] If the composition of the democratic sovereign were heterogeneous, as it must be for a qualified majority to have any utility, then the presence of a two-thirds majority to oppress the minority was even more menacing than a simple majority would be. Moreover, the two-thirds majority could impose limitations that would outlast its own presence: Even if the majority were to slip into the minority, without a new two-thirds vote to modify it, the provision would endure.[38]

The reason to secure certain provisions against the transitory decisions of the ordinary legislature was to protect a "particular matter from an empty, majoritarian functionalism that surrenders up all substantive values to the current majority, while, on the

---

[36] Schmitt (2004: 41).   [37] Ibid., 42.
[38] Ibid., 43.

contrary, parliamentary democracy's legislative process should be open to every content, each opinion, and any aspiration or goal."[39] But constitutional provisions were instead vulnerable to the transitory will of a supermajority. These constitutional laws were protected because of their "value-content," Schmitt argued, but their sacredness was negated by their vulnerability to amendment: "One cannot put marriage, religion, and private property solemnly under the protection of the constitution and, in one and the same constitution, offer the legal means for their elimination."[40]

In the context of Weimar's value neutrality, entrenchment would be impossible: "[A]ny goal, however revolutionary or reactionary, disruptive, hostile to the state or to Germany, or even godless, is permitted and may not be robbed of the chance to be obtained by legal means." The constitution privileged nothing, not even the current form of regime. However, the Second Principal Part of the Constitution nevertheless itemized a list of substantive rights, "introduced in unparalleled scope through countless 'anchorings,' guarantees, inviolability declarations, insurances, and other material-legal entrenchments," Schmitt noted caustically.[41] This was fundamentally inconsistent, Schmitt claimed. Less coherent still was the fact that whereas principles of general freedom and property required a 51 percent majority to change, the rights of religious societies and officials demanded 67 percent. Although Schmitt highlighted this as an example of inconsistency with respect to substantive values, he might have noted instead that this was undoubtedly the outcome of pressure by the Catholic Centre, in particular: the level of protection that these provisions received resulted from bargaining within a heterogeneous constituent assembly.

[39] Ibid., 45–46. [40] Ibid., 46.
[41] Ibid., 39–40.

Citing French constitutional theorist Maurice Hauriou, Schmitt argued that certain fundamental – and unamendable – principles ground each constitution: "When a constitution envisions the possibility of constitutional revisions, the constitution does not intend, for example, to provide a legal method for the elimination of its own legality, still less the legitimate means to the destruction of its legitimacy."[42] At a minimum, constitutions should protect these fundamental clauses from revision, so as not to include within the constitution the means for its own destruction.

In a 1958 afterword to the second edition of *Legality and Legitimacy*, Schmitt cast the essay as a "despairing attempt to safeguard the last hope of the Weimar Constitution." He identified his "core thesis: that the legality of a party can only be denied when the authority to make constitutional amendments is limited," and he castigated critics who had rejected this view as "political fantasy law."[43] In this regard, Schmitt claimed to be the father of entrenchment as an institutional form. As we have seen, such an argument is not without merit. But can he have been the source for the decision to entrench the human dignity clause *per se*? This is less plausible. Schmitt specifically repudiated the notion that democracy can have as its foundation universal human equality or worth – or, further, that human equality could ground any form of concrete political association.[44] Thus, although Schmitt's logic would have influenced the thinking of the Parliamentary Council on constitutional theory – especially given the shadow Schmitt's political turn would have cast on his argument for the apolitical nature of abstract human equality – it remains unlikely that Schmitt would have been the sole influence on the question of entrenching human dignity.

---

[42] Ibid., 58. [43] Ibid., 95.
[44] Schmitt (1985: 10–13); see also Mouffe (1998: 161–63).

Thus, although Schmitt may have provided the intellectual background for the question, the decisive wording may well have originated in the work of Arnold Brecht, a legal scholar who had advocated the entrenchment of rights (but the malleability of the federal structure[45]) in his enormously influential 1945 work, *Federalism and Regionalism in Germany: The Division of Prussia*. Brecht's rationale for the entrenchment of rights was counter-majoritarian; that is, he argued that rights would serve as a bulwark against the "danger that majority rule will once more be abused to abolish the protection of the individual from arbitrary government."[46] Although the rhetorical use of "human dignity" dated to the Frankfurt Parliament,[47] the Holocaust gave the phrase a new resonance. Brecht, occasionally cited as a candidate for the author of the entrenchment clause, identified human dignity as among the fundamental principles worthy of this special status in the following passage.

> [I]t would be advisable for the new German constitution (and for any other democratic constitution to be enacted in the future) to contain certain sacrosanct principles and standards that could not be abolished or suspended by emergency decrees or by any parliamentary or plebiscitarian majorities, either directly or indirectly

[45] Brecht is somewhat unclear in his prescriptions for the federal structure. He argues that certain fundamental states' rights, such as the right to elect their own governments and the right of these governments to be represented in the Federal Council, ought to be immune from "simple national legislation" (1945: 136). I take this to mean that constitutional amendment via qualified majority ought to be possible. Moreover, Brecht writes, "The basis of the German federal system, at least in the greatest part of the country, should be sought in the states' constitutional share in the federal government rather than in any unalterable distribution of jurisdictions between federal and state governments" (Ibid.).

[46] Ibid., 138.

[47] Friedrich Ernst Scheller, President of the High Court at Frankfurt an der Oder in Silesia, argued that the Frankfurt Parliament should abolish the death penalty as a violation of "dignity and human life" (Hucko, 1987: 17).

(as through enabling acts or similar devices). These sacrosanct principles and standards should be distinct from "ordinary" rights stipulated in the Bill of Rights, in that they could not be impaired even by constitutional amendments. They should include fundamental principles regarding respect for the dignity of man, the prohibition of cruelties and tortures, the preclusion of ex post facto laws, equality before the law, and the democratic principle that the law itself cannot validly discriminate for reasons of faith or race.[48]

Thus, whereas Schmitt, and perhaps Thoma, would have shaped the intellectual background of the decision to embrace limits to amendment, the work of Brecht might have provided a justification for the precise formulation that the framers ultimately adopted.[49] In any case, it seems clear that not simply the experience of Weimar's institutions, nor Nazism, shaped decision making in the Parliamentary Council. The jurisprudence that preceded and then responded to the Weimar Constitution – in particular, the central question of the substantive limits to amendment – would have also shaped the decision to entrench.

In this vein, Schmid had argued that rights in the Basic Law should not be used as a protection for antidemocratic activities. At Herrenchiemsee, Schmid had proposed the inclusion of a bill of

---

[48] Brecht (1945: 138). Finn (1991: 188) asserts that this passage had a direct effect on the framers' decision to entrench.

[49] In addition, Article 1 may also reflect the preamble to the Universal Declaration of Human Rights – "Whereas recognition of the inherent dignity and of the equal and inalienable rights of all members of the family is the foundation of freedom, peace, and justice of the world" – and the UDHR's Article 1, which reads, "All human beings are born free and equal in dignity and rights." Available at http://www.un.org/Overview/rights.html (accessed July 6, 2006). Kommers has argued that the "framers lifted this language almost verbatim from the Universal Declaration of Human Rights" (1989 edition: 564, footnote 1). Other sources – including Brecht – seem possible, especially given Kommers's view that this language was sufficiently expansive to encompass Kantian, natural law, socialist, and classical liberal perspectives.

rights, citing "Anglo-Saxon legal thought that a Constitution, even if only provisional, that does not include fundamental rights is no constitutional charter at all."[50] These rights ought to be foundational and serve as genuine guarantees, rather than existing solely as an "annex at the tail end of the Basic Law, as the list of basic rights of the Weimar constitution was a mere annex to it,"[51] but they ought not to extend to the promotion of dictatorship and the ultimate abnegation of freedoms. Schmid's emphasis on the immutable character of these rights ultimately proved decisive in the Committee on Principles and Basic Rights. He pressed the importance of the unwritten inner structure of the constitution in his endorsement of Article 108 of the Chiemsee draft, by which amendments to the democratic and free fundamental order were inadmissible. With virtually no opposition, the Committee decided to entrench.[52]

From the jurisprudential perspective, then, it might seem that the decision to entrench was overdetermined. Was entrenchment the *inevitable* solution to the deficiencies of Weimar, or could a different approach have grounded decision making on the question of constitutional amendment? Was there an alternative intellectual resource constituting a response to Weimar, a competing jurisprudence, to which the framers might have turned?

Hans Kelsen: An Alternative Jurisprudence

David Dyzenhaus has suggested that whereas Schmitt's political theory "positively invited" the fascistic seizure of power in Germany to occur, Hans Kelsen's legal theory "offered no legal resource"

---

[50] *Der Parlamentarische Rat 1948–1949: Akten und Protokolle* 2:75; Steinberger (1990: 213).

[51] Ibid.

[52] *Der Parlamentarische Rat V-I*, "Unverbruchlichkeit der Verfassung (Art. 108 Che.), Neunte Sitzung, Oct. 12, 1948.

to resist such an action.[53] Let us invert this view: If the framers were willing to draw upon Schmitt as a source of an "inviolable core" against constitutional amendment, might they have turned to Kelsen instead for an alternative solution to the apparent problem of constitutional change? Obviously, Kelsen, who as a Jew had been forced out of his position as dean of the law faculty in Cologne, was untainted by Nazism in a way that Schmitt was not. Perhaps more importantly, the Federal Constitutional Court (FCC) was a "Kelsenian tribunal"[54] – that is, it was profoundly shaped by Kelsen's defense of judicial review of legislation and the instrumental role he played in the creation of the Austrian constitutional court. Thus, it is not impossible that the members of the Parliamentary Council could have turned to Hans Kelsen as decisive on the question of entrenchment as well (though it is likely that the perceived vulnerabilities of Weimar-era positivism might not have encouraged such a move).

Kelsen had discussed the use of entrenchment in his 1925 work *Allgemeine Staatslehre* (*General Theory of Law and State*), in which he argued that although there was no reason to hold that the entrenchment of constitutional provisions was necessarily invalid, entrenchment was at best inadvisable. In Kelsen's view, laws should be capable of being revised simply as a means of accommodating changing circumstances. Further, even if formally entrenched, changes are inevitable through what one might term a "hydraulic" mechanism: if modifications cannot occur through the formal amendment process, changes instead will occur through other means, most notably through the interpretive process, even

---

[53] Dyzenhaus is careful in his suggestion that although such theories contributed to the lack of sufficient numbers of people with political commitments capable of withstanding fascism, we cannot ascribe the rise of Nazism to legal theory (Dyzenhaus, 1997: 5; Posner criticizes him – in my view, uncharitably – at 289–90).

[54] Ferejohn and Pasquino (2003: 251).

if it involves completely distorting the meaning of entrenched laws in order to do so.[55]

Likewise, in his 1929 essay *"Die Philosophischen Grundlagen der Naturrechtslehre und des Rechtspositivismus"* ("Natural Law Doctrine and Legal Positivism"), Kelsen's view of entrenchment was unmistakable. Whereas natural law claimed "absolute validity" and presented itself as "a permanent, unchangeable order," the essential nature of positive law was as "an infinitely changeable order which can adjust itself to conditions as they change in space and time."[56] Unlike natural law, positive law possessed "merely hypothetical-relative validity." In Kelsen's view, all decisions must be open to revision: No set of beliefs, and no law, can ever attain the level of absolute and immutable truth.

> Belief in absolute truth and absolute values provides the conditions for a metaphysical, and especially religious-mystical, *Weltanschauung*. But the negation of these conditions, the opinion that only relative truths, only relative values can be attained by human cognition and that every truth and every value ... must thus be ready at all times to retreat and make way for others, leads to a *Weltanschauung* of criticism and positivism, defined as a philosophical and scientific school of thought based in the positive – that is, the given, the perceivable, a changeable and constantly changing *experience* – that rejects the assumption of an absolute transcending this experience.... The metaphysical-absolutist worldview corresponds with an autocratic, the critical relativist with a democratic attitude.[57]

---

[55] Kelsen (1925: 254). In the 1945 English translation of *General Theory of Law and State*, which revised the work, Kelsen cited Article 8, paragraph 4, of the 1875 French Constitution and Article 2 of the amendment of August 14, 1884, which prohibited the revision of the republican form of government. Kelsen (1945: 259–60). See also the discussion in Da Silva (2004: 465). I am grateful to Annie Stilz for her assistance in translating the original German version.

[56] Translated and reprinted in Kelsen (1945: 396–97).

[57] Kelsen (1945: 100–1). English translation by Jacobson and Schlink (2000: 107).

In the wake of Nazism, such relativism, it is true, might have seemed to be tantamount to accommodationism. As such, an argument linking the democratic capacity to modify laws to relativism might have encouraged the adoption of entrenchment. But Kelsen's broader argument on behalf of democratic pluralism and deliberation might have nonetheless encouraged a view that minority protections did not depend upon the permanent reification of minority rights. The fact of pluralism, and of group interests, was not a cause for alarm in Kelsen's reading. Rather, in his view, the presence of heterogeneity demands that deliberation lead to compromise: "For the whole parliamentary process, with its dialectical and contradictory technique of plea and counterplea, argument and counterargument, aims at achieving *compromise*. Therein lies the true significance of the majority principle in actual democracies."[58] The messiness of the public sphere protects us from authoritarianism; deliberation, as it recognizes the fact of pluralism, is an essential characteristic of democracy. On Kelsen's logic, the reciprocal nature of the relationship between the majority and the minority constitutes a source of security for the minority. If the majority fails to accommodate the minority, the minority will withdraw its support, therein depriving the majority of its legitimacy *qua* majority.

An alternative perspective on these matters could in good faith have been adopted; although Kelsenian "relativism" might not have constituted an adequate argument against entrenchment at the time, an argument from democratic pluralism and deliberative revisability could perhaps have served as the basis for rejecting entrenchment in the *Grundgesetz*. How might such an argument have run? In the first place, few members of the Parliamentary Council would have thought that Weimar's lack of an entrenchment

---

[58] Ibid., 57. English translation by Jacobson and Schlink (2000: 102).

clause constituted the primary explanation for the rise of Nazism. That is, following Kelsen, it could have been argued, against the logic of democratic autophagy, that a democracy that needed to protect itself against such a majority *Putsch* was already lost.[59] Entrenchment was a false, perhaps even deceptive, barrier against such incursions: It could lull society into the belief that such incursions were formally excluded and therefore impossible, thus affirming the same sort of "formalistic" logic for which positivism had been widely criticized. Only through constant vigilance to the consequences of institutional choices – which could be generated through a process of ongoing deliberation and scrutiny, retaining the possibility of revising norms in light of potential defects – could a democracy protect itself against dangerous challenges.[60] Finally, recall that the legitimacy of the Basic Law was in jeopardy: There was a substantial risk that the German people would chafe against any norm that seemed to be externally imposed or, further, that they were unable to make their own. Faced with entrenched provisions, the Germans easily could have shucked off the Basic Law on the ground that it sought to impose unalterable conditions. The possibility of altering any of the provisions, combined with the avowedly transitional nature of the "Basic Law," might have enhanced the capability of the Germans to view their failure to amend the constitutions as indeed reflecting their consent, rather than Allied coercion.

---

[59] Kelsen, *Verteidigung der Demokratie*, cited in Jacobson and Schlink (2000: 74).

[60] Note that even Karl Loewenstein, in his famous account of "militant democracy" and the efforts that countries in Europe must take to protect themselves against fascist incursions, did not argue on behalf of entrenchment. Though he denounced the role that the "formalistic" attachment to the rule of law played in preventing democracies from excluding fascist parties (1937: 424), he did not – neither in 1937 nor later on – ever to my knowledge embrace the use of entrenchment. Indeed, in 1961 he specifically wrote of democracies' inability to stave off authoritarianism ("Über Wesen, Technik, und Grenzen der Verfassungsänderung," cited in Da Silva 2004: 458).

Thus, the concept of the "eternity clause" derived, as I have suggested, from the jurisprudential response to Weimar, but this does not mean that entrenchment was the obvious answer. The members of the Parliamentary Council chose to adopt one strand of argument, accepting the idea of limits to change, but there were ample resources for an alternative view. But was the decision to entrench simply one of selecting the right worldview, so to speak? Was it entirely determined by the jurisprudential approach the Parliamentary Council – the Committee on Basic Rights and Carlo Schmid, in particular – had adopted? Schmid, as we have seen, argued that the entrenchment of the conditions of democracy was a necessary (if insufficient) condition for the survival of democracy. Given his opposition to constitution making in the first place, there would have been little reason for him to defend entrenchment for strategic purposes. That is, unless he realized that in doing so he would have granted particular authority to the Federal Constitutional Court. This is a possibility worth considering. Was this an example of institutional or self-interest?

Entrenchment and Interests in the Parliamentary Council

It is conceivable that the choice to entrench may have, in part, reflected strategic considerations on Schmid's part. If he anticipated that elections to the first Bundestag would result in a victory for the center-right coalition, as leader of the SPD he might well have sought to empower an alternative institution in the form of the constitutional court; the institutional features of the FCC were not highly specified in the Basic Law, and so it is indeed possible that he might have preferred to take his chances with the constitutional court. As Georg Vanberg has detailed in his recent work on constitutional review in Germany, the most important political struggle of the first legislative period was over the ratification of treaties establishing sovereignty and the creation of a European Defense

181

Community. The SPD opposed the passage of these treaties; yet given their minority status, they had little recourse except to appeal to the new constitutional court. Schmid was then chairman of the Bundestag foreign affairs committee; in his words, "the only effective break against the determination to create a fait-accompli in an over-hurried fashion is the *Bundesverfassungsgericht.*"[61] The SPD and allies appealed to the FCC for an abstract judicial-review proceeding requesting a determination of "whether a German defense contribution would be constitutionally permissible under the Basic Law."[62] After a protracted conflict over jurisdiction in the two-chamber court (whereas SPD-favorable judges dominated the First Senate, the Christian Democratic Union (CDU) was thought to dominate the Second Senate), the SPD prevailed. Adenauer was finally able to pull together the requisite majority for a constitutional amendment ensuring the constitutionality of the treaties after the second Bundestag election.

Thus, given Schmid's likely concerns about the effect of CDU electoral victories, it is at least possible that Schmid wished to empower a constitutional court. Entrenchment surely would have been a means of doing so, and – especially given the Kelsenian origins of the court – Kelsen's argument that change to entrenched provisions would have had to occur through interpretive means may well have been known. Thus, a view of entrenchment resulting from strategic considerations about the appropriate locus for constitutional change may not be implausible.

At a minimum, it is clear that the entrenchment of federalism did not arise from the view that it constituted a fundamental principle worthy of permanent enshrinement. Instead, the protection of federalism emerged quite late, in the context of compromises and bargains between the SPD and the CDU/CSU (Christian Democratic Union/Christian Social Union), after some late pressure from the

---

[61] Vanberg (2005: 68–69).   [62] Ibid., 69.

American delegation. Throughout the constituent assembly, conflicts arose over the extent and type of *Länder* representation, the legislative independence of the *Länder*, and the fiscal autonomy of the *Länder*. Roughly speaking, the major fault line was between the centralizing tendencies of the SPD and the decentralizing preferences of the CDU/CSU. On the matter of federalism, Schmid appears to have rejected entrenchment.

> Shall the organization of the federal territory remain unchangeable, as it is today? ... I am of the opinion that sound federalism is possible only if there exist reasonably balanced Länder, and not only accidental set-ups which, in many cases, are not older than three years and owe their existence to the coincidence of a line of demarcation between two infantry divisions.... Let us suppose the Ministers President will not succeed (in their task of revising Länder boundaries), must we then forever be satisfied with this state of affairs which the Ministers President were not able to cope with?[63]

However, a move by the military governors on behalf of the *Länder* rendered the situation entirely unstable.[64] On March 2, 1949, the military governors submitted a memorandum criticizing the provisions concerning the federal structure. According to the military governors, the powers of the states were insufficiently protected, including with respect to their sources of revenue. Further, the governors emphasized the continuing problem of the malleability of *Länder* territories, quoting from earlier statements to the ministers-president. General Lucius D. Clay, of the American delegation, in fact threatened to veto the Basic Law if the Parliamentary Council did not enhance the powers of the *Länder* and strengthen the protection of their rights.[65]

---

[63] "Excerpts from the Speech of Dr. Carlo Schmid (SPD), at the Plenary Meeting of the Parliamentary Council held in Bonn, 8 September 1948," in *Documents*, at 80.

[64] Merkl (1963: 62).

[65] Golay (1958: 96).

In an abbreviated draft version of the Basic Law dated April 9, 1949, the SPD bolstered considerably the financial strength of the federal state; yet as a compromise measure, they simultaneously protected the *Länder* by entrenching the federal structure for the first time in Article 64(3). To do so, the SPD used the language of the third reading's Article 106(3), detailed above, but excluded the possibility to amend via a four-fifths majority. After a series of concessions on the parts of both the SPD and the CSU, resolution was reached on April 22 and April 24, and the final readings of the Basic Law took place over the following weeks. Ultimately, the entrenchment of the federal structure was included in the form suggested by the SPD as Article 79(3).

The presence of viable alternatives – and the recognition that entrenchment may have emerged from strategic calculation – may suggest that the decision to entrench was not the sole solution available to the German framers. Further, given its contingency, we might think that it need not serve as a guide for our reflections on the creation of transitional constitutions today. But if the consequences of entrenchment have been generally positive – as the success of the German Basic Law might lead us to infer – there would be little reason to second-guess the decision. Yet the entrenchment of human dignity has granted the constitutional court considerable freedom to interpret these norms without the possibility of reversal, and this has not clearly been for the good.

The Legacy of Entrenchment

As we have seen, when constitutional provisions are made unamendable and constitutional courts have final authority over the interpretation of such provisions, entrenchment does not actually inhibit alterations. Instead, it shifts the locus of change – and the power to determine the legitimate scope of mutability – away from legislatures and toward the court. Constitutional framers, of course, may be well aware of this "hydraulic" mechanism, and they may use it to their advantage if they anticipate that courts will favor the sorts of changes they would like to see in the long run but cannot enact at the time of the constituent assembly. Yet this possible explanation for the creation of entrenchment clauses does not itself constitute a reason for rejecting their usage. Yet two dimensions of this story raise serious normative concerns, both of which hinge on the immunity of entrenched provisions to legislative change.

The first problem relates to the power entrenchment grants to constitutional framers to reify existing inequalities at the time of the framing. Such an inclination is often visible through the effort of states to protect federalism, as we have seen in Germany and in the United States Senate. In Russia as well, the asymmetric distribution of powers in the federation are entrenched.[66] Entrenchment – as the Russian constitution makes explicit[67] – in this form leaves the only redress through the constitutional court (which may itself be an agent of the central authority) or through constitutional revolution.

It may not be transparent how the protection of human dignity also serves this function. However, the entrenchment of such an "open-textured" norm implicitly empowers whoever possesses final interpretive authority – in this case, the constitutional court – to determine its contours, irreversible except by a later decision of this authority. Further, the greater the ambiguity of the provisions, the more power the final interpretive authority will have. If such interpretive authority is anticipated to be sympathetic to a particular faction of the framers – for example, if the constitutional court was expected to be populated by SPD-leaning law professors, for

---

[66] Stepan (1999).

[67] Amendment of Chapters 1 and 9 of the Russian constitution (the former secures the division of power, but not the explicit features of this division) may occur only through the explicit creation of a constituent assembly authorized to write a new constitution.

example – entrenchment could ensure that the SPD's influence over the development of the constitution endured long past the ratification process.

Second, the interpretive decisions of a constitutional court – whether through "abstract" or "concrete" judicial review – regarding entrenched laws cannot be reversed, except by a subsequent court ruling. Whereas constitutional provisions subject to amendment can be revised in light of unintended or undesirable consequences – for example, if Congress wished to reverse a Supreme Court decision deeming cross-burning protected speech on First Amendment grounds – no such recourse is available when laws are entrenched. To amend a hypothetically entrenched First Amendment to prohibit cross-burning might be thus to enact an "unconstitutional" constitutional amendment. In fact, constitutional courts in both Germany and India have exercised their authority to strike down such proposed changes.[68] Indeed, in the first major case adjudicated by the Federal Constitutional Court, *Southwest State Case*, the court asserted its authority to strike down amendments that would conflict with the "inner unity" of the Constitution, that is, the "overarching principles and fundamental decisions to which

---

[68] Note that such power may emerge even in the absence of explicit entrenchment clauses. Although the Indian constitution explicitly specifies that "there shall be no limitation whatsoever on the constituent power of Parliament to amend by way of addition, variation or repeal the provisions of this constitution," the Supreme Court of India developed a "basic structure doctrine" prohibiting amendments to the "framework" of the constitution (*Kesavananda v. State of Kerala*, A.I.R. 1973 S.C. 1461). In an effort to reclaim its authority to amend, Parliament passed the Amendment Act of 1976 removing the Supreme Court's authority to declare constitutional amendments unconstitutional; the Supreme Court then struck down that amendment as harming the basic structure (*Minerva Mills v. Union of India*, 1980 A.I.R. (S.C.) 1789 (India)). For a helpful discussion of this doctrine in the context of entrenchment more generally, see Katz (1996: 269–74); for a discussion of the basic structure doctrine as a means of securing liberal democracy in India, see Jacobsohn (2004: 1794–99).

186

individual provisions of the Basic Law are subordinate," which include democracy and federalism.[69] The court even specifically repudiated "value-free legal positivism," invoking the Schmittian critique, in the *Article 117* Case.[70]

A reader sympathetic to judicial review may respond: What of it? So the constitutional court has been empowered to strike down provisions that are harmful to human dignity or to democracy more generally – why should such an action constitute a violation of democratic principles? Again, the breadth of the principles, combined with the irreversibility of the outcome, should raise concerns even for readers sympathetic to judicial review.

Note that the Federal Constitutional Court itself argued that "any decision defining human dignity in concrete terms must be based on our present understanding of it and not on any claim to a conception of timeless validity."[71] The court, while acknowledging the inevitability of alterations to "human dignity," is asserting its own authority to determine the scope of these changes and, in essence, to give form and content to the concept of dignity. It has done so in many areas,[72] often controversially: It has sacrificed the principle of development of personality for national security;[73] it has upheld the reputations of the dead over artistic freedom;[74] and it has restricted

---

[69] *Southwest State Case*, 1 BVerfGE 14, 32 (1951), cited in Kommers (1997: 76).

[70] 3 BVerfGE 225, 232 (1953), cited in Kommers (1997: 54).

[71] Cited in Benda (1999: 452); see also Eberle (1997: 972) and Kommers (1997) for the account of the Life Imprisonment Case, 45 BVerfGE 187, translated in Kommers 1997: 317.

[72] Eberle (1997) is especially good on this point.

[73] In the Elfes case, cited in Eberle (1997: 980–89) and translated in Kommers (1997: 324–28), the court held that a prominent critic (a member of the CDU) could be denied a passport on national security grounds, despite the court's recognition that the freedom to travel constitutes a distinctive feature of the development of personhood, protected by the human dignity clause.

[74] The famous *Mephisto* case found that the rights of the dead to be free from defamation trumped artistic values: *Mephisto*, 30 BVerfGE, at 195, in Kommers (1997); Eberle (1997).

reproductive autonomy on behalf of the dignity of the fetus. In 1975, the Constitutional Court struck down a federal statute decriminalizing abortion in the first trimester and permitting it afterward if the pregnancy would cause serious damage to the health of the mother, or within 22 weeks if the fetus appeared to have serious birth defects, or in cases of rape or incest. The court held that such decriminalization violated the state duty to protect the life of the fetus as guaranteed by human dignity and the right to life. A center-left coalition had passed the statute against the opposition of the Christian Democrats, who with several *Länder* petitioned the court for abstract review. As Edward Eberle has written, "The Christian Democrats were thus able to accomplish judicially what they were unable to accomplish politically."

In 1993, the court revisited the abortion decision in reviewing the Pregnancy and Family Assistance Act, a response to the effort at unifying the liberalized abortion policy under East Germany with the restrictive West German policies. (Again, deputies of the CDU in combination with the Bavarian government petitioned for abstract review.) Abortion would be permissible on demand in the first trimester after mandatory counseling and a three-day waiting period (though subject to the same constraints as the earlier statute after the third trimester). Although the court this time replaced criminal sanctions in the first trimester with mandatory counseling, it still held abortion to be, in principle, illegal. Again, the court affirmed the dignity of the fetus: "Dignity attaches to the physical existence of every human being...before as well as after birth....Unborn life is a constitutional value that the state is obliged to protect that attaches to each human life, not life generally."[75]

It is widely held that public pressure constituted a primary reason for the decision to shift from the attachment of criminal

---

[75] Abortion II, 88 BVerfGE, at 252, cited in Eberle (1997).

penalties to mandatory counseling for first-trimester abortion. As a judge who participated in the decision told Georg Vanberg, the differences between the 1975 and 1992 decisions "can largely be explained by the desire to find a solution that would be acceptable to everyone.... That was a very conscious effort, we were looking for such a solution. Of course, the court didn't take an opinion poll, but public attitudes did take such a role."[76] This might appear, on my account, to be desirable: The public has a major if indirect role in the specification and therefore alteration of the concept of human dignity. Yet there is an irony here. The reason for entrenchment of human dignity, as we have seen, rests in part on the democratic autophagy argument: In the absence of entrenchment, legislatures or the people as a whole may seek to alter these laws, with disastrous consequences. However, if even judges themselves acknowledge that public opinion shapes their decision making on matters concerning human dignity, the argument that the court's insulation from political pressures makes it a safer locus for constitutional change becomes implausible. Indeed, the very power placed in the court's hands by entrenchment may induce even greater activism, as the court may legitimately take as its mandate the obligation to change rules that have become antiquated or inappropriate.[77] That is, rather than staving off the risk that unfettered democracy will destroy itself democratically, entrenchment may grant unconstrained constitutional courts the authority to harm democracy by undemocratic means.

Conclusion

Here, I have sought to counter a number of widely held views about entrenchment in the German Basic Law. First, it is commonly

---

[76] Vanberg (2005:128); see also Kommers (1997) and Eberle (1997), who emphasize the role that women played in changing social policy.

[77] I am grateful to Jon Elster for this point.

believed that entrenchment was the obvious and even inevitable response to Weimar and to Nazism. I have suggested that the decision to entrench both federalism and human dignity emerged over time and through a complicated combination of ideas and interests, in particular Weimar-era jurisprudence. Entrenchment has shifted the power to specify and modify these laws, especially the open-textured human dignity clause, toward the Federal Constitutional Court. Rather than simply providing a stable core for democracy or inhibiting modifications that might threaten democracy, such a move has had real and controversial political consequences in such areas as abortion rights.

Even the most ardent supporters of the democratic autophagy thesis would likely not believe that the human dignity clause could effectively stave off moral disaster; as such, entrenchment in the Basic Law might be held to be purely hortatory, a lingering textual reminder of atrocities, and dismissed as toothless and therefore harmless. Yet it has given the court an institutionally unchecked authority to determine the nature of changes (although it draws on public opinion in so doing). It also has influenced framers of constitutions, particularly in Eastern Europe, ever since.[78]

As I have suggested, the democratic autophagy argument defending the use of entrenchment to protect democracy is perhaps the most compelling defense of immutable law. Indeed, the most frequent use of entrenchment is likely for regime type; among the constitutions protecting the republican or democratic form of regime include those of Armenia, Brazil, France, Greece, Italy, Portugal, Romania, and Russia. Yet we must bear in mind that entrenchment of a provision as vague as a regime type may empower the constitutional court to determine the contours of what, precisely, a

---

[78] Kokott (1999). For the popularity of the German model among constitutional lawyers, see Holmes and Sunstein, in Levinson, ed. (1995: 305).

"republic" entails, with the distributive consequences and the irreversibility such a decision might entail.

It is worth noting that entrenchment also often serves a role as an element of emergency powers, protecting the constitution for a limited time periods during a crisis. Albania, Belarus, Belgium, Estonia, Georgia, Lithuania, Portugal, Romania, and Spain are among the countries with constitutions that prohibit any amendments during such a period. One may defend entrenchment in such restricted cases on the grounds that the emergency constitutes a break in the ordinary functioning of the regime and that powers expanded during such a period ought not to be permanently granted through constitutional change. In these highly restricted cases, in which democracy faces an imminent, specific threat for a limited period of time, temporary entrenchment of the total constitution may be less liable to abuse than granting the emergency authority power to reshape the constitution at a time of crisis. Whereas the sunset clause used to protect slavery in the U.S. Constitution simply delayed decision making as a gag rule – perhaps as a means to get the Constitution "off the ground," but more likely because of incomplete information about demographic trends – entrenchment of the entire Constitution for a very limited period may be a legitimate means of enabling constitutionalism to endure through a crisis (but without shifting authority to a constitutional court). However, although time-limited total entrenchment during an emergency may be a preferable alternative to enabling constitutional changes to occur through the irregular authority granted to decision makers during these periods, it is also worth noting the probable futility of such a measure. As the Athenian example of the one thousand talents suggests, in cases of profound anxiety, entrenchment is unlikely to stick – even extra-constitutional action may seem to be an attractive alternative during times of crisis.

The fear that democrats will modify law into oblivion – that democracy will cannibalize itself through legal change – has, as we have seen, endured since ancient Athens. Such worry has induced democrats to make certain laws unalterable, but framers have sometimes manipulated this impulse, using entrenchment to lock in advantages or asymmetries in power or to ensure that constitutional courts gain the power to shape laws in ways the framers find themselves politically incapable of doing. The concluding chapter highlights the limitations of entrenchment as a response to the vulnerabilities of democracy, while encouraging us to take comfort in the many arguments – for innovation, political agency, fallibility, and deliberation – that should lead us to embrace the capacity to modify even our most fundamental democratic institutions.

Chapter Six

Conclusion: Defending Democracy Against Entrenchment

In the last four chapters, we have examined four historically salient views of the way in which legal change was understood as a fundamental activity of democracy and the ways in which these views of democracy gave rise to efforts at entrenchment. In providing these accounts of the way in which democracies decided to entrench or to preserve the flexibility of their laws, I hope that I have demonstrated that the capacity to change fundamental laws and institutions is an essential and attractive democratic function. We should not regard the impulse to modify these norms as necessarily rooted in *akrasia*, or passion, but a critical activity of democracy, affirmed repeatedly and justified for good theoretical reasons. Although the choice to entrench norms is understandable, particularly after tragic experiences, there are few reasons to believe that entrenchment will either save us from our worst impulses or improve upon our best. Legislators and constitution framers have extended entrenchment to a variety of provisions since ancient Athens, yet entrenchment's legacy is in no small part the protection of the narrowly instrumental and the manifestly unjust. Entrenchment may hamper moral and legal progress, encouraging citizens to view norms (and framers) as infallible. At its best, it merely shifts the locus of change from legislatures to courts.

Recall that the four defenses of flexible law are as follows: on the grounds of innovation, as we saw in Athens; as a deliberate legislative activity engaged in parliaments, in England; as a means of recognizing human fallibility, as in the American founding; and as a means of ensuring democratic engagement and deliberative legitimacy in the postwar era. When we combine these four accounts, taking together innovation and fallibility, intentionality and deliberation, we see that the arguments in favor of changeable law have engaged some of our deepest democratic commitments. Through studying the theoretical grounds on which democrats have defended legal change, we have also been able to reevaluate some of the fundamental self-conceptions of democrats about their regime and their tendencies. Yet what democrats today can learn from the ways in which past actors have characterized their use of legal change has remained, in part, implicit.

With an eye toward the future, I offer an account of the ways in which a democratic reconsideration of legal change may find traction in contemporary settings; in particular, I draw attention to the broader implications of the critique of entrenchment for constitutional theory, emphasizing the possibility of retaining a commitment to rights without resorting to entrenchment. Abandoning entrenchment does not leave democracy rudderless, vulnerable to arguments from democratic autophagy. That is, although there could be a point at which the institutional prerequisites of collective decision making have been changed to the extent that the regime is no longer democratic, we ought not to put faith in the capacity of entrenchment to save us from this terrible fate. Further, our chances of thwarting such a possibility and ensuring the justice of our institutions from their inception are enhanced through the capacity for revision. In conclusion, I will suggest the broader implications of the defense of flexible law for constitutionalism more generally.

Argument 1: Innovation and Learning

Our first account originated in the study of ancient Athens, where we learned that the Athenians regarded the capacity to change their law as an affirmative good. Though their general proclivity toward "pragmatic innovation" was a source of pride for them and was envied by others, it also generated concern among their allies. The use of entrenchment signaled their intention to abide by a particular commitment – and made their alliances somewhat more credible as a result – but did not actually operate as an effective form of precommitment, given the evidence that the Athenians modified entrenched laws during times of crisis.

In examining the first argument, I shall stylize the benefits of pragmatic innovation emerging from Athens. We might view the claim as a defense of the view that legal change may be an affirmative good because it promotes learning through encouraging institutional experimentation. The Athenians were supposed to have invented everything, after all, and today we may think that democracies that encourage modification of their laws enable their people to view their institutions critically with an aim toward their improvement. The laws themselves may well benefit from such a process (and if they do not, they can be modified again), and the embrace of revision may encourage the sort of progressive experimentation that would be beneficial for society as a whole. In sum: One democratic defense of legal change is because new challenges generate opportunities for us to learn and to innovate, crafting novel institutional solutions to current problems.

Entrenchment, at a minimum, stifles public learning about the entrenched norms themselves. Although an occasional supporter of entrenchment,[1] Stephen Holmes has argued – rightly, in my view – that Locke, Kant, and Mill, "while prohibiting precommitments

---

[1] Holmes and Sunstein, in Levinson (1995: 297).

which obstructed future learning," correctly "endorsed durable – though certainly not unalterable – constitutional rules."[2] A critical faculty toward norms is necessary to enable learning, but in the absence of the capacity to reopen debate on these laws – on this logic, the most fundamental rules of society – such a disposition will be difficult to cultivate. Moreover, these laws themselves would not be responsive to whatever we might learn, either about the consequences of these norms or the moral and political commitments they reflect more generally. It is true, as I have suggested, that entrenchment will not preclude change – it will simply shift the locus of this change away from the people as a whole and their elected representatives and toward courts. One might argue, therefore, that entrenchment will not exclude the possibility of learning, but shift the power to absorb this knowledge to the courts: If one adopts the Rawlsian perspective, holding courts to be the exemplar of public reason, one might have few concerns about such a matter. Yet the capacity to challenge existing political institutions, and to engage in critical reflection about the nature of our political and moral commitments, cannot be enhanced by making the outcomes of public deliberations irrelevant with respect to its effects on the institutional objects of debate.

As Jeremy Waldron has suggested, the capacity for disagreement extends to the formulation and specification of these very liberties ostensibly designed to enhance public learning (for example, the restriction of hate speech or the publication of opinion polls): In other words, the institutions do not simply enable learning, but reify – or shift into the hands of the judiciary – a particular answer to most of these questions.[3] Although we might grant that securing terms of fair debate, such as freedom of the press, might enable a discussion to unfold that would benefit democracy, it would not enable us to learn (except by examples) from deliberation about

---

[2] Holmes (1995: 177).   [3] Waldron (1999b: 279).

what the terms of fair debate should be. If a benefit of changeable law is that it permits learning about the matters regulated by these laws, it is clear that disabling the ability to change law reduces the ability to learn with respect to *those* matters, at least, and perhaps discourages the cultivation of a critical perspective with respect to law in general.

That the desire to innovate and thereby to learn might entice us to change laws for the worse, rather than the better, cannot be denied. As Jon Elster has highlighted, in *De Finibus*, Cicero's Antiochus offers the following account of the Sirens: "For my part, I believe Homer had something of this sort in view in his imaginary account of the songs of the Sirens. Apparently, it was not the sweetness of their voices or the novelty and diversity of their songs, but their professions of knowledge that used to attract the passing voyagers; it was the passion for learning that kept men rooted to the Sirens' rocky shores."[4] But it is undoubtedly better to have the capacity for self-correction and to make "repairable mistakes," in Tocqueville's language, than to be bound permanently to abide by deficient norms. One may reply, however, that in the absence of entrenchment, the institutional preconditions of democracy by which this public learning may occur may themselves be "learned" out of existence, so to speak – eradicating the benefits of legal change and democracy more generally. Because this important challenge will face us whatever the benefits of legal change may be, I shall return to it in a moment.

Argument 2: Deliberate Legislation and Judicial Interpretation

The second defense of legal change places the power of judges to engage in adaptive, incremental, interpretive change against the

---

[4] Cicero, *De Finibus*, V.xviii; Elster (2000: 3).

capacity of legislatures to engage in deliberate legal change. The major implication for a theory of legal change emerging from this analysis has, as we have seen, a consideration of the competing roles of judges and of parliaments in modifying the law. Today, we might think that this distinction has been essentially effaced. Even scholars who are suspicious of the idea that judges must "make" law in the presence of indeterminacy will typically acknowledge that judges alter law through interpretation. As we have suggested, the distinction between "intentionality" and adaptation has also been blurred: Although they may deny "making" law, few judges would insist that they never "change" law, even if in a restorative fashion.[5] Yet Hart's intuition that a key feature of law is its susceptibility to deliberate change – both law in comparison to morality and developed legal systems in comparison to "primitive" societies – is here critical. Whereas a "primitive" society is "static" and the only means by which laws change is through the "slow process of growth... and the converse process of decay," in developed systems there is a means of "deliberately adapting the rules to changing circumstances, either by eliminating old rules or introducing new ones."[6]

Indeed, for Hart, judges could also engage in this activity: The "open-textured" nature of law gave judges some discretion, to the point of gap filling, to determine the law, though constrained by the presence of a "core" of stable meanings. For Waldron, though, the most important feature of Hart's theory is the "dignity" it gives to the concept of "deliberate" legislation, which he believes has been lost in the proliferation of defenses of judicial decision making, particularly in the common-law tradition. In Waldron's view, "the

---

[5] For Scalia, neither judges' capacity to determine what the law "is" nor judges' power to "make law," implies that they have the ability to change law. See *James B. Beam Distilling Co. v. Georgia*, 501 U.S. 549 (1991). (Scalia, concurring in the judgment). For a discussion, see Jill E. Fisch (1997: 1055, n. 127).

[6] Hart (1994: 92–93).

danger of focusing on legislation is that, as a source of law, it is *all too human*, all too associated with explicit, datable decisions by identifiable men and women, that we are to be subject to *these* rules rather than *those*."[7]

More frequently, though, the debate over the proper scope and understanding of judicial authority has been as a subset of the quarrel over the proper role of judges in a democracy, along with the question of judicial discretion. The more difficult the law is to change through legislative (or constitutional) means, the greater the "latitude" to enact these changes those with interpretive authority – notably judges – will acquire.[8] In cases of entrenchment, then, judges will have an exceptionally broad – if not exclusive[9] – power to interpret the law and therefore to change it. What follows from granting judges sole authority to modify entrenched law? One might think that this matter hinges on one's view of judicial review : that is, if one generally accepts the authority of judges to have broad ability to review statutes for constitutionality and to strike down legislation that fails to comply, one may be unconcerned about the power of judges to reject laws that intrude, in their view, on the entrenched constitutional provision. Likewise, if one is concerned about granting judges such latitude in ordinary constitutional cases, one will be horrified by the prospect that they should have unchecked authority to do so with respect to entrenched law.

However, entrenchment raises questions that are distinguishable from the normal matter of constitutional review, and the consequences of entrenchment from an interpretive perspective should

---

[7] Waldron (1999a: 24).

[8] See Knight (2001: 367); John Ferejohn (1998: 504).

[9] In some sense, the power of a legislature to enact law that is within the scope of an entrenched law is the power, indirectly, to shift its "core" meaning. But the power of a judiciary to strike down legislation irrevocably that in their view fails to adhere to this meaning gives judges supremacy in the interpretive realm here.

give even a defender of judicial review pause. One defense of the compatibility of judicial review with democracy – though not the primary justification, certainly – rests on the claim that ultimately the people have authority to modify the constitution if their considered judgment is that the court's interpretation of the constitution is misguided. Although the constitution can only effectively serve as a constraint and guide for the creation of legislation if it its supremacy is upheld through a judiciary, it is argued, in the event that the people believe that the constitutional court is misguided in their determination of constitutionality, they retain recourse to amendment (though this would not be adequate to satisfy opponents of judicial review).[10] Yet entrenchment, by prohibiting revision of the law, disables the capacity of the people and their representatives to check the power of the judiciary in this fashion; the judiciary, in this case, has final say over the content of the law. The ability to check a judicial decision in this realm is permanently excluded.[11]

Argument 3: Fallibility in Legislation and Interpretation

As we saw during the Federal Convention, the appeal to human fallibility constituted a rich and important argument advanced for the inclusion of an amendment clause in the U.S. Constitution. The insight, taken a step further – that law may be wrong and that the people who created it may have had imperfect judgment – constitutes the third defense of legal change. This premise, as I have suggested, has been recognized: Indeed, the argument from fallibility gave the key volume on constitutional change, *Responding*

[10] Eisgruber argues that making amendment more accessible would have a notable effect on judicial decision making, because judges would expect their decisions to be more readily overturned (citing Jacobsohn, *Apple of Gold: Constitutionalism in Israel and the United States* (1993: 24, n.38).

[11] Although in Poland and Romania the legislature may override constitutional court decisions, in the United States and most other countries there is no means of override other than constitutional amendment.

to Imperfection (Levinson, ed., 1995), its title. But the esteem in which constitutions, and constitutional adjudicators, are held today –
ironically, in part because of the success of the U.S. Constitution, from which the account of fallibility emerged – have led
scholars to overlook the turbulent circumstances of constitution
making. Indeed, the entire logic of precommitment in constitution making resides on the belief that the laws created by the
framers embodied reason. The framers, acting rationally, were able
to create laws worthy of great inflexibility, which in turn would
be able to check the passion and interests of majorities and enable
democratic politics. In this view, broadly speaking, constitutions
are a means by which a democracy can commit itself – or commit
future generations – to rules that will facilitate its ability to operate
in an ongoing democratic and just fashion, rules that are protected
against easy change because of the risk "of [people's] own potential
excesses or misjudgments."[12]

Yet no less a theorist of precommitment than Jon Elster notes the
theoretical tension inherent in this concept once applied to constitutions: "There is ... a systematic tendency for constitutions to be
written in turbulent circumstances when judgment is clouded by the
passions of the moment. The conditions under which the *need* for
constitution-making arises tend to hinder the *task* of constitution-
making."[13] In many constituent assemblies – where there is little
consensus about what constitute the fundamental premises of the
regime and where elites seek to lock in interests against the possibility of legislative modification – constitution making is far from a
moment in which the ideal formulation of fundamental democratic
commitments are likely to emerge. Even in a case of what seems to
have been genuine deliberation, the American framing, efforts to
secure interests continuously emerged and bargains were struck,

---

[12] Sunstein (2001: 97).   [13] Elster (2000: 161).

sometimes hastily. Moreover, despite the framers' repeated appeals to their own fallibility, they succeeded in entrenching slavery. The focus on fallibility urges us to retain the possibility of revision not only because we may be "wrong" – our understandings and abilities may be imperfect – but because we may be self-interested, or motivated by "standing passions."

In other words, the empirical conditions of constitution making provide a "common-sense" grounding for the commitment to fallibility: The contentious and highly charged constituent assemblies will not tend to produce infallible documents or even infallible systems of rights. In spite of – or even *because* of – the rational, self-interested, and sometimes passionate nature of constituent assembles, they may indeed generate just and efficient means of political organization. But this cannot be known *ex ante*, nor should we infer from the durability or quality of certain constitutions that their founding moments were paragons of deliberative rationality. Yet the reasons for adopting the standpoint of fallibility with respect to our democratic institutions go deeper.

It may be claimed, for example, that adopting the perspective of fallibility entails that we must take our constitutional commitments lightly – and that this might be profoundly dangerous. First, as Eric MacGilvray has recently argued, rather than foreclosing the bounds of reasonable agreement on constitutional essentials in advance, the commitment to fallibilism enables us, from a morally serious perspective, to regard disagreement about fundamental rights as "a sign of the partiality of human understanding," which will require that "this understanding remain open for revision in the larger interest of seeking the truth."[14] Second, adopting the perspective of fallibility, as we saw in Chapter 4, may indeed induce an outvoted minority to accept the outcome of deliberations.

[14] MacGilvray (2004: 222).

Grounding a defense of flexible law on the grounds that the law may be wrong not only signals to the minority that the outcome of a vote is potentially revisable, but that through argumentation they may be able to persuade the majority of the rightness of their views – indeed, the commitment to fallibility may indeed reflect a norm of equal respect more closely than the entrenchment of rights designed to enshrine such respect.

Yet what if we regard the norm of human dignity, for example, as substantively infallible? When we protect constitutional rights, we do not usually intend them to be purely hortatory: Although some have viewed the protection of human dignity in Bonn in this fashion, once interpreted by a constitutional court such laws have teeth, giving rise to real duties and to real disabilities. Indeed, in Elster's words, "absolute protection requires absolute entrench-ment of the rights, that is, total immunity against amendment."[15] But taking constitutional rights – and the entrenchment of constitu-tional rights – seriously requires us to recognize that in so doing we reify *one particular positive formulation* of such rights. Although many of us would regard norms such as "human dignity" or the "liberty of expression" as so fundamental as to be essentially infal-lible and beyond challenge, it is essential that we remember that we are not protecting these moral concepts *themselves* but the posi-tive instantiation of them, which as the product of a constituent assembly – comprised of human beings – may be imperfect or may have unintended or undesirable consequences once specified through legislation or through judicial interpretation.

Argument 4: Deliberation and the Prospect of Revision

This discussion, in turn, gives rise to the fourth defense of legal change – that is, that because democratic legitimacy derives in part

---

[15] Elster (2000: 131; see also 102).

from the possibility that an outvoted minority may be able to revisit decisions, the ability to modify the law should be affirmed on democratic grounds. Likewise, entrenchment precludes the ability of the minority to reopen debate and thereby threatens legitimacy. For Kelsen, the contentious nature of discussion, arguing and bargaining over legislation, was fundamentally democratic. Against the notion of substantive limits to amendment, Kelsen embraced the ability of a minority to challenge a majority decision and to challenge any norm, no matter how fundamental, as essential to democracy's struggle against absolutism. This logic has had considerable significance for deliberative theory.

For Jürgen Habermas, as well as for Bernard Manin, majority votes serve as a mechanism by which deliberations can be suspended in the face of pressures to decide, though these deliberations may be resumed at a later point.[16] The legitimacy of democratic decisions, on this model, requires that it emerge from a deliberative process open to all, which, by virtue of the nature of the "indeterminacy of justice"[17] and the need for a decision, must be concluded. Its enduring validity, however, depends upon the capacity of the minority to reopen debate at some point in the future and to try again to persuade the majority of the correctness of their perspective.

It may be suggested, though, that the legitimacy of democratic decision making cannot depend exclusively on deliberation, combined with the prospect of revision. Charles Larmore's critique of Habermas – that "discourse principle D" ("Just those action norms are valid to which all possibly affected persons could agree as participants in rational discourses") must be grounded in a moral commitment to equal respect and is therefore thicker than

[16] Habermas (1996); Manin (1987: 359).
[17] Manin (1987: 362).

Habermas wishes to acknowledge – is surely correct.[18] Our capacity to create a just and enduring democracy no doubt depends in part upon such a norm. Yet there is a distinction between recognizing that democracy rests upon some shared commitment to equal respect among its members and entrenching a *law* specifying equal respect as the foundation of the democracy. Further, by enshrining a right to "equal respect," for example, we restrict our ability to give meaningful content – through ongoing deliberation and revision – to such a norm. As I have suggested, there is room for reasonable disagreement about the scope of *who* is entitled to such respect – whether fetuses or primates, for example, deserve equal respect. In the absence of the ability to engage in constitutional revision, we delegate the authority to make these fundamental moral decisions to a constitutional court.

Democracy and the Promise of Constitutionalism

I hope that I have demonstrated that the capacity of democracy to sustain itself does not depend upon entrenchment per se. Although the democratic capacity to modify laws, it is true, may lead to autophagy – to the destruction of democracy by democratic means, as the Athenians knew well – entrenchment will not dissuade a populace bent on injustice or driven by fear. Entrenchment cannot sustain democracy in the absence of a shared commitment to justice, but neither can it bring about such a commitment; further, the ability to challenge existing norms, as democrats have known for centuries, is an essential means by which we can ensure that these laws do, in fact, remain just. In contrast to Bruce Ackerman, I have argued that the absence of an entrenchment clause is no embarrassment for rights foundationalists: We can affirm

---

[18] Larmore (1999); Habermas (1996: 107).

the central status of constitutional rights for democracy without demanding their entrenchment per se. Yet adopting a foundation-alist approach may lead us to sanitize our conception of rights pro-visions: Like any institution, they may reflect efforts by the framers to lock in benefits and reify power asymmetries and, as such, should be subject to revision on these grounds as well.

But what are the more general implications of the democratic defense of changeable law and the rejection of entrenchment? In particular, to what extent does the critique of formal immutabil-ity apply to other forms of entrenchment and to constitutionalism more generally? As I suggested at the outset, we should distinguish between laws that are formally entrenched (e.g., the human dignity clause), laws that are entrenched for a period of time, laws that are *de facto* entrenched through exceptionally stringent amendment procedures (perhaps requiring unanimity), and laws that are taken to be "implicitly entrenched" through their foundational character or their widespread support. In addition, we should consider norms that are merely difficult to change, as is the case with most consti-tutional laws. As suggested in Chapters 1 and 4, the distinction between cases of *de facto* entrenchment, in which the possibility of change is *virtually* excluded – as in the U.S. Constitution, because a state would have to willingly surrender its equal suffrage – and formal entrenchment is insignificant. In neither case will the community derive the benefits associated with mutable law – the capacity to innovate and to correct defects, in particular – and the locus of change will still be shifted toward the judiciary.

Although time-limited entrenchment has, as we have seen, a regrettable legacy from its use to protect slavery, it poses slightly different challenges: The possibility of revision is delayed, rather than excluded entirely. Thomas Jefferson, arguing that constitu-tions should elapse every 19 years – and excluding the possibility of a "perpetual constitution, or even a perpetual law" – saw a def-inite period as a means of ensuring that constitutions reflect the popular will. The mere power of repeal, Jefferson suggested, "is not an equivalent," because the challenges of assemblies, factions, and interests will conspire against change.[19] The passage of the sunset clause may indeed focus attention on the possibility of amendment. Yet the interim period – particularly in transitional moments – may be sufficiently long to permit devious framers to lock in their interests permanently. As a means of stabilizing norms, a sunset clause could ensure that the outcomes have a fair chance to work before revision ought to be embarked upon. However, if the failure of the constitution is imminent, the sunset clause will do little to stave off collapse and may actually hamper efforts to preserve it. The benefit of sunset clauses in the constitution-making process thus remains an open question.

The implications of "implicit limits" to change are likewise complicated. The use of legal change to create norms in fundamental opposition to a constitutional order – either through the creation of new undemocratic institutions or illiberal norms – is indeed a risk. But the doctrine of implicit limits, it seems, will raise similar concerns to those elicited by formal entrenchment. Although we could enable the Supreme Court to strike down amendments in gross violation of the constitutional order, empowering a court to do so would give it remarkable power to shape the boundaries of the constitution. The authority to determine whether a constitutional amendment protecting abortion or prohibiting capital punishment, for example, would not longer reside with the people or their representatives through the power granted to them in Article V; the power would again shift to the courts. Finally, the positive account of "implicit entrenchment," resting on widespread belief in the validity of these norms, is on the one hand attractive – it may reflect the compatibility of the popular will with the fundamental

---

[19] Letter to Madison, Sept. 6, 1789 in Kurland and Lerner, ed. (1987: Vol. 1, Chapter 2, Document 23).

norms shaping its society – but it may also inhibit the critical engagement with constitutional rules that will ensure their future legitimacy as well.

Thus, entrenchment in most forms poses at least some risks. But does the democratic commitment to changeable law pose a challenge to constitutionalism? Constitutionalism is an ingenious solution to the challenge of democratic legal change: At its best, it does secure the institutional preconditions of democratic decision making, while preserving the legal mutability that has been a hallmark of democracy for millennia. Yet to the extent that stringent constitutionalism seeks to restrict democratic agency rather than to enhance it, it may easily fall prey to the pitfalls of entrenchment. However, what type of procedure will constitute excessive stringency will vary from society to society: A three-quarters majority of a popular referendum could be a relatively weak standard in a homogeneous society or a virtually unattainable threshold in a profoundly divided one. Investigations into whether supermajority rules tend to ensure widespread consent to amendments, or secure the ability of minorities (including powerful minorities) to preserve the status quo, or enhance the epistemic quality of proposed changes, for a few possible examples, is thus also an important area for future research. The aim, from the perspective here, should be to determine the circumstances under which constitutions can serve a constitutive function – including ensuring security of expectations and avoiding incoherence and retroactivity – while still retaining a considerable degree of flexibility.

Through approaching these questions from the perspective of political theory, we are able to take a longer view. Here, I hope to have shed light on the relationship between democracy and the rule of law without remaining trapped in the standard terms in which such matters are addressed: the dichotomy between "popular sovereignty" or majoritarianism and constitutionalism. Instead, through historical and theoretical inquiry, we have examined the implications of particular legal formulations, of the distinction between judicial and legislative agency, and of the impulse toward self-binding and the benefits and vulnerabilities of democratic deliberations.

The broader lesson from the historical investigations has been to embrace the value of pragmatic experimentation with respect to law in democracies. The capacity to respond to contingencies with new institutional solutions was a source of pride for Athens. Likewise, efforts at asserting the power to enact deliberate legal reform comprised a hallmark of seventeenth-century republicanism. Regarding our constitutional commitments as fallible – recognizing that our most fundamental norms may turn out to be flawed, and only through the process of subjecting these norms to meaningful challenge can we retain our faith in them – is the legacy of the American framing; likewise, the commitment to pluralism and to the benefits of deliberation is a distinctive contribution of the postwar era. Although these distinctive efforts to create and to defend flexible law should inspire us, we should remain wary of the corresponding impulse to entrench that we have seen emerge in response to the essentially unbounded character of democratic change.

In this book, I have aimed to retrieve and to defend the democratic pedigree of legal change. The goal has been, primarily, to demonstrate the seminal role that legal change has played in democracy, something often overlooked in the contemporary focus on the rule of law. Moreover, I have sought to show that not just any form of constitutional rigidity can be rendered compatible with democracy: Entrenched, or unamendable, law may pose a challenge, and, as suggested, even rigid forms of constitutionalism may have harmful consequences for democratic legitimacy.

To engage in constitutional change is both an exhilarating and a frightening activity: It is to acknowledge the human origins, and the frailty, of our law. That we would seek to avoid this confrontation and to help our children and grandchildren to evade this recognition by entrenching is understandable and in many ways laudable: Stability, particularly after turbulence, is a source of comfort. But the promise of democracy rests, in part, on the ability to confront its challenges. Constitutionalism surely enables us to secure democratic freedoms. But these liberties must also extend to the capacity to remake the laws constituting the democracies in which some of us are fortunate enough to live.

References

Abbott, W. C. *The Writings and Speeches of Oliver Cromwell*. 4 vols. Cambridge, MA: Harvard University Press, 1937–47.

Ackerman, Bruce. *We the People: Foundations*. Cambridge, MA: Harvard University Press, 1991.

Ackerman, Bruce. *We the People: Transformations*. Cambridge, MA: Harvard University Press, 1998.

Aeschines, trans. Chris Carey. Austin, TX: University of Texas Press, 2000.

Amar, Akhil Reed. "Philadelphia Revisited: Amending the Constitution Outside Article V." 55 *University of Chicago Law Review* 1043 (1988).

Amar, Akhil Reed. "Popular Sovereignty and Constitutional Amendment." In *Responding to Imperfection*, ed. Sanford Levinson. Princeton, NJ: Princeton University Press, 1995.

Antiphon and Andocides, trans. Michael Gagarin and Douglas M. MacDowell. Austin: University of Texas Press, 1998.

Aquinas, Saint Thomas. *Treatise on Law*, trans. Richard J. Regan. Indianapolis: Hackett, 2000.

Aristotle. *Rhetoric*, trans. W. Rhys Roberts. In *Complete Works of Aristotle*, vol. 2, ed. Jonathan Barnes. Princeton, NJ: Princeton University Press, 1984.

Aristotle. *The Politics and the Constitution of Athens*, ed. Steven Everson. Cambridge: Cambridge University Press, 1996.

Aristotle. *The Nicomachean Ethics*, trans. David Ross. Oxford: Oxford University Press, 1998.

Aristotle. *Politics*, trans. Ernest Barker. Oxford: Oxford University Press, 1998.

Bacon, Sir Francis. *The Essayes or Counsels, Civill and Morall*, ed. Michael Kiernan. Oxford: Clarendon Press, 2000.

Barber, Sotirios A. *On What the Constitution Means*. Baltimore: Johns Hopkins University Press, 1984.

Barber, Sotirios A., and Robert P. George. *Constitutional Politics: Essays on Constitution Making, Maintenance, and Change*. Princeton, NJ: Princeton University Press, 2001.

Benda, Ernst. "The Protection of Human Dignity (Article 1 of the Basic Law)." 53 *SMU Law Review* 443–53 (1999).

Bentham, Jeremy. *Rights, Representation, and Reform*, ed. P. Schofield, C. Pease-Watkins, and C. Blamires. Oxford: Oxford University Press, 2002.

Bernstein, Richard B. with Jerome Agel. *Amending America: If We Love the Constitution So Much, Why Do We Keep Trying to Change It?* Lawrence, KS: University Press of Kansas, 2000.

Boardman, Roger Sherman. *Roger Sherman: Statesman and Signer*. New York: Da Capo Press, 1971.

Bork, Robert H. *The Tempting of America: The Political Seduction of the Law*. New York: Free Press, 1990.

Brandon, Mark E. "The 'Original' Thirteenth Amendment and the Limits to Formal Constitutional Change." In *Responding to Imperfection*, ed. Sanford Levinson. Princeton, NJ: Princeton University Press, 1995.

Brecht, Arnold. *Federalism and Regionalism in Germany: The Division of Prussia*. New York: Oxford University Press, 1945.

Burgess, Glenn. *The Politics of the Ancient Constitution*. University Park: Pennsylvania State University Press, 1992.

Burns, J. H., ed., with Mark Goldie. *The Cambridge History of Political Thought 1450–1700*. Cambridge: Cambridge University Press, 1996.

Caldwell, Peter C. *Popular Sovereignty and the Crisis of German Constitutional Law: The Theory and Practice of Weimar Constitutionalism*. Durham, NC: Duke University Press, 1997.

Cicero. *On the Commonwealth and On the Laws*, ed. James E. G. Zetzel. Cambridge: Cambridge University Press, 1999.

Cohen, Jean L., and Andrew Arato. *Civil Society and Political Theory*. Cambridge, MA: MIT Press, 1994.

Coke, Sir Edward. *The First Part of the Institutes of the Laws of England, or, A Commentary upon Littleton*. Union, NJ: Lawbook Exchange, 1999.

Coke, Sir Edward. La Sept Part Des Reports Sr. Edw. Coke Chiualer, Chief Justice del Common Banke, 1608.

Collier, Christopher. *Roger Sherman's Connecticut: Yankee Politics and the American Revolution*. Middletown, CT: Wesleyan University Press, 1971.

Cooley, Thomas M. "The Power to Amend the Federal Constitution." 4 *Michigan Law Journal* 117 (1893).

Cotterell, Mary. "Interregnum Law Reform: The Hale Commission of 1652." 83 *English Historical Review* 689–704 (1968).

Currie, David. *The Constitution of the Federal Republic of Germany*. Chicago: University of Chicago Press, 1994.

Da Silva, Virgílio Afonso. "A Fossilized Constitution," 17(4) *Ratio Juris* 454–73 (2004).

Demosthenes. *Against Meidias, Androtion, Aristocrates, Timocrates, Aristogeiton*. Cambridge, MA: Harvard University Press, 1935.

Dodd, Walter. *Revision and Amendment of State Constitutions*. Baltimore: Johns Hopkins University Press, 1910.

Dow, David R. "The Plain Meaning of Article V." In *Responding to Imperfection*, ed. Sanford Levinson. Princeton, NJ: Princeton University Press, 1995.

Dworkin, Ronald. "Equality, Democracy and Constitution: We the People in Court." 28 *Alberta Law Review* (1990).

Dworkin, Ronald. *Freedom's Law*. Cambridge: Harvard University Press, 1996.

Dyzenhaus, David. *Legality and Legitimacy: Carl Schmitt, Hans Kelsen and Hermann Heller in Weimar*. Oxford: Oxford University Press, 1997.

Eberle, Edward J. "Human Dignity, Privacy, and Personality in German and American Constitutional Law." *Utah Law Review* 963 (1997).

Eisgruber, Christopher. *Constitutional Self-Government*. Cambridge, M.A.: Harvard University Press, 2001.

Elliot, Jonathan, ed. *The Debates in the Several State Conventions on the Adoption of the Federal Constitution as Recommended by the General Convention at Philadelphia in 1787. . . .* 4 vols., 2nd ed. Washington: Taylor and Maury, 1836; vol. 5, Washington: Taylor and Maury, 1845.

Elster, Jon. *Ulysses and the Sirens*. Cambridge: Cambridge University Press, 1984.

Elster, Jon. *Ulysses Unbound*. Cambridge: Cambridge University Press, 2000.

An Experimental Essay Touching the Reformation of the Lawes of England. Aug. 17 1648 (E 541).

Farrand, Max, ed. *The Records of the Federal Convention of 1787*, vol. 1–3. New Haven, CT: Yale University Press, 1966.

Ferejohn, John. "The Politics of Imperfection: The Amendment of Constitutions." 22 *Law and Social Inquiry* 501–31, at 504 (1998).

Ferejohn, John and Pasquale Pasquino. "Rule of Democracy and Rule of Law." In *Democracy and the Rule of Law*, eds. José María Maravall and Adam Przeworski. New York: Cambridge University Press, 2003.

Finkelman, Paul. *Slavery and the Founders: Race and Liberty in the Age of Jefferson*. Armonk, NY: M. E. Sharpe, 2001.

Finley, Moses. *The Use and Abuse of History*. New York: Viking Press, 1975.

Finn, John E. *Constitutions in Crisis: Political Violence and the Rule of Law*. New York: Oxford University Press, 1991.

Fisch, Jill E. "Retroactivity and Legal Change," 110 *Harvard Law Review* 1055 (1997).

Fleming, James E. "We the Exceptional American People." In *Constitutional Politics: Essays on Constitution Making, Maintenance, and Change*, eds. Sotirios A. Barber and Robert P. George. Princeton, NJ: Princeton University Press, 2001.

Foreign Relations of the United States 1946, vol. 8: *The Far East*. Washington, DC: U.S.G.P.O., 1971.

Fornara, Charles W. *Archaic Times to the End of the Peloponnesian War*. Cambridge: Cambridge University Press, 1983.

Fortescue, Sir John. *On the Laws and Governance of England*, ed. Shelley Lockwood. Cambridge: Cambridge University Press, 1997.

Fox, Gregory, and George Nolte. "Intolerant Democracies." 36 *Harvard International Law Journal* 1 (1995).

Freehling, William W. "The Founding Fathers and Slavery," 77 *American Historical Review* 81–93 (1972).

Freeman, Samuel. "Ordinary Meaning, Democratic Interpretation, and the Constitution." 21(1) *Philosophy and Public Affairs* 3–42 (1992).

Friedrich, Carl. "Rebuilding the German Constitution, I." 43(3) *American Political Science Review* 461–82 (1949).

Gagarin, Michael. *Early Greek Law*. Berkeley: University of California Press, 1986.

Gartzke, Erik, and Kristian Skrede Gleditsch. "Why Democracies May Actually Be Less Reliable Allies." 48(4) *American Journal of Political Science* 775–95 (2004).

Gaubatz, Kurt Taylor. "Democratic States and Commitment in International Relations." 50 *International Organization* 109–39 (1996).

Golay, John Ford. *The Founding of the Federal Republic of Germany*. Chicago: University of Chicago Press, 1958.

Gomme, A. W. *A Historical Commentary on Thucydides*, vol. 1. Oxford: Oxford University Press, 1945.

Gooch, G. P. *English Democratic Ideas in the Seventeenth Century*. New York: Harper Torchbook, 1959.

Gray, Charles. "Parliament, Liberty, and the Law." In *Parliament and Liberty from the Reign of Elizabeth to the English Civil War*, ed. J. H. Hexter. Stanford: Stanford University Press, 1992.

Greenberg, Janelle. *The Radical Face of the Ancient Constitution: St. Edward's 'Laws' in Early Modern Political Thought*. Cambridge: Cambridge University Press, 2001.

Habermas, Jürgen. *Between Facts and Norms*. Cambridge, MA: MIT Press, 1996.

Habermas, Jürgen, with William Rehg. "Constitutional Democracy: A Paradoxical Union of Contradictory Principles?" 29(6) *Political Theory* 766–81 (2001).

Hale, Sir Matthew. "Considerations Touching the Amendment or Alteration of Laws." In *A Collection of Legal Tracts Relating to the Law of England*, vol. 1, ed. Francis Hargrave. London: Printed by T. Wright, 1787.

Hamilton, Alexander, James Madison, and John Jay. *The Federalist Papers*, ed. Clifford Rossiter. New York: Penguin Books, [1788] 1961.

Hansen, Mogens Herman. *The Athenian Democracy in the Age of Demosthenes*. Oxford: Blackwell, 1991.

Hansen, Mogens Herman. "Nomos and Psephisma in Fourth-Century Athens," 19 *Greek, Roman, and Byzantine Studies* 315–30 (1978).

Hardin, Russell. *Liberalism, Constitutionalism, and Democracy*. Oxford: Oxford University Press, 1999.

Harding, Phillip. *From the End of the Peloponnesian War to the Battle of Ipsus*. Cambridge: Cambridge University Press, 1985.

Harrington, James. *The Political Works of James Harrington*, ed. J. G. A. Pocock. Cambridge: Cambridge University Press, 1977.

Harris, William F. *The Interpretable Constitution*. Baltimore: Johns Hopkins University Press, 1993.

Harrison, A. R. W. "Law-Making at Athens at the End of the Fifth Century BC." 75 *Journal of Hellenic Studies* 26–35 (1955).

Hart, H. L. A. *The Concept of Law*. Oxford: Oxford University Press, 1994.

Hayek, F. A. *Law, Legislation, and Liberty, vol. 1: Rules and Order*. Chicago: University of Chicago Press, 1973.

Heath, G. D., III. "Making the Instrument of Government." 6 *Journal of British Studies* at 31 (1967).

Hedrick, Charles W., Jr. "Democracy and the Athenian Epigraphic Habit." 68(3) *Hesperia* 387–439 (1999).

Herodotus. *The Histories*, trans. Aubrey de Selincourt. London: Penguin Books, 1972.

Hirst, Derek. *England in Conflict, 1603–1660*. London: Arnold, 1999.

Hirst, Derek. "The Lord Protector, 1653–1658." In *Oliver Cromwell and the English Revolution*, ed. John Morrill. London: Longman, 1990.

Hobbes, Thomas. *Leviathan*. Cambridge: Cambridge University Press, 1991.

Holmes, Stephen. *Passions and Constraint*. Chicago: University of Chicago Press, 1995.

Holmes, Stephen, and Cass Sunstein. "The Politics of Revision." In *Responding to Imperfection*, ed. Sanford Levinson. Princeton, NJ: Princeton University Press, 1995.

Hornblower, Simon. *The Greek World 479–323 B.C.* London: Routledge, 1992.

Huber, Gregory, and Sanford Gordon. "Accountability and Coercion: Is Justice Blind When It Runs for Office? 48(2) *American Journal of Political Science* 247–63 (2004).

Hucko, Elmar M., ed. *The Democratic Tradition: Four German Constitutions.* Leamington Spa, England: Berg Publishers, 1987.

Hutchinson, William T., William M. E. Racahl, Robert Rutland, et al., eds. *The Papers of James Madison* (17 vols.). Chicago and Charlottesville: University of Chicago Press and University of Virginia Press, 1962–1991.

Jacobsohn, Gary Jeffrey. "Symposium: Borrowing: The Permeability of Constitutional Borders," 82 *Texas Law Review* 1763 (2004).

Jacobsohn, Gary Jeffrey. *Apple of Gold: Constitutionalism in Israel and in the United States.* Princeton, NJ: Princeton University Press, 1993.

Jacobson, Arthur J., and Bernhard Schlink. *Weimar: A Jurisprudence of Crisis.* Berkeley: University of California Press, 2000.

Jacobsohn, Gary Jeffrey. "Symposium: Borrowing: The Permeability of Constitutional Borders," 82 *Tex.* L.R. 1763.

Johnson, James. "What the Politics of Enfranchisement Can Tell Us About How Rational Choice Theorists Study Institutions." In *Preferences and Situations: Points of Intersection between Historical and Rational Choice Institutionalism*, eds. Ira Katznelson and Barry R. Weingast. New York: Russell Sage Foundation, 2005.

Karpen. Ulrich. *The Constitution of the Federal Republic of Germany: Essays on the Basic Rights and Principles of the Basic Law With a Translation of the Basic Law.* Baden-Baden: Nomos Verlagsgesellschaft, 1988.

Katz, Elai. "On Amending Constitutions: The Legality and Legitimacy of Constitutional Entrenchment," 29 *Columbia Journal of Law and Social Problems* 251–92 (1996).

Kelly, Duncan. *The State of the Political: Conceptions of Politics and the State in the Thought of Max Weber, Carl Schmitt and Franz Neumann.* Oxford: British Academy/Oxford University Press, 2003.

Kelsen, Hans. *Allgemeine Staatslehre.* Berlin: Julius Springer, 1925.

Kelsen, Hans. *Vom Wesen und Wert der Demokratie.* Tubingen, Germany: Verlag von J. C. B. Mohr, 1929.

Kelsen, Hans. *General Theory of Law and State,* trans. Andres Wedberg. Cambridge, MA: Harvard University Press, 1945.

Kennan, George F. *At a Century's Ending: Reflections 1982–1995.* New York: Norton, 1996.

Knight, Jack. "Institutionalizing Constitutional Interpretation." In *Constitutional Culture and Democratic Rule*, ed. John Ferejohn, Jack N. Rakove, and Jonathan Riley. Cambridge: Cambridge University Press, 2001.

Knight, Jack. *Institutions and Social Conflict.* Cambridge: Cambridge University Press, 1992.

Koch, Adrienne, and William Peden. *The Life and Selected Writings of Thomas Jefferson.* New York: Modern Library, 1993.

Koch, H. W. *A Constitutional History of Germany in the Nineteenth and Twentieth Centuries.* London: Longman, 1984.

Kokott, Juliane. "From Reception and Transplantation to Convergence of Constitutional Models in the Age of Globalization." In *Constitutionalism, Universalism, and Democracy: A Comparative Analysis*, ed. Christian Starck. Baden-Baden: Nomos Verlagsgesellschaft, 1999.

Kommers, Donald P. *The Constitutional Jurisprudence of the Federal Republic of Germany*, 2nd edition, Durham, NC: Duke University Press, 1997; 1st edition, 1989.

Kommers, Donald P. "Germany: Balancing Rights and Duties." In *Interpreting Constitutions: A Comparative Study,* ed. Jeffrey Goldsworthy. New York: Oxford University Press, 2006.

Kurland, Philip B., and Ralph Lerner. *The Founders' Constitution*, vol. 4. Chicago: University of Chicago, 1987.

Larmore, Charles. "The Moral Basis of Political Liberalism." 96(12) *Journal of Philosophy* 599–625 (1999).

Law's Discovery, June 27, 1653, E 702 (18).

The Lawyers Bane or the Laws Reformation and New Model, Aug. 13, 1647, E401 (36).

Letters of Delegates to Congress, 1774–1789, ed. Paul H. Smith. Washington: Library of Congress, 1976–2000.

Levinson, Sanford. "How Many Times Has the United States Constitution Been Amended? (A) 26; (B) 26; (C) 27; (D) >27: Accounting for Constitution Change." In *Responding to Imperfection*, ed. Sanford Levinson. Princeton, NJ: Princeton University Press, 1995.

Lewis, David. "The Athenian Coinage Decree." In *Selected Papers in Greek and Near Eastern History*, ed. P. J. Rhodes. Cambridge: Cambridge University Press, 1997.

Lewis, David M. "Entrenchment-Clauses in Attic Decrees." In *Phoros: Tribute to Benjamin Dean Meritt,* ed. Donald William Bradeen and Malcolm Francis McGregor. Locust Valley, NY: J. J. Augustin, 1974.

Lilburne, John. *The Just Man's Justification,* June 6, 1646, E 340 (12).

Loewenstein, Karl. "Militant Democracy and Fundamental Rights I." 31(3) *American Political Science Review* 417–32 (1937).

Loewenstein, Karl. *Über Wesen, Technik, und Grenzen der Verfassungsänderung*. Berlin: De Gruyter, 1961.

MacDowell, Douglas M. "Law-Making at Athens in the Fourth Century B.C.," 95 *Journal of Hellenic Studies* 62–74 (1975).

MacDowell, Douglas M. *The Law in Classical Athens*. Ithaca, NY: Cornell University Press, 1978.

MacDowell, Douglas M. *Spartan Law*. Edinburgh: Scottish Academic Press, 1986.

Macedo, Stephen. *Liberal Virtues*. Oxford: Oxford University Press, 1990.

MacGilvray, Eric A. *Reconstructing Public Reason*. Cambridge, MA: Harvard University Press, 2004.

Madison, James. *Writings*, ed. Jack Rakove. New York: Library of America, 1999.

Maltz, Earl. "Slavery, Federalism, and the Structure of the Constitution." 36 *American Journal of Legal History* 466–98 (1992).

Manin, Bernard. "On Legitimacy and Political Deliberation," 15(3) *Political Theory* 338–68 (1987).

Marbury, William. "The Limitations upon the Amending Power." 33 *Harvard Law Review* 223–35 (1919).

Matthews, Richard K. *If Men Were Angels: James Madison and the Heartless Empire of Reason*. Lawrence: University Press of Kansas, 1995.

Mattingly, Harold. *The Athenian Empire Restored*. Ann Arbor: University of Michigan Press, 1996.

McCormick, John P. *Carl Schmitt's Critique of Liberalism: Against Politics as Technology*. Cambridge: Cambridge University Press, 1997.

McIlwain, Charles Howard. *The High Court of Parliament*. New Haven, CT: Yale University Press, 1910.

Meier, Christian. *Athens: A Portrait of the City in Its Golden Age*. New York: Henry Holt, 1993.

Meiggs, Russell, and David Lewis. *A Selection of Greek Historical Inscriptions to the End of the Fifth Century B.C.* Oxford: Clarendon Press, 1969.

Merkl, Peter H. *The Origin of the West German Republic*. Westport, CT: Greenwood Press, 1963.

Mill, John Stuart. *The Collected Works of John Stuart Mill*, ed. John M. Robson. Toronto: University of Toronto Press; London: Routledge and Kegan Paul, 1963–91.

Mill, John Stuart. *On Liberty and Other Essays*. Oxford: Oxford University Press, 1991.

Mouffe, Chantal. "Carl Schmitt and the Paradox of Liberal Democracy." In *Law as Politics: Carl Schmitt's Critique of Liberalism*, ed. David Dyzenhaus. Durham, N.C.: Duke University Press, 1998.

References

Müller, Jan-Werner. *A Dangerous Mind: Carl Schmitt in Post-War European Thought*. New Haven, C.T.: Yale University Press, 2003.

Murphy, Walter. "An Ordering of Constitutional Values." 53 *Southern California Law Review* 703–60 (1980).

Murphy, Walter F. "Merlin's Memory: The Past and Future Imperfect of the Once and Future Polity." In *Responding to Imperfection*, ed. Sanford Levinson. Princeton, NJ: Princeton University Press, 1995.

Nedham, Marchamont. *Mercurius Politicus*, no. 73, Oct. 23–30, 1651. E644 (5).

Nedham, Marchamont. *True State of the Commonwealth*. 1654. E728 (5)

Ober, Josiah. *The Athenian Revolution*. Princeton, NJ: Princeton University Press, 1996.

Ober, Josiah. *Mass and Elite in Democratic Athens*. Princeton, NJ: Princeton University Press, 1989.

Ober, Josiah, and Charles Hedrick. *Demokratia: A Conversation on Democracies, Ancient and Modern*. Princeton, NJ: Princeton University Press, 1996.

Office of Military Government for Germany (United States), Civil Administration Division. *Documents on the Creation of the German Federal Constitution*. Sept. 1, 1949.

Orfield, Lester Bernhardt. *The Amending of the Federal Constitution*. Ann Arbor: University of Michigan Press, 1942.

Ostwald, Martin. *From Popular Sovereignty to the Sovereignty of Law*. Berkeley: University of California Press, 1986.

Der Parlamentarische Rat 1948–1949: Akten und Protokolle, ed. Johannes Volker Wagner. Boppard am Rhein, Germany: Boldt, 1995.

Plato. *The Laws*, trans. Trevor J. Saunders. London: Penguin Books, 1970.

Plato. *Statesman*, trans. J. B. Skemp; revised and introduced by Martin Ostwald. Indianapolis: Hackett, 1992.

Plutarch. *Lives*, ed. Arthur Hugh Clough, trans. John Dryden. New York: Mondern Library, 2001.

Pocock, J. G. A. *The Ancient Constitution and the Feudal Law*. Cambridge: Cambridge University Press, 1987.

Pocock, J. G. A. *The Machiavellian Moment*. Princeton, N.J.: Princeton University Press, 1975.

Posner, Richard A. *Law, Pragmatism, and Democracy*. Cambridge, MA: Harvard University Press, 2003.

Preuss, Ulrich K. "Political Order and Democracy: Carl Schmitt and His Influence." In *The Challenge of Carl Schmitt*, ed. Chantal Mouffe. London: Verso, 1999, pp. 155–79.

Rakove, Jack N. *Original Meanings: Politics and Ideas in the Making of the Constitution*. New York: Vintage Books, 1997.

Rawls, John. *Political Liberalism*. Cambridge, MA: Harvard University Press, 1993.

Reed, William. "Alliance Duration and Democracy: An Extension and Cross-Validation of 'Democratic States and Commitment in International Relations.'" 41 *American Journal of Political Science* 1072–78 (1997).

Rhodes, P. J., with David Lewis. *The Decrees of the Greek States*. Oxford: Clarendon Press, 1997.

Robinson, Henry. *Certain Proposals in Order to a New Modelling of the Lawes and Law-Proceedings*. London: Printed by M. Simmons, 1653.

Rosenfeld, Michel. "Can Rights, Democracy and Justice Be Reconciled Through Discourse Theory? Reflections of Habermas's Proceduralist Paradigm of Law." 17 *Cardozo Law Review* 791–824 (1996).

Ross, Alf. "On Self-Reference and a Puzzle in Constitutional Law." 78 *Mind* 1–24 (1969).

Ruhm von Oppen, Beate. *Documents on Germany under Occupation, 1945–54*. London: Oxford University Press, 1955.

Ryder, T. T. B. *Koine Eirene*. London: Oxford University Press, 1965.

Sanderson, John. *Biography of the Signers to the Declaration of Independence*. Philadelphia: R. W. Pomeroy, 1823–27.

Saxonhouse, Arlene W. *Athenian Democracy: Modern Mythmakers and Ancient Theorists*. Notre Dame, IN: University of Notre Dame Press, 1996.

Schmitt, Carl. *Verfassungsrechtliche Aufsätze aus den Jahren 1924–1954: Materialien zu einer Verfassungslehre*. Berlin: Duncker and Humblot, 1958.

Schmitt, Carl. *Political Theology*, trans. George Schwab. Cambridge, MA: MIT Press, 1985.

Schmitt, Carl. *The Crisis of Parliamentary Democracy*, trans. Ellen Kennedy. Cambridge, MA: MIT Press, 2000.

Schmitt, Carl. *Legality and Legitimacy*, trans. Jeffrey Seitzer. Durham, NC: Duke University Press, 2004.

Schwartzberg, Melissa. "Jeremy Bentham on Fallibility and Infallibity." *Journal of the History of Ideas*. Forthcoming.

Seaberg, R. B. "The Norman Conquest and the Common Law: The Levellers and the Argument from Continuity." 24 *Historical Journal* 791–806 (1981).

Sealey, Raphael. *The Athenian Republic: Democracy or Rule of Law?* University Park: Pennsylvania State University Press, 1986.

Sealey, Raphael. "On the Athenian Concept of Law," 77 *Classical Journal* 289–302 (1982).

Shapiro, Barbara. "Law Reform in Seventeenth Century England." 19 *American Journal of Legal History* 280–312 (1975).

Shapiro, Barbara. "Sir Francis Bacon and the Mid-Seventeenth Century Movement for Law Reform." 24 *American Journal of Legal History* 331–362 (1980).

Sharp, Andrew, ed. *The English Levellers*. Cambridge: Cambridge University Press, 1998.

Sheldon, Garrett Ward. *The Political Philosophy of James Madison*. Baltimore: Johns Hopkins University Press, 2001.

Skinner, Quentin. *Visions of Politics: Volume 3: Hobbes and Civil Science*. Cambridge: Cambridge University Press, 2002.

Sommerville, J. P. "Cromwell and His Contemporaries." In *Oliver Cromwell and the English Revolution*, ed. John Morrill. London: Longman, 1990.

Sommerville, J. P. *Politics and Ideology in England 1603–1640*. London: Longman, 1986.

Steinberger, Helmut. "Historical Influences of American Constitutionalism upon German Constitutional Development: Federalism and Judicial Review." 36 *Columbia Journal of Transnational Law* 189 (1997).

Steinberger, Helmut. "American Contitutionalism and German Constitutional Development." In *Constitutionalism and Rights: The Influence of the United States Constitution Abroad*, Louis Henkin and Albert J. Rosenthal, eds. New York: Columbia University Press, 1990.

Stepan, Alfred. "Federalism and Democracy: Beyond the U.S. Model." 10(4) *Journal of Democracy* 19–34 (1999).

Stroud, Ronald S. *The Athenian Grain-Tax Law of 374/3 B.C.* Princeton, NJ: American School of Classical Studies at Athens, 1998.

Suber, Peter. *The Paradox of Self-Amendment*. New York: Peter Lang, 1990.

Sunstein, Cass R. *Designing Democracy: What Constitutions Do*. Oxford: Oxford University Press, 2001.

Takayanagi, Kenzo, Ichiro Ohtomo, and Hideo Tanaka. *The Making of the Constitution of Japan*, vol. 1: *Documents*. Tokyo: Yuhikaku, 1972.

Thoma, Richard. "The Reich as Democracy," trans. Peter C. Caldwell. In *Weimar: A Jurisprudence of Crisis*, eds. Arthur Jacobson and Bernhard Schlink. Berkeley, CA: University of California Press, 2000.

Thucydides. *The Landmark Thucydides*, trans. Richard Crawley, ed. Robert B. Strassler. New York: Free Press, 1996.

Tocqueville, Alexis de. *Democracy in America*, trans. and eds. Harvey C. Mansfield and Delba Winthrop. Chicago: University of Chicago Press, 2000.

Tod, M. N. *A Selection of Greek Historical Inscriptions*, 2 vols. Oxford: Oxford Uniiversity Press, 1946, 1948.

Todd, S. C. *The Shape of Athenian Law*. Oxford: Clarendon Press, 1993.

Tuck, Richard. *Natural Rights Theories*. Cambridge: Cambridge University Press, 1979.

Urbinati, Nadia. *Mill on Democracy: From the Athenian Polis to Representative Government*. Chicago: University of Chicago Press, 2002.

Vanberg, Georg. *The Politics of Constitutional Review in Germany*. New York: Cambridge University Press, 2005.

Veall, Donald. *The Popular Movement for Law Reform, 1640–60*. Oxford: Clarendon Press, 1970.

Vile, John R. *The Constitutional Amending Process in American Political Thought*. Westport, CT: Praeger, 1992.

Vile, John R. *Constitutional Change in the United States*. Westport, CT: Praeger, 1994.

Vile, John R. "The Case against Implicit Limits on the Constitutional Amending Process." In *Responding to Imperfection*, ed. Sanford Levinson. Princeton, NJ: Princeton University Press, 1995.

Vile, John R. *Encyclopedia of Constitutional Amendments, Proposed Amendments, and Amending Issues, 1789–2002*, 2nd ed. Santa Barbara, CA: ABC-Clio, 2003.

Waldron, Jeremy. *The Dignity of Legislation*. Cambridge: Cambridge University Press, 1999a.

Waldron, Jeremy. *Law and Disagreement*. Oxford: Oxford University Press, 1999b.

Warr, John. *The Corruption and Deficiency of the Lawes of England Soberly Discovered*. June 11, 1649. London: T. Osborne.

Weston, Corinne. "England: Ancient Constitution and Common Law." In *The Cambridge History of Political Thought 1450–1700*, ed. J. H. Burns, with Mark Goldie. Cambridge: Cambridge University Press, 1996.

Wood, Gordon S. *The Creation of the American Republic 1776–1787*. Chapel Hill: University of North Carolina Press, 1998.

Woolrych, Austin. *Commonwealth to Protectorate*. Oxford: Oxford University Press, 1982.

Wootton, David. "Leveller Democracy and the Puritan Revolution." In *The Cambridge History of Political Thought 1450–1700*, ed. J. H. Burns, with Mark Goldie. Cambridge: Cambridge University Press, 1996.

Wootton, David, ed. *Divine Right and Democracy*. Middlesex, England: Penguin Books, 1986.

Worden, Blair. "Republicanism, Regicide, and Republic: The English Experience." In *Republicanism*, vol. 1, ed. Martin van Gelderen and Quentin Skinner. Cambridge: Cambridge University Press, 2002.

Worden, Blair. *The Rump Parliament: 1648–1653*. Cambridge: Cambridge University Press, 1974.

Xenophon. *Xenophon in Seven Volumes*, vol. 7, trans. E. C. Marchand. Cambridge, MA: Harvard University Press, 1984.

References

Yack, Bernard. *The Problems of a Political Animal*. Berkeley: University of California Press, 1993.

Zaret, David. *Origins of Democratic Culture: Printing, Petitions, and the Public Sphere in Early-Modern England*. Princeton, NJ: Princeton University Press, 2000.

Index